T0193879

Manipulating
the last Pure Godly
DNA

The Genetic Search for God's DNA on Earth

E.A. JENSEN

Order this book online at www.trafford.com
or email orders@trafford.com

Most Trafford titles are also available at major online book retailers.

Printed in the United States of America.

ISBN: 978-1-4669-6105-0 (sc)
ISBN: 978-1-4669-6107-4 (hc)
ISBN: 978-1-4669-6106-7 (e)

Library of Congress Control Number: 2012918175

Trafford rev. 03/27/2013

www.trafford.com

North America & international
toll-free: 1 888 232 4444 (USA & Canada)
phone: 250 383 6864 ♦ fax: 812 355 4082

CONTENTS

This book is dedicated to my father and grandfather, both born with enough common sense to be able to decipher the precious truth, with the limited information available to them, in order to help and encourage me to see through the thick fog of reality and truth.

INTRODUCTION

It is amazing how little we understand about whom we are, where we came from and what is to become of the human race . . . . even if the information is available?

Is this because of misinformation, deliberate brainwashing by society and the fight for numbers in different religious groups, or just a lack of interest in knowledge?

If you start talking about history, time and times past, people tend to be totally misinformed, or don't realise how it all fits together. The main problem is that 9 out of 10 people's conception of time and the vast expansion of it involving earth, humans and religion is totally out of synchronisation.

It is no wander that the lords of science and religion hardly ever see eye to eye. The big hype about who's right or wrong is totally unnecessary.

Big bang, evolution, Homo erectus, Adam and geological anomaly's billions of years ago is to much for the untrained brain to file and the result or tendency is to discard it all as useless information . . . .

In this book I will try and explain to you the "time line" of events. We will use archaeological, paleontological and scientific facts together with ancient Biblical historical and mythological manuscripts to state events and happenings.

We will also have a look into the legends and theory's that are more controversial in our age like what psychic's have to say and legends like Atlantis and UFO sightings.

I will use the correct scientific, Biblical and mythological names, quote scriptures and try and explain in layman's terms to make it more "street friendly" and understandable.

You may call this a "theory" just the same as if we would speak about, "evolution", also just a "theory".

To get this, or, as we would like to say . . . to "click" what I am about to explain and show you, I would need you to cage your normal borders of intellect, your way of thinking and your way of understanding, for the duration of this book.

We have been learned or manipulated not to think further than certain times and to see these times as different events. This is wrong according to the Bible and science . . . . it never really stopped . . . . time was ticking Eon's ago . . . .

The Bible is also one of the most correct historical and religious document available for studying the topic of earth's history during its time. It is also important to understand that the Bible was created (written) only for certain people, a certain seed line with a specific DNA code. It also gives us hints of peoples, nations and other interesting information about the earth and the times which the bible relates to.

I also make use of the complete works of Josephus. There are millions of people not using the Bible as reference and therefore these works supply us with a lot of early earth information during these same times.

Therefore I will be using the correct historical names of God, Jesus and Christ as written in the original Aramaic scriptures as well as the correct names and wording as used in geology and the palaeontology sciences.

Aramaic was the official language spoken during Biblical times and it is ancestral to both the Arabic and Hebrew alphabets.

Many questions are asked and so many misconceptions arise regarding all these, sometimes mystic, theories and ideas. It creates serious confusion on questions regarding Pre Adamic and Pre historical times.

When dinosaurs, fallen angels, mythology, Nephilim or Noah's flood is mentioned in a conversation, it almost always ends up in as many view points as people around the table.

This flustering state was and still is one of the main reasons why Biblical and scientific students and believers don't see eye to eye. It also doubles as the spark, creating total disbelievers in both theory and doctrine.

Keep in mind that this book does not claim to be a complete work of any specific area of science or Biblical doctrine.

I am using as much as possible information on specific sciences and doctrines to bring my point over, but it is at no means a full or complete work of any of them.

Believing or disbelieving my point or angle of approach on this matter will also not have a magical effect of guaranteeing your way, either to Heaven or Hell . . . . but it is nice to have an opinion that make sense.

It is also important to think of how you view your Creator . . . . and in a Biblical sense I we will be talking about YHWH ELOHIM.

Do you see Him as a magician waving his wand around creating by change, on a whim or the drop of a penny, spending no thought on what's to happen or the consequences of the deed, or do you see Him as a **"Super Engineer"** with superior knowledge on what we know today in all sciences, creating and organising with deliberate reason, intelligence and knowledge?

The way you interpret your view on the Creator will drastically change your conception on what is to come in this book.

The earth and everything on and around it has order, meticulously planned and placed in minute detail and wonder and in some cases we still don't have answers to it all.

My personal point of view is that YHWH can create by just speaking a word and it will be scientifically perfect up to the molecular level.

The time period we will be looking at will be from 13.5 billion years ago up to Noah's flood and up to the calling of Abraham.

It is important for people to understand the chronology of events and times. For years I battled with questions and uncertainties of what happened where and when . . . . was it real or just the figment of some ones imagination?

In time as all the real and correct answers to these questions fell into place within my personal understanding the more I was able to see the light and understand the imposable chaos that was whirling around in my head.

My main concerns was firstly, why I was not taught about some of these crucial **"bomb shell"** facts about geology, Biblical and mythological facts earlier in life? What are they trying to hide . . . or is it just the fact that nobody has a clear understanding and don't agree on how it all fits together?

It took me a lifetime of searching and filtering through mountains of useful and useless information to reach the critical point of understanding, created out of facts in all these fields.

I hope that my point of view may light or spark your knowledge and understanding in these matters.

There are a couple of chapters that are very technical. Feel free to skip them if you are familiar or not really interested in the technical side of the story. I had to include it however to have the information available should you want to double check on certain statements or theory's.

The main objective of this book is to make believers on both sides of the Biblical and natural sciences debate, showing both that we all were right from the start and that we basically just need to see the "missing link" we all are looking for. What we need to see or understand is that the time line of earth's history and the Biblical events must be seen as one continuous event, not separate.

The creation of earth took place long before Adam, It was created by ELOHIM, it became destroyed a couple of times and it was rectified a couple of times, (3 times) every time ELOHIM added whatever he wanted and tested His creation. With the Biblical creation the main addition to the new earth was the Adamic man, his knowledge of writing and other crucial sciences for us to start recording events and knowledge as we understands it today.

Adam was added to the earth situation to become the new ruler "manager" of planet earth, because of the mismanagement by Lucifer and his fellow fallen angels.

The plan went astray as Satan intervened and we need to understand these hidden events. The minute you except these truths about our history it is if a curtain pulls back and reveal the Bible into an understandable book that can be red and experienced as it should have been. At the same time your understanding to the sciences opens up and your current believe system and who you are and what you believe in gets new meaning.

So what did Satan mismanage or what exactly went wrong for all this to happen? Why was this not mentioned or recorded? The evidence of these facts is there for us to find and explore. The effect on the human race acquiring this knowledge are huge, it has such a dramatic effect on the way we reason that it had to be hidden until the end times when it is said that knowledge will increase.

It was there from the beginning of time, nothing new, just hidden until time ripens to release the knowledge.

With this statement I am not saying that I am the first person to see or understand these truths.

It has been recognised and discussed in the past. The main problem however was the wall of lack of time for evidence to open up the picture on the sciences and historical events with facts and the accumulation of knowledge in these fields.

We are now entering the era where knowledge and information is increasing with dramatic speed and effect around the world.

Slowly the picture starts to focus and take shape, the longer you study these facts, the longer you focus on this hidden picture until suddenly, the light bursts into your thoughts and mind.

This book should answer the three fundamental questions asked around the world at some stage of everybodys life.

Why are we on earth, where are we from and where are we going to? Please note the style of writing, I make use of short paragraphs to help highlight and understand statements better, rather than lengthy drawn out paragraphs.

Enjoy this intellectual and spiritual rollercoaster ride with me, but please buckle up and be prepared to see and experience dramatic and frightening knowledge and insight on events that shaped, and is shaping, your world and mine.

CHAPTER 1

Geology and Time

VAST PERIODS OF TIMES

Geologists, archaeologists and **palaeontologists** have divided and named the geological history of earth time into 4 main groups; **Eon's, Era's, Period's and Epoch's or Ages.**

Geologist: Is a scientist who studies the solid and liquid matter that constitutes earth as well as the processes and history that has shaped it.

Archaeologist: Is a scientist who studies human activity through the recovery and analysis of the material culture left behind over time.

Palaeontologist: Is a scientist who studies prehistoric life making use of fossils to determine organisms' evolution and interactions with each other and their environments.

Eon's are half billion years or more ago.

Era's are several hundred million years ago.

Periods are tens of millions years ago.

Epoch's or Ages are millions of years ago.

"Phylum or Phyla" describes a grouping of organisms based on general specialization of body plan.

Life-Domain-Kingdom-Phylum-Class-Order-Family-Genus-Species

The old European scientists, working on a broad division of the earth's history, recognised groups of rocks or systems separated by major earth-movements, and the succession worked out by them, thought altered in detail, have formed the basis of historical geology in all countries where the science of the earth has been studied.

As knowledge increased they build a time scale of the events forming earth. This scale is used as a chronological schema relating stratigraphicaly to time to describe the timing and relationships between events that have occurred during the history of the earth.

Different spans of time on this time scale are usually delimited by major events such as meteorites hitting earth, global ice ages and, volcanic eruptions and floods leading to mass extinctions, in other words, each era, period or age on the scale are separated by major cataclysmic events on earth.

Further on you'll find a graphic time sequence table explaining in more detail all that's been said above.

Take some time to study it. Please notice that it starts at the top of the page at 100 thousand years ago and then 1 and 1.8 million years ago at the Holocene Era which we are in now.

It does not include the last 100 thousand years which we will have a look at later on.

Also . . . please note the Precambrian Eon . . . The moment the years reach 1000 million it equals 1 billion years. We will be using the USA and French formula to calculate a billion where a billion is a thousand x a million. In other parts of the world a billion equals a million x a million. Please take a minute to contemplate the enormity of 1 billion years, if taking in consideration that Adam is only +/- 6000 years ago from today.

So how did they do it . . . . how sure are they that these "times" and the science behind how to calculate the "time" are correct?

Let's look at some dating techniques.

CARBON 14 DATING

This technique is widely used on recent artefacts, but you should note that this technique will not work on older fossils (like those of the dinosaurs which are over 65 million years old). Carbon dating is used to determine the age of biological artefacts up to 50,000 years old. This technique is not restricted to bones; it can also be used on cloth, wood and plant fibres. Carbon-14 dating has been used successfully on the Dead Sea Scrolls, Minoan ruins and tombs of the pharaohs among other things.

Carbon-14 has a half-life of about 5,730 years, it is a radioactive isotope of carbon. The short half-life of carbon-14 means it cannot be used to date extremely old fossils. Levels of carbon-14 become difficult to measure and compare after about 50,000 years.

Carbon-14 is created from nitrogen-14 in the upper atmosphere of the earth. Radiation from the sun collides with atoms in the atmosphere. These collisions create secondary cosmic rays in the form of energetic neutrons. When these neutrons collide with nitrogen-14 in the atmosphere carbon-14 can be created. Nitrogen normally occurs in a seven protons, seven neutron, nitrogen-14 state.

The carbon on Earth exists as carbon-12. Carbon-14 is an isotope of carbon, which exists only, in small amounts in the environment (1 in one trillion carbon atoms is carbon-14). The ratio of carbon-14 to carbon-12 in the atmosphere and on earth is nearly constant, although there has been some change in carbon-14 concentration over the last 10,000 years.

Carbon-14 formed in the atmosphere can combine with oxygen to form carbon dioxide (CO_2). This carbon-14 labelled carbon dioxide is taken up by plants in their normal process of photosynthesis. Animals and people that eat these plants take the carbon-14 into their bodies as well.

Carbon-14 in the bodies of animals and plants is constantly decaying to lower levels, but the decaying carbon-14 is constantly being replaced as the plant or animal consumes more carbon-14 from the air or through its food. At any given moment all living plants and animals have approximately the same percentage of carbon-14 in their bodies. When a plant or animal dies it stops consuming new carbon-14. However, the carbon-14 already in the organism's body continues to decay and lower at a constant rate. The amount of carbon-14 in an artefact decreases at a predictable rate while the amount of carbon-12 remains constant.

By comparing the ratio of carbon-14 to carbon-12 in an artefact to the ratio of carbon-14 to carbon-12 in living organisms' scientists can determine the age of an artefact.

RADIO CARBON DATING

Radiocarbon dating has been one of the most significant discoveries in 20th century science. Renfrew (1973) called it 'the radiocarbon revolution' in describing its impact upon the human sciences. Oakley (1979) suggested its development meant an almost complete re-writing of the evolution and cultural emergence of the human species.

Desmond Clark (1979) wrote that were it not for radiocarbon dating, *"we would still be foundering in a sea of imprecision's sometime bred of inspired guesswork but more often of imaginative speculation"* (Clark, 1979:7). Writing of the European Upper Palaeolithic, Movius (1960) concluded that *"time alone is the lens that can throw it into focus".*

The radiocarbon method was developed by a team of scientists led by the late Professor Willard F. Libby of the University of Chicago in immediate post-WW2 years. Libby later received the Nobel Prize in Chemistry in 1960:

> **"For his method to use Carbon-14 for age determinations in archaeology, geology, geophysics, and other branches of science."**

According to one of the scientists who nominated Libby as a candidate for this honour;

> **"Seldom has a single discovery in chemistry had such an impact on the thinking of so many fields of human endeavour. Seldom has a single discovery generated such wide public interest."** (From Taylor, 1987).

Today, there are over 130 radiocarbon dating laboratories around the world producing radiocarbon assays for the scientific community.

The C14 technique has been and continues to be applied and used in many, many different fields including hydrology, atmospheric science, oceanography, geology, archaeology and biomedicine.

It follows from this that any material which is composed of carbon may be dated. Herein lies the true advantage of the radiocarbon method, it is able to be uniformly applied throughout the world. Included below is an impressive list of some of the types of carbonaceous samples that have been commonly radiocarbon dated in the years since the inception of the method:

The historical perspective on the development of radiocarbon dating is well outlined in Taylor's (1987) book "Radiocarbon Dating: An archaeological perspective". Libby and his team initially tested the radiocarbon method on samples from prehistoric Egypt.

They chose samples whose age could be independently determined. A sample of acacia wood from the tomb of the pharaoh Zoser (or Djoser; 3rd Dynasty, ca. 2700-2600 BC) was obtained and dated. Libby reasoned that since the half-life of C14 was 5568 years, they should obtain a C14 concentration of about 50% that which was found in living wood (see Libby, 1949 for further details).

The results they obtained indicated this was the case. Other analyses were conducted on samples of known age wood (dendrochronologically aged). Again, the fit was within the value predicted at ±10%. The tests suggested that the half-life they had measured was accurate, and, quite reasonably, suggested further that atmospheric radiocarbon concentration had remained constant throughout the recent past.

In 1949, Arnold and Libby (1949) published their paper "Age determinations by radiocarbon content: Checks with samples of known age" in the journal *Science*. In this paper they presented the first results of the C14 method, including the "Curve of Known's" in which radiocarbon dates were compared with the known age historical dates (see figure 1). All of the points fitted within statistical range. Within a few years, other laboratories had been built. The activity ratio relates to the carbon 14 activity ratio between the ancient samples and the modern activity. Each result was within the statistical range of the true historic date of each sample.

In the 1950s, further measurements on Mediterranean samples, in particular those from Egypt whose age was known through other means, pointed to radiocarbon dates which were younger than expected. The debate regarding this is outlined extensively in Renfrew (1972). Briefly, opinion was divided between those who thought the radiocarbon dates were correct (i.e., that radiocarbon years equated more or less to solar or calendar years) and those who felt they were flawed and the historical data was more accurate.

In the late 1950's and early 1960's, researchers measuring the radioactivity of known age tree rings found fluctuations in C14 concentration up to a maximum of ±5% over the last 1500 years. In addition to long term fluctuations, smaller 'wiggles' were identified by the Dutch scholar Hessel de Vries (1958).

This suggested there were temporal fluctuations in C14 concentration which would necessitate the calibration of radiocarbon dates to other historically aged material. Radiocarbon dates of sequential dendrochronologically aged trees primarily of US bristlecone pine and German and Irish oak have been measured over the past 10 years to produce a cylindrical/radiocarbon calibration curve which now extends back over 10 000 years (more on Calibration). This enables radiocarbon dates to be calibrated to solar or calendar dates.

Later measurements of the Libby half-life indicated the figure was *ca.* 3% too low and a more accurate half-life was 5730±40 years. This is known as the **Cambridge half-life**. (To convert a "Libby" age to an age using the Cambridge half-life, one must multiply by 1.03).

The major developments in the radiocarbon method up to the present day involve improvements in measurement techniques and research into the dating of different materials. Briefly, the initial solid carbon method developed by Libby and his collaborators was replaced with the Gas counting method in the 1950's. Liquid scintillation counting, utilising benzene, acetylene, ethanol, methanol etc, was developed at about the same time.

Today the vast majority of radiocarbon laboratories utilise these two methods of radiocarbon dating. Of major recent interest is the development of the Accelerator Mass Spectrometry method of direct C14 isotope counting. In 1977, the first AMS measurements were conducted by teams at Rochester/Toronto and the General Ionex Corporation and soon after at the Universities of Simon Fraser and McMaster (Gove, 1994).

The crucial advantage of the AMS method is that milligram sized samples are required for dating. Of great public interest has been the AMS dating of carbonaceous material from prehistoric rock art sites, the Shroud of Turin and the Dead Sea Scrolls in the last few years.

The development of high-precision dating (up to ±2.0 per mille or ±16 yr) in a number of gas and liquid scintillation facilities has been of similar importance (laboratories at Belfast (N.Ireland), Seattle (US), Heidelberg (Ger), Pretoria (S.Africa), Groningen (Netherlands), La Jolla (US), Waikato (NZ) and Arizona (US) are generally accepted to have demonstrated radiocarbon measurements at high levels of precision).

The calibration research undertaken primarily at the Belfast and Seattle labs required that high levels of precision be obtained which has now resulted in the extensive calibration data now available.

The development of small sample capabilities for LSC and Gas labs has likewise been an important development—samples as small as 100 mg are able to be dated to moderate precision on minigas counters (Kromer, 1994) with similar sample sizes needed using minivial technology in Liquid Scintillation Counting.

Carbon 14: Thousands of years
Radio Carbon: Millions of years

GEOLOGICAL TIME TABLE

EON	ERA	PERIOD		EPOCH		Ma
Phanerozoic	Cenozoic	Quaternary		Holocene		0.01
				Pleistocene	Late	0.8
					Early	1.8
		Tertiary	Neogene	Pliocene	Late	3.6
					Early	5.3
				Miocene	Late	11.2
					Middle	16.4
					Early	23.7
			Paleogene	Oligocene	Late	28.5
					Early	33.7
				Eocene	Late	41.3
					Middle	49.0
					Early	54.8
				Paleocene	Late	61.0
					Early	65.0
	Mesozoic	Cretaceous		Late		99.0
				Early		144
		Jurassic		Late		159
				Middle		180
				Early		206
		Triassic		Late		227
				Middle		242
				Early		248
	Paleozoic	Permian		Late		256
				Early		290
		Pennsylvanian				323
		Mississippian				354
		Devonian		Late		370
				Middle		391
				Early		417
		Silurian		Late		423
				Early		443
		Ordovician		Late		458
				Middle		470
				Early		490
		Cambrian		D		500
				C		512
				B		520
				A		543
Precambrian	Proterozoic	Late				900
		Middle				1600
		Early				2500
	Archean	Late				3000
		Middle				3400
		Early				3800?

So before we get to technical I would like to explain and get you to understand the enormity of this **"time"** problem, just for your own sake of grasping it I will do it point by point.

From today backwards in time it is 2012 years to the birth of YAHSHUA (Jesus).

This last 2000 years is broken up into different times and dark ages. Most people will be able to give you some sort of rundown of events in this era. Let us just say that our world with our modern times started around the 16 centaury (400 years ago) where transport in the form of larger sailing ships starts to develop our knowledge of foreign lands and peoples as they got discovered for the "first time".

Knowledge of our planet and the stars became available and it is during this time that we discover or except that the earth is round and that it is gravity holding us down . . .

It is in the last 60 years that science and technology start to lift human kind and knowledge to the heights it reached today. We may call it the Quaternary or Holocene knowledge explosion depicting the end of our current period in the geological time scale.

Comparing to the speed of large cataclysmic events that happened in earth's history on our geological time frame, it is extraordinary and frightening to realize that this knowledge explosion can be compared to those older major cataclysmic events that happened in the past that normally indicated the end of an era or Epoch.

It is also interesting to note that it is the case with nature as well. For long periods of time things tend to change very little and slowly, and then for some apparent reason things start to speed up and go wrong, the global change can all of a sudden be measured in years and not hundreds or thousands of years.

Everything starts changing with cataclysmic speed, like we experience today, to end in complete chaos and destruction.

If we look at the population growth of planet earth we see the same tendency.

Our population problem started in around 1850 when oil came into its own in our technological age. From Adam to 1850 which is approximately 5850 years the world population never exceeded 1 billion people. since 1850 we have doubled in population six fold in the last 150 years comparing to the last six thousand years.

"As we reached the fifth billion, in 1987, humans became the most numerous species on earth in terms of total biomass. Around 1990, we became the most numerous mammalian species on the planet, outnumbering rats at six billion. There is now more human flesh on the planet than there is of any other single species".

"We now consume more than 45% of the world's total "net primary productivity", which is the measure of the sum total of food and energy available to all species on earth under normal circumstances".

"We humans consume more than 50% of the planets available fresh water. This means that every other species of plant and animal life on planet earth must now compete against one another for what little is left."

At 2010 we are aiming at the 8 billion mark and still growing.

Scientists have established that the earth has got about 45 years of oil reserves left to feed the beast. What will happen next . . . . will the bubble burst naturally, will the earth's population return to its normal earth sustainable level of less than 1 billion?

How will this happen, and how close are we to this point?

It is clear for all that wants to know and those willing to make the study that the earth is speeding up on all fronts to an enormous cataclysmic event awaiting us in the near geological future.

From YAHSHUA's birth to Noah's flood is approximately another 2200 years back, nearly the same length in time as we had after His birth.

The half a page in the Bible covering the period from Noah to Adam constitutes for another nearly 2000 years totalling from today to Adam about 6000 years.

Have a look at the time line in chapter 6 to see the ages of the people in this first 2000 years after the Adamic creation and the astonishing fact that they all knew each other will come to light. The accumulation of knowledge must have been enormous in those times.

Another interesting fact about this time is that Noah was building the ark for the coming deluge for about 150 years before it started to rain. Can you imagine what a mammoth task it was and how society and other people reacted to this half crazy old man building a boat high and dry for some coming event? Can you imagine the commitment in his believes and the word of YHWH?

FROM ADAM BACKWARDS WE WILL LOOK AT IT IN THE FOLLOWING WAY

6000   Beginning of Bronze age

7000   Earth is a wasteland

8000   Mastodons and other giant mammals go extinct

9000   First evidence of melting of metals

10 000   End of Wurm/Wisconsin ice age . . . see level rise with 91 meters

Now we will start jumping by the 10 000's of years:

(one complete Adamic age plus an additional 4000 years with each jump)

20 000   See level 130 meters lower than today

30 000   Neanderthal disappear

40 000   Cro-Magnon man appears, first cave paintings depicting gods.

50 000   Mega fauna die out

60 000   Oldest male ancestor of human

70 000   Toba volcanic eruption

80 000   Non African humans interbreed with Neanderthals

90 000   Beginning of seed collection and planned crops

Now we jump by the 100 000's of years:

(nearly seventeen complete Adamic ages with each jump)

100 000   Stone age

200 000   Homo sapiens

300 000   Controlled fire

400 000   Hunting with tools

500 000   Speech

600 000   Yellowstone eruption
700 000   Human & Neanderthal split
800 000
900 000   (167 complete Adamic ages at one million years ago)
1 MIL   So when you reach one million of these "1 million" years you will reach your first 1 billion years.

(167 million complete Adamic ages in one billion years)

GEOLOGICAL AND BIOLOGICAL
TIMELINE OF THE EARTH

THEORY A

Astronomical and geological evidence indicates that the Universe is approximately 13,700 million (13.7 Billion) years old, and our solar system is about 4,567 million years old. Earth's Moon formed 4,450 million years ago, just 50 million years after the Earth's formation.

The composition of the rocks retrieved from the Moon by the Apollo missions is very similar to rocks from the Earth, the Moon formed as a result of a collision between the Earth and a Mars-sized body, also called Orpheus or Theia, which accreted at a Lagrangian point 60° ahead or behind the Earth.

A huge meteorite bombardment of the Moon and the Earth happened 3,900 million years ago. It is thought to have been caused by the debris of a planetary collision beyond the earth or by asteroids whose orbits were destabilized and were sent toward the inner solar system during the formation of planets beyond the Earth.

The Mars Reconnaissance Obiter and the Mars Global Surveyor have found evidence that the Borealis basin in the northern hemisphere of Mars may have been created by a huge impact with an object +/- 2000 kilometres in diameter around 3900 million years ago.

This probably caused the debris for the cataclysmic meteorite bombardment of the Earth and Moon.

Approximately 3,000 million years ago, the earth has cooled enough for the crust to form and land masses to start settling. The supercontinent Rodinia was formed about 1100 million years ago, and it broke into several pieces that drifted apart 750 million years ago.

They collided back together about 600 million years ago, forming the Pan-African Mountains in a new supercontinent called Pannotia. Pannotia started breaking up again at about 550 million years ago to form Laurasia and Gondwana. Laurasia included what are now North America, Europe, Siberia, and Greenland. Gondwana formed what are now India, Africa, South America, and Antarctica. Laurasia and Gondwana came together approximately 275 million years ago to form the continent of Pangea.

Where we reach our present situation where Pangea is still barking up today, contributing to the formation of the Atlantic Ocean.

Further on you will find a time line of life forms associated with the different time zones to give a better idea of what happened when as far as life is concerned.

THEORY B

Young Earth Creationist, theory.

The theory mainly works on the assumption that dating techniques are wrong and not that accurate since the rocks or fossils used for dating are not closed systems and could have been contaminated by neighbouring minerals and climatic events, thus implying that the earth is much younger than anticipated in theory A.

It states that all fossils should be seen as living in the same time frame, existing simultaneously.

The theory is strengthened by the fact that our main body of fossils, 98%, are marine fossils and that the "floaters and bloaters" missed fossilisation.

To explain the theory rather quick and accurate you may see it in the following way.

Imagine a pond in your back garden . . . . At the bottom you get a thin layer of mud with small microscopic creatures, some small other snail like phyla and organisms share this muddy habitat with some creepy crawly's of different, but mostly the same phyla.

You also have a couple of water lilies and other aquatic plants, grasses and reeds in the one corner. A few frogs' and other fish share the pond with some ducks breeding just alongside in the reeds of the pond . . . .

Now . . . . if we create a small cataclysmic event where a bucket of dirt falls into the pond we will get fossilization on the bottom but the rest will go on as if nothing happened.

Should we get a little more dirt into the pond we will have fossilization of the fish and plants as well . . . maybe the ducks (floaters and bloaters) will die of loss of habitat but they won't fossilize because the destruction is below them in the water . . . . maybe they could float away to the edges of the pond and be deposited on the shore and maybe the situation can occur for some of them to fossilize if there should be another bucket spilled into the pond creating a huge mud burial effect of everything . . . . Get the picture??

It is rather difficult getting a fixed time frame on this theory . . . . some takes it as early as 6000 years (Adam, biblical creation) to at most 10 000 years ago.

DEVELOPMENT OF LIFE
DURING THE ERAS

Paleozoic Era

Period	MYA	Life Forms
Cambrian	600-500	Algae and simple invertebrates, like jellyfish & worms. Arthropods, brachiopods, & trilobites.
Ordovician	500-440	Graptolites, Orthocerous, & primitive fish. The first vertebrates begin to appear.
Silurian	440-395	The first true plants appear. Crinoids & eurypterids are abundant. The first air breathers.
Devonian	395-345	Fish evolve into more complex animals. Sharks and amphibians multiply.
Carboniferous	345-280	Plentiful ferns. Reptiles evolve. Spiders, cockroaches, & scorpions appear. Life on dry land.
Permian	280-225	Reptiles become abundant. Pine-like trees develop. Trilobites become extinct.

Mesozoic Era

Period	MYA	Life Forms
Triassic	225-190	The beginning of the dinosaurs. Plant eaters, meat eaters, flying reptiles, and crocodiles.
Jurassic	190-136	Giant dinosaurs develop. Abundant plant life & shellfish, like ammonites, lobsters, and shrimp.
Cretaceous	136-65	The peak of development. Downfall of the great dinosaurs, like triceratops, t-Rex, & pterodactyls. Deciduous trees develop.

Cenozoic Era

Period	MYA	Life Forms
Tertiary	65-2	Mammals develop, such as camels, bears, cats, monkeys, rodents, and dogs. Grasses & fruits like today appear.
Quaternary	2-Present	More mammals develop, like the sabre-toothed tiger and mastodon. Modern man appears.

GEOLOGICAL POINTS TO PONDER

"There is another and allied difficulty, which is much more serious. It alludes to the manner in which species belonging to several of the main divisions of the animal kingdom **suddenly appear** in the lowest known fossiliferous rocks." (Darwin The Origin of Species, p. 348)

"The **abrupt manner** in which whole groups of species suddenly appear in certain formations, has been urged by several palaeontologists like, Agassiz, Pictet and Sedgwick as a fatal objection to the believe in the transmutation of species. If numerous species, belonging to the same genera of families, have really started into life at once, the fact would be fatal to the theory of evolution through natural selection." (Ibib. p. 344)

"To the question why we do not find rich fossiliferous deposits belonging to these assumed earliest periods prior to the Cambrian system, I can give **no satisfactory** answer." (Ibib. P. 350)

"The most famous such burst, the Cambrian explosion, marks the inception of modern multicellular life. Within just a few million years, **nearly every major kind** of animal anatomy appears in the fossil record for the first time. The Precambrian record is now sufficiently good that the old rationale about undiscovered sequences of smoothly transitional will no longer wash." (An asteroid to die for, Stephen J Gould, Discover, October 1989, p. 65)

"We find many Cambrian fossils already in an advanced state of evolution, the very first time they appear. **It is as though they were just planted there**, without any evolutionary history." (R Dawkins, The blind watchmaker, London: W.W. Norton 7 Company, 1987, p. 229)

"One of the major unsolved problems of geology and the evolution theory is the occurrence of diversified, multicellular marine invertebrates in lower Cambrian rocks on all the continents and their absence in rocks of greater age." (I. Axelrod, "Early Cambrian Marine Fauna," Science, Vol. 128, 4 July 1958, p. 7)

"Evolutionary biology's deepest paradox concerns this strange discontinuity. Why haven't new animal body plans continued to crawl out of the past hundreds of millions of years? **Why are the ancient body of plans so stable?**" (J.S. Levinton, "The Big Bang of Animal Evolution," Scientific American, Vol. 267, November 1992, p. 84)

"The evolutionary origin of the main groups of animals, and the absence of any record whatsoever of a single member of any of the phyla in the Precambrian rocks remains as explicable on orthodox grounds as it was to Darwin." (T.N. Geoge, Professor of Geology, Glasgow, "Fossils in Evolutionary Perspective," Science Progress, Vol. 48, No. 189, January 1960, p. 5)

THE CAMBRIAN EXPLOSION

A fascinating aspect of the Cambrian Explosion is its apparent speed over some 5 to 10 million years. (Short time for these events to form)

Most textbooks hardly ever or never mention it. This phenomenon is so profound in the fossil record that Scientific America called it, **"Life's Big Bang."**

It is considered one of the biggest challenges to the evolutionary theory. Many reputable and highly accomplished scientists say it is an insurmountable challenge to the theory of evolution and our understanding of Pre Adamic time and the understanding of synchronized events as it happened from roughly 14 billion years ago.

This "Explosion" refers to the great quantity and diversity of life found in what is called the Cambrian layer of the geological column. The Cambrian age is dated by scientists as being about 530 million years old.

What really are interesting is not just what is found in this layer, but what **is** found in the layers above (earlier), and what **is not** found in the layers under (older) it.

"The Cambrian layer has virtually every phyla known to man, all major body plans and enormous varieties of each all coexist in this layer . . . . No evidence of life in the layers underneath (Proterozoic) except microscopic fossils of 2mm and smaller. In the layers above (Ordovician) a steady decline to nearly nothing, the only phylum with an adequate fossil record to appear after the Cambrian was the phylum Bryozoa, (Aquatic invertebrate animals) which is not known

before the early Ordovician" . . . . No evolutionary sequence here, they all coexistent and died simultaneously . . . . Wow!!!! This sounds like creation to me.

At this point I would like to draw your attention back to the four main Eras' in our geological column namely the **Achaean, Palaeozoic, Mesozoic and Cainozoic**.

These different periods of time is separately identified by scientist in accordance with major cataclysmic events that had total or near total extinction of all life as a result . . . . you may say back to back . . . . That is why we have a fossil record.

A fossil record in a certain time frame is nothing more of the evidence of death, or the evidence of the end of that particular period . . . evidence of a sudden cataclysmic event that had lead to the end of that era, period or age for that matter.

That also explain the fact that so many animals and plants died all at once . . . and quick. Remember, for a living organism to become a fossil it need to be embodied, frozen, dried or buried before decaying or the decomposing process starts . . . we are talking immediately, seconds, minutes and at most maybe hours . . . .

Some animals were found with food or pray still in the process of being swallowed . . . indicating rapid burial or one of the above mentioned states . . . completing the first and most important step into fossilisation.

THE K-T EVENT

Sixty-five million years ago about 70% of all species then living on Earth disappeared within a very short period. The disappearances included the last of the great dinosaurs.

The Triassic, Jurassic, and Cretaceous periods known together as the Mesozoic came to an abrupt end.

Palaeontologists speculated and theorized for many years about what could have caused this "mass extinction," known, as the K-T event (Cretaceous-Tertiary Mass Extinction event). Then in 1980 Alvarez, Alvarez, Asaro, and Michels reported their discovery that the peculiar sedimentary clay layer that was laid down at the time of the extinction showed an enormous amount of the rare element iridium.

First seen in the layer near Gubbio, Italy, the same enhancement was soon discovered to be worldwide in that one particular 1-cm (0.4-in.) layer, both on land and at sea. The Alvarez team suggested that the enhancement was the product of a huge asteroid impact.

On Earth most of the iridium and a number of other rare elements such as platinum, osmium, ruthenium, rhodium, and palladium are believed to have been carried down into Earth's core, along with much of the iron, when Earth was largely molten. Primitive "chondritic" meteorites (and presumably their asteroidean parents) still have the primordial solar system abundances of these elements. A chondritic asteroid 10 km (6 mi.) in diameter would contain enough iridium to account for the worldwide clay layer enhancement. This enhancement appears to hold for the other elements mentioned as well.

Since the original discovery, many other pieces of evidence have come to light that strongly support the impact theory. The high temperatures generated by the impact would have caused enormous fires, and indeed soot is found in the boundary clays.

A physically altered form of the mineral quartz that can only be formed by the very high pressures associated with impacts has been found in the K-T layer.

Geologists who preferred other explanations for the K-T event said, "Show us the crater." In 1990 a cosmos chemist named Alan Hildebrand became aware of geophysical data taken 10 years earlier by geophysicists looking for oil in the Yucatan region of Mexico.

There a 180-km (112-mi.) diameter ring structure called "Chicxulub" seemed to fit what would be expected from a 65-million-year-old impact, and further studies have largely served to confirm its impact origin. The Chicxulub crater has been age dated (by the 40Ar/39Ar method) at 65 million years! Such an impact would cause enormous tidal waves, and evidence of just such waves at about that time has been found all around the Gulf.

One can never prove that an asteroid impact "killed the dinosaurs." Many species of dinosaurs (and smaller flora and fauna) had in fact died out over the millions of years preceding the K-T events. The impact of a 10-km asteroid would most certainly have been an enormous insult to life on Earth.

Locally, there would have been enormous shock wave heating and fires, tremendous earthquakes, hurricane winds, and trillions of tons of debris thrown everywhere. It would have created months of darkness and cooler temperatures globally. There would have been concentrated nitric acid rains worldwide. Sulphuric acid aerosols may have cooled Earth for years. Life certainly could not have been easy for those species which did survive. Fortunately such impacts occur only about once every hundred million years.

PROOF ABOUT PRE ADAMIC
TIMES AT THIS STAGE?

1. Life is shown to exist spontaneously in certain Era's.
2. Earth has been destroyed a couple of times just to be populated again and again.
3. All life did not go extinct between eras, periods or ages.
4. Some life forms made it to the next period or ages, others not.
5. Cataclysmic events ended all of these time frames. (Earthquakes, Meteorites etc.)
6. It is unclear how long these periods of total destruction lasted.
7. According to science, evolution does not fit the evidence everywhere or always.
8. There was beginnings and ends of times . . . eras, periods and ages.
9. The rate of evolution is undetermined and sometimes not present.
10. Earth is much older than 6000 years.
11. Different phyla occurred at different times and did not necessarily repeat in following eras, but some could and did.
12. The main body of phyla tend to evolve from small to very large and back again.
13. Life expectancy for dinosaurs was between 75 to 300 years.
14. Landmasses moved away and reformed three times in geological history.
15. Monkeys and apes appear only 65-2 million years ago after the KT event.
16. Modern manlike creatures only appear 2 million years ago.
17. There were a couple of total extinctions on earth.
18. The KT extinction event was 65 million years ago. (End of Mesozoic)

CHAPTER 2

Brain teasers, Psychic's and the Unexplained

PSYCHICS AND OTHER
CONTROVERSIAL VIEWPOINTS

To bring everything into perspective we will have to have a look on what other theory's and myths have to say about the earlier history of mankind and bring some of the evidence into our point of view. This will include Atlantis, the Anunnaki and even life on Mars. To do this we will touch on certain subjects and statements that will be mentioned later in the book again.

Keep in mind that the following chapter are all related to an accumulation of myth, legends, science and folklore at this point. We are also touching on the unexplained.

Various myths, legends, ancient writings and scriptures, works of art, and structures from around the world all tell their own part of the story. Because it is not always clear what the "ancients" meant and for what reason they did certain things, we will shed some light on these mysteries with the aid of esoteric knowledge and the insights of certain known and lesser known psychic intuitive. As mentioned before, in the Bible, the Thora, the Quran and the Mesopotamian myths there is the mention of angelic or godly beings, also called the sons of God, which once came from the heavens and bred with the humans, whose descendants (called: "Nephilim") were described as "giants", which were bigger and stronger compared to the ordinary humans from those times. According to various psychics intuitive these angelic beings originally came from other parts of the universe. A certain group of these beings would once have colonized the planet Mars when life was still possible, but would have fled to earth because of a devastating catastrophe, where they bred with the pre Adamic humans on earth which led to their existence in the current population of modern man. The pyramidal structures on Mars would speak for themselves, which one placed according to a so called planetary electromagnetic grid on the planet, just like in later time's specific pyramids and temples were built according to the grid of the earth.

Various psychics say that these descendants became extinct at the beginning of the last ice age 10 to 5000 before Adam, except for some remnants of some species that are now extinct but would still have lived during medieval times according to the legends from that time.

Descendants of these "giants" became known as "gods" in other civilizations, because they were not only bigger and stronger, but also had superior intellect compared to most of the other people who lived a more primitive life. They could have had their home in the technologically advanced civilization of Atlantis, situated in the Atlantic Ocean and they could also have colonized other parts of the world including Egypt, Peru, and Mexico.

They had a great understanding of nature and because of this they also developed flying machines (which could also move under water like a submarine) by the means of anti-magnetic forces and the planetary electromagnetic grid that was laid out on the planet.

This is why there is the mention among various ancient cultures of "gods" who could fly through the air in what had been described as flying chariots. (The Biblical story of Ezekiel possibly also described such a chariot.)

Before the use of written language, people knew of their past from stories of much older times, which are now known to us as the old myths and legends. The term "myth" is often used to refer to a false or fabricated story, but according to the academic use of this term it only concerns a tradition from the oldest known times of a certain group of people and does not pass judgement on its truth or falsity. Though there are different versions of one certain myth, due to the retelling of the story, it is up to you to consider if such a myth could have a certain base of truth. Some myths are likely not to be meant literal, but mere symbolic, to communicate a message in the form of a story that would be difficult to tell in the literal sense.

The city of Troy was always previously thought of being merely a legend with no basis in reality until it had been found in the year 1870 in Turkey by Frank Calvert and Heinrich Schliemann, on the base of clues from the ancient Hittite and Egyptian texts. As of the year 1998, Troy was added to the UNESCO World Heritage list. Atlantis, which was ever been described in painstaking detail by the most influential Greek philosopher Plato, could be approached in the very same way, for it is remarkable that there are a number of similar myths from various cultures which supposedly never had any form of contact with each other. The ancient Egyptians, Hindus, Chinese, Greeks, and the old Meso-American tribes (Mayas, Aztecs, Incas), all believed that they were the descendants of a lost civilization that disappeared after a natural disaster, what often concerned a huge flood.

MESOPOTAMIAN SCRIPTURES

Ancient Mesopotamia is the land area corresponding to modern-day Iraq and to a lesser extent North-Eastern Syria, South-Eastern Turkey and smaller parts of South-Western Iran. It is also known as the 'land of rivers" because it is located in the area between the two rivers the Tigris and the Euphrates, which were already mentioned as early as in the book "Genesis" from the Tanakh (Hebrew Bible). Later, the Tanakh was adapted by Christianity in the Old Testament and therefore its content is, with the exception of a few passages from the Book of Daniel which had been written in Aramaic, hardly different from the original Old-Hebrew text.

There are certain ancient Mesopotamian myths, including the myths of the, Akkadians, Assyrians, Sumerians and Babylonians, have remarkable similarities with the stories of the Tanakh and the Old Testament. It is known that these Mesopotamian stories are much older and sometimes even more detailed. For example: The story about the person Utnapistim from the Gilgamesh epic is very similar to the flood story that is mentioned in the book of Genesis in the Bible and the Tanakh. This would imply that, these "Bible stories", in all likelihood could have their roots in those earlier myths, instead of beings a diversion, what was previously thought.

The Bible is mainly a compilation of ancient texts, selected by the early church fathers. Texts that people weren't supposed to read, because they were not in accordance to the general Christian orthodox belief, were labelled as uneconomical and were purposely left out in the Bible, and this includes all works that were seen as Apocryphal and Gnostic's, like the "Book of Enoch", even though the Canonical text Genesis 5:24 makes a very shortly reference to Enoch,

"Enoch walked with God; then he was no more, because God took him away."

The full version of the book of Enoch was once thought to be lost, but fortunately this book was later found again in the Ethiopian version of the Bible, where this book previously never was excluded.

In 1945 a jar had been found within the ruins of an ancient monastery in the Egyptian place called Nag Hammadi. Within this jar were found manuscripts that dated from the early days of Christianity, which are now known as the Nag Hammadi writings. Besides the well-known stories from the New Testament there were also found ancient writings that had never been found before, like the Gospel of Mary Magdalene and the Gospel of Thomas. These texts were never included to the Bible because the Christian church considered the contents of these gospels as typical Gnostic, and Christian orthodox belief does not acknowledge the Gnostic views and concepts.

One might think that it could affect the stability and integrity of the Christian community as these books, which are still criticized within the orthodox community, were to be officially added to the Bible.

Within the traditional Christian conceptions of God, there is an unbridgeable distance between man and God, what is quite different in Gnosticism. The fundamental difference between the traditional Christian view and Gnosticism is that not only Jesus Christ is God's son, but each being, and that everything and everyone is part of a total unity that is known in the Gnosticism as the "All", the "Source" or also "the Father". The Father and the Son are symbolic representations where the Father represents the total being while the Son is what is derived from the Father. In Gnostic texts, for example, it is described:

"Like a beam of light is related to the sun, so man is also related to the Source",
"We have 'the features of the Father'",

"We are the heirs of the Father"

"Because you, a mere man, claim to be God" (John 10:33).

Yashua then answered them by quoting Psalm 82:6 which say:

"I have said, ye are gods; and all of you are children of the Most High."

SUMERIAN MYTHS AND LEGENDS

According to scriptures the Sumerians had a flourishing culture and wrote all kinds of things like we would do today on clay tablets in cuneiform script, including: rules, laws, poetry, and stories (myths). These are currently the earliest recognized forms of writing. It is characterized by a composition of wedge-shaped formations and was used by the Sumerians, Akkadians (Assyrians/Babylonians) and Persians. In the 1760s, Karsten Biebuhr brought back bricks with cuneiform from a dig in Egypt, Arabia, and Syria. In 1802, Georg Friedrich Grotefend, a German school teacher, was the first to decipher cuneiform.

According to the Hebrew Bible—all Israelites were descended from Abraham, who was born in the Sumerian city of Ur, and later migrated with his family to Canaan (which is now roughly corresponding to modern-day Israel, Palestine, Lebanon, and the western parts of Jordan and Syria.) This could mean that Abraham could have heard of these myths, possibly he was even grown up with it, which he later could have written down in the Torah; the first five books of the Tanakh.

German psychic intuitive Ute Kretzschmar (who assumedly channelled the groups of ascended masters known as "Confucius" and "Kuthumi") described the "Elohim" in her book: "Die Seele in den Meisterjahren" (2003), as an exalted, re-fused complete being existing of souls that completed their cycles of incarnation in the "dual universe" (part of the universe were "duality" exists). It was the further development of the ascended masters and arch-angels. They are called "angels" because in that state they are fused with the dimension of angels.

This re-fused total being bears the experiences of many in "himself". "Eloah" does not know the experience of being divided into multiple beings and is the only non-divided total being that can enter the dual universe.

Genesis 1:26 implicates mankind was created to the likeness of its creators: the Elohim, instead of one sole being, as it very clearly states:

"God (Elohim) said: Let us make man in our own image."

This message also echoes through Greek mythology, where it is stated that man was created in the image of the "gods", and the section of the early Sumerian epic of creation: the "Enûma Eliš", in which the "gods" did create mankind (ch. 6:4).

Also, in the story from the Bible where the Israelites sing at the crossing of the Red Sea: "Who is like you, O YHWH, among the gods?" (Exodus 15:11), actually could imply that YHWH wasn't the only known god, and that people believed that other gods did exist, though these people considered the "Lord" being the One Almighty and most righteous and powerful among the "gods".

From the Book of Exodus:

> "Who is like you, O YHWH, among the gods?
> Who is like you, majestic in holiness, awesome in glorious
> deeds, doing wonders?"—Exodus 15:11

These observations eventually overthrew the belief that Israel had always worshipped no other god but the God of Israel known as Yahweh (YHWH) in the Tanakh and Jehovah (JHVH) in the English and Greek Bible.

THE ANUNNAKI

"Anunnaki" is generally believed to mean something to the effect of "Those of Royal Blood" (Leick, Gwendolyn: "A Dictionary of Ancient Near Eastern Mythology"), but linguists are actually divided about its true meaning. The name is composed of the following words:

Anun: Is the name of the Anunnaki's supreme god: Lord; leader; king. His kingdom was "in the expanse of the heavens", and he is known—like the god Uranus—as a personification of the heaven/sky. (note the resemblance with the Pharaoh's names: <u>Amon</u>otep and Tutank<u>amon</u>)

na: Meaning "to send". In many Acadian, Sumerian, Assyrian and Old Babylonian texts and inscriptions, "Na" was written as "Ina", and meant in, from within, so on.

ki: means "earth" in Acadian and Sumerian, but also means "the underworld", "the netherworld", "the world of death". They regarded earth sometimes as the "world of death" because everything in the earthly "material word" eventually perishes.

In the book "The Twelfth Planet" (1976), author and expert in ancient languages Zechariah Sitchin translated this word as: "those who from heaven to earth came." The word "Anunnaki" may also be translated as: "the descendants of An (u) on earth" or "the descendants of the gods of heaven on earth", which in turn is similar to the term "sons of God" as mentioned in the book Genesis. Because of the similarities between the Anunnaki from the Mesopotamian myths and the Elohim from the Holy Scriptures, it is possible that they are both and the same groups.

The word Anunnaki is also similar to the name of the group of giants who are called "Anakim" in old Hebrew or Enkaites in the Biblical book Numbers, 13:32-33, which translates to "long neck ones". The Anakim would be one of the many names for the giants or pointing to a certain group of giants.

The word Anunnaki is similar to the word: "annunagi" which is usually translated as: "the shining ones" (shining with glorious light, as seen by those who could perceive their magnificent radiating auras), probably meant in the sense of: "the magnificent ones".

The names Anunnaki and Annunagi are variations of each other. It is considered that the word for the "Nagas"; the word for the serpent gods/people, who are mentioned in the ancient Vedic scriptures from India, could be derived from the Sumerian word "Anunnagi". The Nagas called themselves "Devas", a term for all beings that which are on a higher plane of existence, compared to earthly humans. The Avestan word "Daeva" means: "being of shining light".

EXTRATERRESTRIAL VISITORS

Certain myths seem to be interpretations of what people, in these ancient times, believed what had happened, according to their own understanding and frame of reference. Most of the times words to explain what happened were just not invented at the time and the lack of understanding and the inability to describe the event ends up to sound like myths to us.

They tried to describe an experience they could not explain any other way than that they must have been in contact by a "Supreme Being", gods or angels; Messengers from the "Divine". Many texts talks about beings that came from the "heavens" known as gods, angels or star beings. In some sense we could regard them by modern language as being from extraterrestrial origin; beings from other parts in the universe.

Today, there exists the understanding that "heaven" is the place where one goes after death, but the word "heaven" originally referred specifically to the sky and all that is above, including space and the "heavenly bodies", which includes the planets and the stars. Thus, the Sumerian and Akkadian words for "heaven" could be replaced with "above", and this would mean that, according to these stories, these beings came from the skies.

The theory that the "gods" from ancient mythology were possibly beings of extraterrestrial origin was popularized with the books of Italian journalist and writer Peter Kolosimo (most notably: "Non e terrestre" (1968); which translates to "Not of this World"), and the later Swiss author Erich von Däniken with "Chariots of the Gods? (1968)", and was later dubbed as the "Ancient Astronaut Theory".

American writer Zechariah Sitchin (1920-2010) studied old and new Hebrew, and all sorts of Semitic and European languages, and had great knowledge of the Old Testament. Sitchin's work is about his own translation and re-interpretation of the ancient Sumerian clay tablets and seems to fuel some more credibility to the ancient astronaut theory. His hypotheses are not widely accepted by scientists and academics, which often dismiss his work as pseudoscience and pseudo history.

At the time Sitchin wrote his first book: "The 12th Planet" (1976), only specialists could read the Sumerian writings. Using his knowledge of ancient texts, he researched and re-translated the ancient Sumerian writings according to his own interpretations which happened to differ at certain points from the previous translations of others.

According to him these tablets are about the long story of technologically advanced humanoid beings from another planet outside our solar system they referred to as "Nibiru", who came to earth some hundreds of thousands of years ago with the purpose to mine gold to save the atmosphere of their dying home planet. In ancient texts they were referred to as the "Anunnaki".

The operations on earth were in charge of two half brothers with the titles of Enlil "Lord of Heaven" and Enki, "Lord of the earth". Because the work was too heavy for the small workforce, they genetically altered the most intelligent and capable species available at that time on earth, which were ape-like human beings (presumably the "Homo-Erectus"). Over the last 500 years, thousands of ancient gold mines where found in Africa, including a 200,000 years old metropolis dubbed as "Adam's Calendar" which had been discovered in the year 2009. It is possibly relevant to this story, because mining for gold was very hard work and needed organisation.

The idea was to create a type of worker that was capable enough, but not too intelligent to question and resist their work. Later however, Enki—against the will of Enlil—decided to make this species more intelligent, and so a species closer to modern man came into existence. This could be the reason why archaeologists are still not able to find the supposed "missing link" between upright walking ape-man "Homo-Erectus" and modern man "Homo-Sapiens".

If this theory is correct, it would mean that modern man is actually a hybrid being, genetically altered by these technologically advanced extraterrestrial beings that mixed some of their own genes with the genes of the earth's ape-man. In that view, the ape-man but also the extraterrestrial beings to some degree, could both be our genetic ancestors.

After time things got out of hand with the human race when the daughters of man produced offspring from the so-called fallen angels from the sons of God, a lot of sin and suffering had been done on earth. Enlil was therefore convinced that the tempering with "man" from earth was a terrible sin against the Cosmos and that it had to be undone, which led to the great flood or the Deluge. His brother Enki however secretly saved one pius man and his family, against the will of Enlil, though probably more people would have survived this great disaster.

The Gnostic text, "The Apocalypse of Adam", also tell about a certain sub creator, referred to as the "demiurge", who created Adam and Eve. In these Gnostic texts, the demiurge is seen as the fashioner of the materialistic world.

Various Gnostic systems view both the demiurge and material world however as evil creations and the immaterial (spirit) world as being good; the reason for this is probably because of the attempts of the sub creator to destroy mankind in the great Deluge. Because of this conflicting ideology, Gnostic texts were not included in the Bible.

Since the principal evidence for Sitchin's claims lies in his own personally derived etymologies and not on any scholarly agreed interpretations, his theories remain at most pseudoscience to the majority of academics. Sitchin's work has been criticized for some flawed methodology and mistranslations of ancient texts as well as for incorrect astronomical and scientific claims.

Many scholars today disagree with Sitchin's translations of specific terms like Anunnaki as: "those who from heaven came to earth", and Nephilim as: "people of the fiery rockets". He also uses the word "Nephilim" synonymous with the word "Anunnaki", though in the Bible this term is only applied to these so-called "giants"; the offspring of the "sons of God and daughters of men". At present we know more about the ancient Mesopotamian languages compared to the time when Sitchin wrote his first books, and therefore he had to rely more on his own speculation.

The depictions like cylinder seal VA 243, in which he sees all the planets of our solar system (including Pluto) and the extra planet which he believes is Nibiru has been regarded as highly controversial.

A lot of scientists and astronomers believe his translations are incorrect about the theory of another planet, called Nibiru, outside our solar system. The word "Nibiru" is Akkadian and the meaning is uncertain. As the word "Hiburu" or "Niburu" could be a variation of the word "Nibiru" or "Niburu", it might be that the word "Hebrew" originated from the similar sounding word: "Hiburu". Nibiru was known as the celestial body or region which was sometimes associated with the god Marduk. While certain researchers believe that "Marduk" was the ancient name for the planet Jupiter, Sitchin believed that this planet that was known as "Marduk" in Babylonian and Nibiru in Sumerian times was a planet outside our solar system.

He saw evidence for his theory in depictions of things which he thought could be rockets, but these were more likely depictions of mountains, pillars, obelisks or menhirs. Personally I don't think this "evidence" is not very convincing at all, but was often shown at his presentations.

In contrast to currently generally accepted translations, he has his own interpretation of the Enûma Eliš: the Babylonian creation myth, in which he is convinced this myth is about celestial bodies instead of Sumerian gods.

He is criticised to have used many other sources and mythologies besides the Sumerian myths to construct a story, like in his controversial book "The Lost Book of Enki". Many scholars think these myths are generally unrelated to each other, but it is undeniable though, that certain myths from various ancient civilizations share a lot of similarities with each other, especially these myths which are about a great flood.

Although Zechariah Sitchin's theories are now proven to be certainly not 100% correct; as a fore-runner in ancient Mesopotamian languages he brought forth some refreshing new interesting theories, views and insights, and added to the popularity of both the "ancient astronaut theory" and the ancient Sumerian gods; the Anunnaki. Basically, Sitchin's translations seem to be quite similar to those from others, including world leading Assyriologist Samuel Noach Kramer (1897-1990), with the distinct difference however that these gods weren't just being regarded as "divine" beings, but as beings which came from another planet.

This seems to support the vision of numerous psychics intuitive who state that the "humanoid" life form does not only exists on planet Earth and that it had its origins from other places in the universe. To name but a few psychics who mentioned humanoid extraterrestrial beings:

Dutch trance medium Daan Akkerman (www.esoterischgenootschap.nl) explained in his book "Lanto 1: Atlantis", that these "visitors" who had been mentioned on the Sumerian clay tablets, were "advanced spiritual beings" which came from the star constellation of Orion and needed gold to restore or save, the planet Mars, instead of Sitchin's hypothetical planet Nibiru.

According to Daan Akkerman: On far away planets it shall be discovered that huge buildings, like those megalithic pyramids on the earth, would have existed for a long time and that these buildings are actually reflections and mirages of something that actually exists for a long time in the Cosmos. (See the chapter "Life on Mars in the Ancient Past" for some examples.)

Scientists would be once convinced that man is in fact not from the earth, and that he only became into its current form because of the earthly structures, and that there were times when man could travel as a transparent being between the many planets. Man was ever capable during the ages of Atlantis and Lemuria, to travel completely as a transparent being in so-called space ships, which were made from a transparent material and did have a form which currently not known on earth.

Daan Akkerman described these angels as extraterrestrial beings that already visited planet Earth since the early times of Lemuria. During the times of Atlantis they were frequent visitors to mankind, offering knowledge. Atlantis was actually in contact with so-called "space ships" from various solar systems. Mankind also, was able to travel to various solar systems by the means of the non-physical astral body.

According to the readings of trance medium Rev. Douglas James Cottrell (PhD) (www.douglascottrell.com), who connects with his "soul mind" to the Akashic Records by "deep trance meditation" (DTM), there had been intelligent "human" life on Mars some 30 billion years ago, but had to flee to other planets, including earth, because of a great catastrophe.

The name "Mardock" is quite similar to "Marduk"; who was generally known as an ancient Babylonian god/ruler, son of Ea/Enki, but also the later Babylonian name for the planet which was earlier known by the Sumerians as the planet Nibiru. (According to Zechariah Sitchin's theory, Nibiru was a planet outside our solar system. Quite possibly the planet Nibiru was renamed to Marduk since the reign of the god/ruler Marduk.)

THE SONS OF GOD

According to Edgar Cayce, these "sons of God"; these "angels", were spiritually advanced beings from other parts of the universe who consisted of those souls led by Amilius: the Christ soul, who voluntarily became entrapped in materialism in order to assist the first wave of trapped souls to free themselves and find their way back to their original state of consciousness; to God. They accomplished this by steering the process of physical evolution in a way that created more appropriate physical forms for these souls.

When at last the desired physical human form was created, Amilius physically incarnated as the first "Adam" in the Garden of Eden in Mesopotamia. This of course is reminiscent of the ancient Mesopotamian myths regarding the creation of modern man by the "Anunnaki". The Christ soul would later have been re-incarnated as: Enoch, Hermes (Thoth), Melchizedek, Joseph, Joshua, Asaph, Yashua, Zend and ultimately Jesus; the man who was first to attain complete "at-one-mint" as the perfect divine-human unity known as the "Christ".

The "sons of God" followed when they came down from the heavens and saw that the "daughters of men" were beautiful. And indeed; as a result many became entrapped in materialism. The few that remained faithful to good and righteousness started to call themselves the "children of the Law of One", while those were in opposition to their law, called themselves the "sons of Belial".

Douglas James Cottrell (PhD) spoke during his sessions regarding the planet Mars, about humanoid beings which once lived on Mars but eventually escaped to other planets, including the earth, because of a huge disaster that made the planet inhabitable. The Martians that arrived on earth survived and became Earthlings. From his sessions it was however not clear if there already were humans that lived on the earth at, and before that time, but if that was the case it would be possible that these refugees from Mars were the "sons of God" (Bene Elohim/Igigi/Grigori) that had been mentioned in the ancient scriptures. According to Zechariah Sitchin's translation of the Sumerian clay tablets, the Igigi had a station on Mars (Sumerian: Lahmu), what could mean that the Igigi actually were colonists of Mars.

The book: "A Dweller on two Planets" (1894) by Phylos the Thibetan (claimed to have been received through channelling by Frederick S. Oliver) also mentioned the term "the Sons of God" in accordance with the lost continent of Atlantis. (More about this book in the chapter about Atlantis.) Quoted from page 204:

> "Atl, known through the olden earth as Atlan, Queen of the Seas," and her people as "Children of Incal," i. e., "Of the Sun," and as the "Sons of God." How are the mighty fallen!"

In the book "Initiation" by Elisabeth Haich, she tells the story of her own life where she recalls a past life experience in Egypt. She mentions the pharaoh from that time as being from a lineage of people called "the sons of God". These could have been the same people Edgar Cayce referred to as the "children of the Law of One", as both the "children of the Law of One" and the "sons of Belial" were the descendants of the "sons of God".

According to them, the family of this seed line, "left their bodies" just before the coming "age of darkness". The book mentions that these sons of God "de-materialized" their advanced technology and left the earth plane to enter into the Spirit realm, from where they could offer better aid and guidance to the still evolving human's beings. These beings already were part of the group dedicated to the spiritual evolution of mankind.

LEGENDARY CREATURES

One of Edgar Cayce's sessions speak of half-human beasts, varying from the size of midgets to giants, that began to populate earth from some point in time, but were mostly wiped out after the great flood; According to his readings, this eventually became the basis for the legendary creatures of Greek and Roman mythology; like the unicorn, mermaid, minotaur, Cyclops, and the satyr.

Lytle Robinson also mentioned these mixtures based on the Edgar Cayce readings in his book "Edgar Cayce's Story of the Origin and Destiny of Man (1972)":

> "Overcoming the monstrosities, the mixtures and the animal influences was accomplished through rebirth, surgery and evolution towards a more divine purpose. The animal influences finally disappeared about 9000 B.C. Remnants of these creatures, with their appendages of wings, tails, feathers, claws and hooves were later depicted accurately in Assyrian and Egyptian art. The sphinx is a notable example of one of the earlier monstrosities."

Jon Peniel, author of the book: "Children of the Law of One & the Lost Teachings of Atlantis (1998)", wrote the following:

> "You have probably heard of mythological beings such as the Minotaur, Centaur, Mermaid, etc . . . The Minotaur had a bull's head and a human body, the Centaur, a human head and torso with a horse's body. You may also have seen pictures of Egyptian 'gods' with animal heads and human bodies, or

animal bodies and human heads (like the Sphinx). In the Pacific regions, ancient drawings and carvings of 'bird headed' humans can be found on both sides of the ocean. Why do you think so much of this exists? Many legends and myths have some foundation in fact, and this is no exception. The ancient teachings from Atlantis reveal that such creatures did indeed exist and that their origins were not what you might expect—they were the fallen angelic beings from the 'first wave' of materialization on earth."

Winged reliefs which often are given descriptions like "Winged Genie", or "Genius". The general thought is that these reliefs depict "genies" or spirit beings, doing certain rituals. Like in the depictions of the Ishtar Gate, the symbol of the Chamomile flower is apparent on the wristbands they are wearing on both wrists. There are "beings" seen here who seem to have two sets of wings, while others are depicting with none. These eagle heads doesn't seem to be masks, because of the clearly human styled hair, and at some reliefs like the one below-left even beard growth is seen below the beak. Who wants to put styled hair and even a beard on a mask if its purpose was to faithfully represent the head of an eagle?

In his readings, Edgar Cayce mentioned the so-called "Temple of Sacrifice", which was a spiritually based hospital or health centre, and the "Temple Beautiful", which was a school of higher learning and vocational training. According to Edgar Cayce's material, these temples had nothing to do with human or animal sacrifices but instead the sacrifice of the ego and selfishness was meant, to develop oneself in the way to a more divine purpose. These centres gave hope to humanity that their bodies could be transformed, to heal the body and soul and also to get rid of the animalistic influences which had perverted mankind on a large scale. These reliefs seen above may have to do with the rituals performed in those centres.

". . . for, in the period, there was the Temple of Sacrifice; or that wherein the body was shed of the animal representations through the sacrificing of the desires of the appetite, through the changing of self in the temple service."

(Source: Reading 275-33)

Treatments for correction of bodily and mental deformities were accomplished not only through the use of surgery, medicines, electrical therapy, massage, spinal adjustments and the like; but by diet, the vibrations of music, colours, dancing, song, chanting, and most important, by the use of meditation for raising the spiritual vibration within the body. There is actually a high relation between mind and matters where scientists are in present time are just scratching the surface with their theories about quantum mechanics.

"The passage of individuals through the experiences in the Temple of Sacrifice was much as would be in the hospitalization, or a hospital of the present day, when there have become antagonistic conditions within the physical body, such as to produce tumours, wins[cysts], warts or such.

Magnify this into the disturbances which were indicated, or illustrated in conditions where there was the body or figure of the horse, or the head of the horse with the body of man; or where there were the various conditions indicated in the expressions by the pushing of spirit into physical matter until it became influenced by or subject to same. Such influences we see in the present manifested as habits, or the habit-forming conditions.

Then there are, or were the needs for the attempts to operate, as well as to adhere to diets and activities to change the natures of the individuals; that their offspring, as well as themselves, might bring forth that which was in keeping with—or a pattern of—those influences in which there were souls or spirits with the idea, or ideal, of seeking light."

During one of his sessions, deep trance medium Douglas James Cottrell described the temple complex of Angkor Wat in Cambodia as a health centre similar to the "Temple Beautiful" and the "Temple Sacrifice", that was built by those that had migrated from Atlantis (Poseidon) and settled in this region. It would originally have been constructed some 10,000 years ago. At these temple complexes there are also depictions of humans with animalistic features, like people who are seen with the tail of a snake in place of human legs. (Source: Douglas James Cottrell PhD: Secrets of Angkor Wat, by Rammsteinregeln.)

THE GREAT DELUGE

There is many ancient myths from many different cultures over the world concerning a great flood. However, this does not have to mean that every myth was talking about the same disaster.

In the Mesopotamian myths; The "gods" either created or foresaw the coming flood. The Lord Enlil saw this happening as an opportunity to undo their creation, which they thought was huge failure because of the corruption and lawlessness of the people which started with the interference of the "fallen angels" and the birth of the giants.

The god Enki (Ea), regarded as a co-creator and protector of mankind, didn't want to destroy his creation so, despite the agreement of the gods to let mankind perish, he told a pious man known as Ziusudra (Sumerian), Utna-pishtim (Old Babylonian), and Noah (both Babylonian and Hebrew "Book of Genesis") about the coming flood and instructed him to build a giant wooden ark to save him and his family.

According to Sumerian mythology, Enki also assisted humanity to survive the Deluge designed to kill them. In the Legend of Atrahasis, Enlil, the king of the gods, sets out to eliminate humanity, the noise of whose mating is offensive to his ears.

He successively sends drought, famine and plague to eliminate humanity, but Enki thwarts his half-brother's plans by teaching Atrahasis about irrigation, granaries and medicine. Humans again proliferate a fourth time. Enraged, Enlil convenes a Council of Deities and gets them to promise not to tell humankind that he plans their total annihilation.

Enki does not tell Atrahasis, but instead tells the walls of Atrahasis' (a.k.a. Utnapishtim, Ziusudra, Noah) reed hut of Enlil's plan, thus covertly rescuing Atrahasis by either instructing him to build some kind of a boat for his family, or by bringing him into the heavens in a magic boat.

After the seven day Deluge, the flood hero frees a swallow, a raven and a dove in an effort to find if the flood waters have receded. On the boat landing, a sacrifice is organised to the gods. Enlil is angry his will has been thwarted yet again, and Enki is named as the culprit. As the god of what we would call ecology, Enki explains that Enlil is unfair to punish the guiltless Atrahasis for the sins of his fellows, and secures a promise that the gods will not eliminate humankind if they practice birth control and live within the means of the natural world.

The threat is made, however, that if humans do not honour their side of the covenant the gods will be free to wreak havoc once again. This is apparently the oldest of the surviving Middle Eastern Deluge myths."

According to Edgar Cayce, the biblical "Deluge" would have happened around 22,006 BCE. Because of the cataclysm, the Atlantean land broke up into three large and two smaller islands. It is not to be confused with the final demise of Atlantis which happened around 9,900 BCE, when it finally sunk and disappeared into the Atlantic Ocean.

The book: "A Dweller on two Planets" by Phylos the Thibetan and claimed to be channelled through Frederick S. Oliver, described various previous lives of a soul called Phylos, including one where he lived in Atlantis, and he also described some insights from the "Book of Life", which is also known as the "Akashic Records" in New Age terminology. At page 404 of this book, the author wrote that he saw in the Book of Life that the vessel of "Nepth" (apparently Noah), was carried by the great flood from Atlantis into Africa, from where it at finally came to a halt in Asia.

Noah's story also bears some similarities with both the Chinese "Fu Xi" (or "Fohi"), who was the very first ruler of China according to Chinese mythology, and "Manu"; known in various Hindu traditions as the progenitor of mankind and the very first king to rule this earth.

THE TOWER OF BABEL

Before the Tower of Babel event the whole earth was speaking one understandable language, the people in the land of Shinar, started to build a city with a large tower that would have its top in the heavens to save them next time a flood occurs, so that they wouldn't be scattered abroad upon the face of the earth. We can assume that, for this reason, it could have served as a large marker that still would be seen at very large distances. In Genesis 11:6-8, the LORD saw what they were up to and said:

> "If as one people speaking the same language they have begun to do this, then nothing they plan to do will be impossible for them. Come, let us go down and confuse their language so they will not understand each other. So the LORD scattered them from there over all the earth, and they stopped building the city."

There is a Sumerian myth that is similar to that of the story of the Tower of Babel, called Enmerkar and the Lord of Aratta. This myth talks about the building of a massive ziggurat in Eridu by Enmerkar; the king of Uruk. (According to Sumerian mythology, Enmerkar was the mortal son of the god Utu and Aia.) Here he demanded a tribute of precious materials from Aratta for its construction, at one point reciting an incantation imploring the god Enki to "disrupt" (according to Samuel Noah Kramer's translation) the linguistic unity of the inhabited regions—named as Shubur, Hamazi, Sumer, Uri-ki (Akkad), and the Martu land.

The part of the Sumerian epic entitled "Enmerkar and the Lord of Aratta" seems to be related to the story of the Tower of Babel and the confusion of tongues:

"Once upon a time there was no snake, there was no scorpion, there was no hyena, there was no lion, there was no wild dog, no wolf, there was no fear, no terror, and man had no rival. In those days, the lands of Subur (and) Hamazi, harmony-tongued Sumer, the great land of the decrees of prince ship, Uri, the land having all that is appropriate, the land Martu, resting in security, the whole universe, the people in unison to Enlil in one tongue [spoke]. (Then) Enki, the lord of abundance (whose) commands are trustworthy, the lord of wisdom, who understands the land, the leader of the gods, endowed with wisdom, the lord of Eridu changed the speech in their mouths, [brought] contention into it, into the speech of man that (until then) had been one."

Today in the place of Al-Mahawil in Bābil (Babel), Iraq, we can find the remains of a ziggurat dedicated to Marduk in the city of Babylon of the 6th century BCE, known as the "Etemenanki"; which translates to: "temple of the foundation of heaven and earth". In 1913, archaeologist and architect Robert Koldewey started its excavation after it had been rediscovered by the native Arabian population. It had been regarded to be the ruins of the Tower of Babel.

The structure was also known as the "Tower of Jupiter Belus" (Belus translates like Bêl to "Lord") and had been Hellenised by Herodotus to "the Tower of Zeus Belus". A cuneiform tablet from Uruk, written in 229 BCE, states that the tower was made up of seven terraces. After the fall of Babylon it never had been restored. Its ruins can be found with Google Maps at coordinates: 32 32'10N, 44 25'14E.

ATLANTIS, LOST CIVILIZATION

Greek philosopher, Plato wrote about Atlantis in his dialogues that it was told by the character Critias that his grandfather heard about the story of Atlantis hundred years ago from Solon, a well-known Athenian poet and politician. Solon heard about the story during his stay in Egypt in 565 BCE. The story tells us that before the advanced Greek civilization, there once was another highly advanced civilization called "Atlantis", they were an island nation. Plato's account is regarded by many as the most credible account of these peoples and their lost civilization.

Plato wrote that Atlantis was situated beyond these "Pillars of Hercules", somewhere in the Atlantic Ocean. For generations its people lived virtuous lives until greed and power began to corrupt them. Its final destruction happened some 9,500 years ago; In a single day and night; the land of Atlantis disappeared in the depths of the sea due to violent earthquakes and floods. Many scholars today believe Plato's story about Atlantis was a fictional account, a possible metaphor, for the reason that there is no known land or civilization which fits its descriptions; however Plato himself did imply in his own story, even multiple times, that it once really existed. The earlier ancient Greek historian Herodotus used the name "Atlantis Sea" for the sea past the "Pillars of Heracles" (the Strait of Gibraltar), which may imply that Herodotus also knew something about Atlantis.

In "Timaeus and Critias", Plato wrote that Atlantis was founded by Poseidon, known as "the god of the sea", who according to the myths fell in love with a mortal woman named Cleito. Cleito gave birth to five sets of twin boys, and the domain was divided amongst them. The eldest, named Atlas became the first king of Atlantis. Poseidon had his own temple within the citadel of Atlantis City. Its exterior was entirely covered with silver and its pinnacles with gold, and the interior of the temple was of ivory, gold, silver, and orichalch, even to the pillars and floor. The temple contained a colossal statue of Poseidon standing in a chariot drawn by six winged horses, about him a hundred mermaids riding on dolphins. Arranged outside the building were golden statues of the first ten kings and their wives.

The great library of Alexandria in Egypt was possibly the greatest library that has ever existed on earth according to legend, a large source of ancient literature, which for thousands of years had been the Western world's most important centre of learning. Historians tell us that it was conceived and opened either during the reign of Ptolemy I (323-283 BCE) or his son Ptolemy II (283-246 BCE), but its literature could have been much older, and could have contained more evidence for the ancient continent and society of Atlantis.

The Roman historian Ammianus Marcellinus (330-400 CE) wrote that the intelligentsia of Alexandria regarded the story and destruction of Atlantis a historical fact, It was described as a class of earthquakes that suddenly, by a violent motion, opened up huge mouths and so swallowed up portions of the earth, as once in the Atlantic Ocean a large island was swallowed up.

Julius Caesar "accidentally" burned down the library, but probably not completely. In this time, a neighbouring library in the Serapeum temple still existed. It was finally completely destroyed during the conquest of Egypt by the Arabs in the year 642 AD. In 2004, a Polish-Egyptian excavation team announced its discovery of the remains of the long lost lecture halls, or auditoria of the library, which proved without any doubt that this great library truly had existed. According to Edgar Cayce the library was initially established in the year 10,300 BCE.

The loss of these ancient writings that possibly included these that were on the subject of Atlantis, as historical fact, is the reason why we have known so little about it? There is a lot been written about Atlantis, even in this day and age; It is even said that it is the most documented subject in the history of literature. It is possible that it is referred to in ancient Hindu texts and it also became the subject of numerous esoteric, occult and the official works, and clairvoyant readings. However, many of the presented claims about Atlantis still remain to be proven for it to be regarded as factual evidence. Personally I recommend reading the book "Atlantis: Insights from a Lost Civilization" (1997) by Shirley Andrews which summarises geologic and metaphysical evidence that makes it likely that it really had existed.

"Atlantis" is a remarkable name; It is often thought to be connected to the god Atlas from Greek mythology: one of the sons of the god Poseidon and the first king of Atlantis. The name is actually not Greek but probably originates from Nahuat: the language of the Aztecs. The name seems to be a composition of several words from the Nahua language; "atl" is the word for "water" and "atlan" means: in the middle of the water. (On its own, "antis" means "copper".) "Aztec" is the Nahuatl word for "people from Aztlán". According to the history of the Aztec people of Meso America, they originally came from a now lost land called "Aztlán".

Mexican polymath and writer Carlos de Sigüenza y Góngora (1645-1700) came into possession of an unique collection of manuscripts and paintings from the indigenous Mexican people, which he inherited from his friend Don Juan de Alva; the son of Fernando de Alva Cortés Ixtlilxochitl and a direct descendant of the kings of Texcoco. Ixtlilxochitl was a learned man and wrote for the first time the history of Mexico into Spanish. In 1668, Sigüenza began the study of Aztec history and Toltec writing, and concluded that there had been another race of people before the Toltec's named the Olmos. He believed that these Olmos came from the mythical island of Atlantis and that they were responsible for the building of the pyramids at Teotihuacán. Later, after his death, his work was partly destroyed by the inquisition and another part was lost.

Luckily, the Italian adventurer and traveller Gemelli Careri (1651-1725), with whom de Sigüenza also did share his information, included de Signüenza's information about Atlantis and the ancient Mexican calendar in his own book: "Giro del Mondo". (Source: "The Mayan Prophecies"

(1995) by Adrian Gilbert and Maurice Cottrell.) In New Spain, Careri had the opportunity to study the pyramids carefully and their affinity to the Egyptian pyramids led him to believe that the ancient Egyptians and the Amerindians both descended from the inhabitants of Atlantis.

OTHER REFERENCES TO ATLANTIS

The Greek historian and rhetorician Theopompos (c. 380 BCE) wrote of the huge size of Atlantis and its cities of Machimum and Eusebius and a golden age free from disease and manual labour.

Greek historian Diodorus Siculus (flourished between 60 and 30 BCE) made a reference about Phoenicians had been to the immense "Atlantic island". He also wrote that these "Atlanteans" were engaged in war with the Amazonians.

Greek historian Timagenus recorded the war between Atlantis and Europe. Tribes in ancient France said that Atlantis was their original home. Proculus (reigned c. 280 CE) visited the islands of Africa (Canaries or Azores) where the natives told him of the destruction of Atlantis.

The Norse mythology mention of "Asgard"; a land or capital city situated in the centre of the world where the gods lived. It may be that this Asgard was in fact the central situated capital of Atlantis which was named: "Atlantis City" by Plato and that the gods could be the Ashvins/Asvins who are mentioned in the old Indian texts as Vedic gods who symbolised the rising and setting of the sun and appeared in a golden chariot. These chariots or aircraft of the Ashvins from the old Vedic texts were more or less described in the same manner as the aircraft described in the book "A Dweller on Two Planets" (1894). This could mean that the Atlanteans, the citizen of Atlantis City, were known by the people of ancient India as the Ashvins and as "the gods" in Northern-Europe.

The ancient "Oera Linda Book" from the Netherlands mentions the submerged Atlantic island known as "Atlan" by volcanic eruptions, earthquakes and rapid sea level changes. Its group of habitants who were followers of the goddess Freya, fled to the place they later called "Fray's Land", currently known as the Dutch region of Friesland.

In the ancient writings of the Aztecs and Mayans, the Chillum Balaam, Dresden Codex, Popular Vouch, Codex Cartesian's and Torino Manuscript also had been interpreted as histories of the destruction of the lost continents of both Atlantis and Lemuria. The Aztecs even mention the name of the place of which they came as "Aztlán", a possible reference to Atlantis.

English occult writer and inventor James Churchyard (1851-1936) wrote several volumes of books documenting ancient writings he claims to have translated in Southeast Asia concerning Atlantis and Mu, while geologist William Given claimed to have excavated identical tablets in Mexico.

Many ancient writings and stories from Greece, Egypt, the Mayans and the Aztecs, the Basques from Spain, the Gaul's from France, the tribes of the Canary and Azores islands, the Frisians from the Netherlands, and many Amerindian tribes all speak of their origins from a large sunken land in the region of the Atlantic Ocean.

The psychic Edgar Cayce (1877-1945) referred to Atlantis as fact - not fiction. In a number of his readings, he spoke about past lives, travelled to in a heighten state of Hypnosis and trance, people once had lived in Atlantis. Among Edgar Cayce's 14,306 documented readings, exactly 700—which is less than 5% mentioned Atlantis.

According to Cayce, in the beginning, Atlantis was not a mere island but a large continent of the size of Europe, including Asia in Europe that stretched from the Gulf of Mexico to the Mediterranean Sea. Evidences of this lost civilization could be found in the Pyrenees and Morocco at one side and in British Honduras, Yucatan and America on the other side. Some parts including the British West Indies and the Bahamas once were part of that huge continent, and the islands of the Azores once were its large mountain tops.

Edgar Cayce suggest that 52,000 years ago, volcanic eruptions and earthquakes started to cause a shift of the magnetic poles of the earth which resulted in the loss of land in Atlantis and eventually became an archipelago of five islands. With the upheavals, the initial migrations from Atlantis took place in small numbers to the east and west. The earliest settlements were in the region of the Pyrenees in France and Spain and later in Central and South America.

The "Encyclopaedia Britannica", the original Canary Island Gouaches: "are thought to have been of Cro-Magnon origin". Archaeology tells us that Cro-Magnon man "invaded" the western shores of Europe and North Africa, in several waves around 35,000 BCE. According to the theories of Scottish folklorist Lewis Spence and theosophical writers like Walter Scott-Elliot, these people were immigrants from the continent of Atlantis.

From "The History of Atlantis (1927)" by Lewis Spence:

> "The discovery of this race [Cro-Magnon]. . . . At once aroused profound interest in the scientific world, for the height and brain-capacity remarked in the skeletal specimens recovered was so extraordinary as to force anthropologists to the conclusion that at one time a much higher type of man must have dwelt in Europe." (p. 80)"

Within the period from 28,200 to 18,000 BCE, there was another shift of the magnetic poles of the earth, which caused volcanic eruptions which led to great earth changes and the start of the last known glacial age.

During this period Atlantis lost land again and became one island that was connected by a chain of islands to the land of North-America. Because of the upheavals, there were large movements of people who were migrating to other, safer parts of the earth including: the Americas, Egypt, India, Persia and Arabia (Cayce 364-13).

The remaining principal land areas in this part of the world were the islands of Poseidon in the North (West Indies area), Aryan in the central

Atlantic and Peru in the west (then known as the land of Go). Also, two smaller islands that were known as Antalya and Eyre, which were ruled by Aryan. The Mahabharata, one of the ancient Sanskrit texts of India (estimated from 600 BCE), actually refers to "Attalla, the White Island", which was situated in the far west. Often this description is believed to mean an island covered with snow like Greenland or Antarctica, but did this text actually intended to refer to the white colour of the people's skin, and could this be the same island as the once Atlantic island: "Antalya"?

From section CCCXXXVII of the Mahabharata:

> "The men that inhabit that island have complexions as white
> as the rays of the Moon and they are devoted to Mahayana . . .
> Indeed, the denizens of White Island believe and worship only
> one God."

Among Hindu nationalists, the name "Aryan" refers to the Hindu/Indian people, and is derived from the Sanskrit "Aria" meaning "Noble". According to certain occult texts (possibly from Helena Blavatsky) which were also known by Adolf Hitler, the Aryan race originated in Atlantis (island of Aryan). Hitler believed that the Aryan race was the most exalted among the human races. In the Sanskrit texts, people are usually called Aria or Anaya (not-noble) based on their behaviour. The name "Iran", which was called Persia in the past, roughly translates to "Land of the Aryans".

After the great upheavals, Atlantis was fully destroyed in 17,400 BCE, which he called the first destruction of Atlantis. (Cayce 364-11) The second and final destruction happened in 9,900 BCE, where another shift of the magnetic poles caused the final demise of Atlantis, and also the end of the last glacial age. During this period the last remaining great islands of Atlantis sank into the sea. Only its scattered mountain peaks remained, which are now known as the islands of the Azores. The people that were able to escape at that time, fled to places including: Egypt, Yucatan and Mexico. (Cayce 364-1 and 288-1.)

ATLANTEAN TECHNOLOGY

Based on the readings from Edgar Cayce; It took the Atlanteans some "200,000 years" to advance to a technologically high level of development. (Cayce 364-4) Early on, they already learned to use gas for transport balloons made from animal skins, discovered electricity, and at later times they developed flying "ships", advanced forms of communication, and a "power plant" which operated through the use of a "great crystal" that could capture and store the energy gathered from the sun, the moon and other cosmic energies.

The energy of the "great crystal" had been used as a spiritual tool for those who could handle the great energy. Later it was used for rejuvenation of the human body, and the transmission of energy throughout the land - like radio waves - which powered crafts and vehicles that traversed the land, through the sky and under the sea at the speed of sound. They were also able to levitate huge stones by altering and nullifying gravity, through a higher understanding of the workings of nature, sound and vibrations.

This crystal had been referred to as the "taxi stone" or "firestone", had been described as huge in size, six sided, cylindrical in length, prismatic in shape, and opalescent (almost transparent), and could be tuned to various levels to produce power. The crystal was housed in a dome where insulation materials, "akin to asbestos" where used. This probably means that the crystal could generate a large amount of heat and the scattered conserved light issuing forth from all the facets would mean that the crystal would be glowing with light, thus the name "firestone" would be appropriate. Edgar Cayce described the construction of this stone in Reading 440-5:

> "As to describing the manner of construction of the stone,
> we find it was a large cylindrical glass (as would be termed

today), cut with facets in such a manner that the capstone on top of same made for the centralizing of the power or force that concentrated between the end of the cylinder and the capstone itself."

In the Biblical book Ezekiel, there is the mention of "fiery stones" which were located at the "mount of God". No one knows for sure what is meant by the term "fiery stones", but may very well refer to these "firestones"" which were used in Atlantis. (See Ezekiel 28:14 and 28:16.)

The second period of disturbances, starting around 28,000 BCE, was due to the overturning, or overcharging, of their largest crystal generator which was located near the so-called "Bermuda Triangle" in the area of the islands of Bermuda in the Atlantic Ocean.

Incredible amounts of energy were stored inside something like an underground battery and eventually got overloaded and caused a massive explosion, one can imagine that would lead to some major disturbances within the earth crust, and the disappearance of landmasses.

This damaged generator would periodically trigger a massive shift of unfocused electromagnetic energy which could de materialize its direct surroundings, which can cause both ships and planes to go astray. The current scientific theory is that this place is dangerous because of gasses that are emerging from the bottom of the ocean which nullify the natural carrying capacity of water and air, causing both ships and planes to crash into the bottom of the ocean. But it is still highly unnatural for such a great amount of natural gasses to be released at once, and even leaks or drillings could probably not release such a great amount at once, especially in such a wide area, so I think the possibility of dematerialization is still viable.

The mention of a ship in the form of a whale is also a very interesting detail what could mean that the fish or whale that swallowed Jonah in the Biblical story of Jonah, could have been in fact an Atlantean ship or submarine which looks like a whale, instead of a real whale. It is actually impossible to survive within the belly of a real whale, and certainly not as long as the mentioned "three days and three nights", as its stomach acids would be fatal to any human. Also, it could be that such an airplane in the form of a eagle or hawk is seen at these ancient bas-reliefs from ancient Mesopotamia, that are known currently known as depictions of the "Farohar" or simply, the "winged disk".

The book: "A Dweller on two Planets" (1894) (by Phylos the Thibetan, channelled through Frederick S. Oliver) describes many aspects of the Atlantean civilization at a certain point in time, including geological situation, buildings, religion, education, technology and politics. There was a caste system in Atlantis, which lead to great competition among the people. For this reason, many people where highly educated, which allowed them to acclaim higher functions, better opportunities and civil rights. Lower educated people ended up in lower classes which and could have a hard time possibly while living in poverty. In Atlantis City, each class of the population lived in a different area of Atlantis.

The book describes various kinds of technology that had still not yet been invented during 1894, the year this book had been written. It includes a portable communication device like today's wireless mobile phone which could also transmit pictures, a kind of gun that used electricity instead of bullets, flying machines that worked through the means of anti-gravity, and even some devices that are unknown to current modern society. In this book, the "advanced" technology was already lost nine centuries prior to the final demise of the Atlantis, due to the destruction of Marzeus: the city of manufacturing arts, by the "Navaz" forces (explained as "earth-currents" at page 37) which they had "forgotten how to control" (page 211). This is particularly reminiscent of Edgar Cayce's readings about the overturning of the Great Crystal.

From page 205 of "A Dweller on Two Planets":

> "And when manhood suffers decadence, degradation, all nature with which he has to do also sensibly alter for the worse. Marzeus, the city of manufacturing arts, was no more; it had gone down before corruption. Art had not suffered so much as

had science. But the science which drew upon the mysterious forces of Nature the "navaz" - this had so far disappeared that airships were forgotten, or at most were semi-mythical history".

Some other technology is mentioned by Zailm, the naima, "those wonderful wireless, combined telephonic and photographic image transmitters". And the vocaligrapha, the caloriveyant instruments ["a device which would save fuel, energy to be converted into heat for cooking and other purposes" (page 37)] and the water-generators – all were lost in the night of time. "But the men of the twentieth century shall find them all again."

When Plato described Atlantis in his writings, most of this advanced technology had already been lost for many centuries. It was not possible for Plato to have knowledge about this technology during these times, the Atlanteans relied once again on more primitive transport, like wooden ships to sail the sea. He described that Atlantis waged many wars with other civilizations to conquer more land for colonization. The Atlanteans still had a powerful army, but were humiliated when they were defeated in their attempt to penetrate to "Athens"

Signs of various kinds of lost technology, which according to legend, possibly could have originated from Atlantis and maybe even further back in time to the times of Lemuria, are evident in and around many ancient megalithic structures around the globe such as in Machu Pichu, Egypt, Baalbek, England and many others. These structures are often built with a frame of huge stone blocks which sometimes are weighing multiple hundreds of tons, therefore it is unthinkable how they could have moved and more importantly, lifted them without the use of modern technology.

It is apparent that at some point in time, people stopped to use these large and heavy stones for construction purposes, which could mean that they lost the technology at this point, or that people changed physically from giant to normal body frame. This seems evident in the restoration work at certain megalithic sites in Meso-America were smaller stones were used to fill in the gaps between the stones which were formed by earthquakes. Also, at certain constructions like in Egypt and Baalbek, there are some very heavy stones which are just lying around, as if they were never had been put to into place. Could this be because they just weren't able to move the many more?

These ancients were also able to carve and deform the hardest types of stone with such accurate precision as if they where laser cut. This curious kind of stone masonry is found at those megalithic sites from Egypt, Puma Punku and Cuzco.

These achievements could be considered as the smoking guns for the evidence of ancient lost technology and should be receiving more serious attention and research.

Building with great blocks of stone may be considered primitive by some but stone is actually one of the most durable materials for construction. The advantage of using very heavy stones is that they have far superior resistance against earthquakes and violent storms.

The other side of the coin should also be looked at, if the people were much larger, or gigantic, in proportion to today at about 39 feet high which is 12 meters tall, these large stones should then fit their proportions perfectly. For them to build with something smaller would be the same as building a house today with bricks the size of "Lego bricks".

Materials like metals, plastics and wood, which are abundantly in use in modern times, aren't actually very durable at all. If there would be remains to be found, made of these not-so-durable materials, after a time period of 10,000 years, it would have to be exceptionally well conserved and protected from natural influences like humidity, corrosion and erosion, because otherwise there would be nothing left of it today.

ATLANTEAN FLYING MACHINES

The book also describes a certain Atlantean cigar-shaped flying machine which is much like a modern passenger aircraft, though without wings and a tail. It doesn't rely on aero-dynamic forces, but instead uses the forces that could be considered gravitational/anti-gravitational. The machine is called a "vailx" and is actually the same name given to the flying craft of the Aswin people who had been mentioned in many ancient Sanskrit texts from India. This would mean that the Atlanteans were known as the Aswins in the Sanskrit texts.

It is said that when the 18 year old author of "A Dweller on Two Planets" channelled this information, he could impossibly have known of these ancient Sanskrit texts. Also, besides some early experimentation, airplanes weren't invented until 1899, at the time when the American Wright Brothers designed their first aircraft.

"Our vailx was of the middle traffic–size, these vessels being made in four standard lengths: number one, about twenty–five feet; number two, eighty feet; number three, something like one hundred and fifty–five feet, while the largest was yet two hundred feet longer than the third size. These long spindles were in fact round, hollow needles of aluminium, formed of an outer and an inner shell between which were many thousands of double T braces, an arrangement productive of intense rigidity and strength. All the partitions made other braces of additional resistant force. From amidships the vessels tapered toward either end to sharp points. Most vailxi were provided with an arrangement allowing, when desired, an open promenade deck at one end. Windows of crystal, of enormous resistant strength, were in rows like portholes along the sides, a few on top, and others set in the floor, thus affording a view in all directions."

According to the descriptions, these craft could fly very fast, so maybe Atlantean technology was able surpass the speed of light, which might cause a time-flex in space-time according to certain theories, and thus might allow for some form of time travelling. So, could it possibly have been that these ancient Atlanteans were once so technologically advanced that they could not only travel through space, but time as well? Or could it possibly be that some of these ships actually had been found and taken for a test flight, while still kept as military secret?

Psychic, Paul Solomon also mentioned and described these Atlantean flying machines in one of his "Source Readings" (reading #5, March, 1972).

> "Now this is Poseidon, and this is fantastic. It's like a different world altogether because there are flying machines all over. I see so many of them flying. Now you (Harry Snipes, the conductor) were a pilot of a machine, a flying machine that worked in this way, the power of this machine comes from two sources, from above and from the earth side. There is a magnetism from the Sun or from the celestial forces that draws upon the ship and there is magnetism from the earth that draws upon the ship. These ships operate by creating a balance between the two forces. Solar energy is used to counteract the magnetism of the earth. The power that provides the thrust is on the nature of what we would call a laser beam that operates through a copper conductor that runs in two long channels along the base of the ship. The ship has a shape like a long cylinder, no wings, only these two runners along the bottom that appears as copper."

In the next part of his reading he also mentioned another type of flying machine described as small winged aircraft:

> "Channel: I see another unusual flying machine. I don't know where this is. I assume this must be part of the Atlantean existence. This is a one-man craft. It is ridden similar to the manner of the motorcycle without wheels, but it has curved

wings; that is, the wings extend outward and curve downward at the tips, just slightly longer than a man's arms, maybe two feet longer on each side. Now these machines are black; the legs of the man wrap around a cylinder which produces the propelling force, but I see nothing of fire or smoke vapour. This is an electro-magnetic force. It's activated by a copper core that runs about three quarters of the length. It appears hollow in the back. It relates to another force on the other side and they seem to develop some sort of polarity in relation to each other to equalize pressure or magnetic force on both sides of the ship. Now the body would seem to be in direct contact with this core that runs along the topside of the machine and the body is lying upon the machine facing forward. The controls are operated by the hands and fingers on either side of the machine as the arms reach around the machine and forward. Now the protective shield in front of the face again is not transparent, but would seem transparent from the side on which the operator reclines, for it has a sensitive screen that reveals images of that which it is approaching. They seem to be capable of going high into space, somehow, with no harmful effects to the rider."

This description sounds similar to these small objects, 8-12 cm in length, dubbed by some as "golden airplanes", which originated from the Tolima Indians in Colombia, and are believed to be at least 1,500 years old. Museums from Germany and Colombia, who have these objects on display, claim these objects to be fictitious sculptures related to flying fish, insects and birds.

By closer inspection however, these seem to be models of machines build with advanced technology and aerodynamics. These models are equipped with both a horizontal and a vertical stabilizer and looking at certain models, we can even make out rudders and elevators, while other designs were built in a way that the stabilizers themselves could act as rudders and elevators. Further we can see what looks like a seat of a motor cycle; a wind shield, and cylinders which could be related to its way of propulsion.

It seems to match quite well with the description that Paul Solomon gave about these flying machines which he assumes must be part of the Atlantean existence. Erich von Däniken, known for his "ancient astronaut" hypothesis in his book, "Chariots of the Gods", once undertook experiments to build scale models of these statues out of plastic, of about a meter in size, and only being powered by a front propeller. These models were being proven aero dynamic and able to fly through the air.

Daan Akkerman mentioned in one of his readings that those extraterrestrial "angels" were able to manifest and de materialize or "shape shift" at will, during the Atlantean times, and were able to time travel between dimensions of time, with the aid of small airplane-like craft.

This could be related to the ancient Mesopotamian depictions of the "winged disk", also known as "Farohar". These angels weren't been around anymore (in physical form) during the later era of technological advancements, so if these flying machines were built during this era.

Eklal Kueshana, author of the book "The Ultimate Frontier", described yet another type of Atlantean craft. He wrote in an article from 1996 that the vailixi were first developed in Atlantis around 18,000 BCE. During this time, the most common ones had the shape of what we know today as a flying saucer.

"They used a mechanical antigravity device driven by engines developing approximately 80,000 horse powers."

The chariot or device, that had been witnessed and described by the Biblical prophet Ezekiel might have been such a saucer shaped Atlantean aircraft. The description of "wheels within wheels" suggests a saucer shaped craft. Our earliest accounts of flying "machines" had already been mentioned in the ancient texts from India called the Vedas, especially in the Mahábhárata, Bhágavata Purána and Rámáyana, by the name of "Vimana". These craft's could even travel in space as there is the mention of a battle on the moon between two of these craft's. They were described in various shapes and sizes: cigar shaped, blimp-like, saucer-shaped, triangular, and double-decked.

As mentioned earlier, the Atlanteans where possibly described in the Vedic scriptures from India as the "Asvins or Ashvins".

HUGE BEASTS

Edgar Cayce also told in his readings about "huge beasts" and "giant lizards", which lived in the times of Atlantis. He mentioned that the first ape-like human beings, which were living in caves, existed as early as 10,500,000 BCE (Cayce reading 2665-2). In the times of Atlantis, around 50,000 BCE, enormous carnivorous beasts were threatening man in many parts of the world. Mankind did built gigantic architecture to partially keep the large animals from entering a city and partially for earthquake stability. At a later time there had been a gathering of people from five nations around the world, where they decided to exterminate these beasts, because otherwise people may have not been able to survive (reading 262-39).

They used poisonous gas in the caves where they dwelled, but this wasn't a huge success, because of sudden wind changes these gasses came back to the people and it often only made the beast come out enraged. They ultimately coped with them with explosives and by "sending out super-cosmic rays from various central plants". In 1932 he said: "These rays will be discovered within the next twenty-five years." This could have been referred to the later rediscovery of the anti-neutron beam. There was another ray which created a radiating force by storing up energy in a small insulating crystal of special magnetic properties, so that the crystal passes on more energy that it receives. This sound very much like the laser, which also wasn't discovered until the sixties.

The gas pockets were blown open in the lairs of the animals which precipitin volcanic eruptions and earthquakes in the still slowly cooling earth, and caused the first continental catastrophe which affected both Lemuria and Atlantis; The axis of the world started to shift, which led to the beginning of the last great ice age. Lemuria was the first to be affected while Atlantis followed shortly. After the cataclysm, the huge beasts did become nearly extinct.

Could it be possible that these animals still have survived up to the early times of Atlantis? Various psychics intuitive made the mention of large, currently extinct animals, which lived in the same time frame as mankind. Trance medium Daan Akkerman asserted that most of current modern scientist wrongly dated the remains of these animals back to millions of years; it would have concerned animals that lived "only" 25,000 years ago.

Trance medium Rev. Douglas James Cottrell (PhD) was asked "what killed off the dinosaurs?", and his answer was:

First: the climatic changes that would be similar to this, but as such there would be the shift at the planets' rotation, and as such, those that would be existing in humid climates - as most of these beasts did - they would have been shifted or put into very cold climates, and this would have caused their demise, but primarily it would be large masses of water sweeping across the continent itself.

Evidence of this would be the caches of bones found along hills or mountain ranges or ridges, in which their carcasses would have been swept and deposited as you would say. When you find them in large groupings, these are not pawns that they have fallen into, it is that their bodies had been swept across the mass of land as large waves have come across the landmass, and they would have drowned, you would say."

(Source: Rev. Douglas James Cottrell DTM Session: Ezekiel's wheel, the Garden of Eden, and the Dinosaurs' demise, by Rammsteinregeln)

Dragons are mentioned in the Norse, Greek and Chinese mythology and in medieval legends such as St. George and the Dragon. According to description and illustrations these were often slender, serpent- or lizard like creatures, often with four paws and sometimes with wings, and while they were not exceptionally huge proportions, they still were deadly predators. Some medieval depictions of dragons are looking much like the dragons as depicted in Chinese art. The dragon is also part of the animals from the Chinese zodiac, where the other animals are non-mythological creatures, which could suggest that the dragon was also once seen as a non-mythological creature.

Spanish Conquistadors brought back stories from South America that there were stones with strange creatures carved on them found in a cave near Ica, Peru. They were believed to be ceremonial burial stones from the Nazca culture. Some of the stones were even brought back to Spain. In his work: "Relation de antique dades d'este reyno del Peru", Indian chronicler Juan de Santa Cruz Pachucuti Llamgui already wrote in the year 1571 about these strange engraved stones from Ica, long before the very first remains of a dinosaur were recognized in the early 19th century. These stones were called "Manco" and were found in the "Kingdom of Chperu"-tomb in Chinchayunga.

These Inca stones were popularized in 1970 by Dr. Javier Cabrera, a Peruvian medical doctor who received an engraved stone as a birthday gift. In thirty-five years, he had collected over 11,000 engraved stones. The clearly illustrated andesitic stones are depicting humans, dinosaurs and even humans riding and fighting with dinosaurs, advanced technology like telescopes, maps of the earth, rituals and sexual depictions.

Research has shown that erosion of the images on the stone was minimal, therefore it is believed by many they couldn't be very old. However, the oxidisation in the carvings of one of the Inca stones has been dated to at least 55,000 years old, which places its origins right within the time frame given by Edgar Cayce when dinosaurs still would have roamed on the earth and co-existed with man.

In Acámbaro, Mexico, there had been found several thousands of small ceramic figurines in the form of dinosaurs, and humans riding them. They are generally regarded as a hoax, because it was rumoured that these kinds of figures were still being made by traditional artists in more recent and modern times. Though, this does not exclude the possibility that these kinds of figures could be based on much older ones.

It is often said that there is no reliable evidence for the validity of these figures as actual ancient artefacts. In 1955, outcomes of radio-carbon dating of these figures in New Jersey showed an age between 1,600 BCE and 1,110 CE. More surprisingly, an additional 18 pieces were dated by the University of Pennsylvania at around 2,500 BCE. (Source: http://mexicanarcheology.tripod.com)

At the ruins of an ancient Buddhist temple called Ta Prohm, near Angkor Wat in Cambodia, there is a certain stone relief depicting humans, various animals and what seem to be mythological creatures. Around these animals we can see decorations that may represent cycles of creation, possible related to the evolution of these animals. Among these animals, there is one particular animal which seems to have plates on his back, just like a Stegosaurus.

However, the head of the animal is too large for any kind of stegosaurus that we know of today, as all known species of Stegosaurus actually had a proportionally small head. Some assume that these plates are part of the surrounding ornaments, but this does not seem to be the case as the forms of these plates are actually similar to those of a stegosaurus and do not fully match the shapes of the ornaments, and also, these kind of plates or ornaments are missing in the depictions if the animals above and below the stegosaurus.

Apart from the plates, the animal looks somewhat like a rhinoceros instead, especially the Sumatran rhinoceros because of its short horn. The rhinoceros however, always has a very thin and short tail, unlike the thick tail in the pictures above.

Because of the large head, the heavy build and the seemingly absence of a horn, it also shares some characteristics of the toxodon, which was a mammal which looked like a rhino without a horn, that according to archaeology became extinct at the end of the Pleistocene, which was around 12,000 years ago. But like the rhinoceros, the toxodon also had a thin and short tail.

GEOGRAPHICAL EVIDENCE

Cedric Leonard pointed out in his book: "A Geological Study of the Mid-Atlantic Ridge" (1979) that Wegener's theory about the shifting of continents, now known as "plate tectonics", does not mean that a mid-Atlantic continent was impossibility, as this is often thought. Leonard shows that even if all continents were once part of one single huge continent 200 million years ago, there would be still sufficient room for another large continent in the northern part of the Atlantic Ocean.

". . . Poseidon will be among the first portions of Atlantis to rise again. Expect it in sixty-eight and sixty-nine ('68 and '69); not so far away!"

The "Bimini Road" is an underwater rock formation near North Bimini island in the Bahamas, off the coast of Florida. It consists of a 0.5 mile (0.8 km) long, northeast-southwest linear feature, composed of roughly rectangular to sub rectangular limestone blocks. It looks like a long, artificially created stone wall that once could have been above the sea level.

Many researchers dismiss the Biminis Road as a fully natural formation, any structure that would be affected by a thousand years of water erosion and the growing of sea weed would look naturally, of course. But the curious things are there were found large stones that were piled up onto each other, that certain blocks were cut in a rectangular form, and what seems to be tool marks on numerous blocks, which adds to the evidence that these possibly were artificial, man-made structures.

Because of its discovery by plane in 1968, various authors that had written about the Edgar Cayce readings erroneously assumed that these formations in this area must have been once part of the island of Poseidon. However, the Edgar Cayce reading clearly stated that, after the island of Poseidon had sunk, its mountain tops had became the islands of the Azores, and not those of the islands of Biminis. Poseidon would have lain largely a little south and west of the Azores. Also, the sea levels around the Azores islands are known to be slowly rising since at least 1939, while the Bahamas have not.

Edgar Cayce mentioned that in the Biminis area there could be found records of some kind were kept which would be specific to the methods of construction of the "great crystal", or "firestone". From Cayce Reading 440-5:

MEGALITHIC STRUCTURES

Many large monuments and megalithic structures had been built across the globe. Thought to be build by different cultures, there are certain similarities between them which could prove there ever was a global civilization or organisation in the ancient past. Many ancient cultures did build pyramids or pyramid-like structures; There have been found large pyramids in North and South America, Egypt, China, and some smaller ones in Greece, the Canary Islands and Indonesia.

Pyramids are generally thought of to be tombs for the kings, but there is a serious problem with that idea. Never has an extant mummy been found in any pyramid, nor have any parts of a mummy been identified with certainty as those of a king. Nobles and pharaohs like the famous Tutankhamen had been buried into the "Valley of the Kings", not inside any pyramid.

Mummification had been practiced all over the world, not only in Egypt, but also in South America, China and the Canary Islands. There are researchers who think that, because of the building of the pyramids and the practices of mummification at the Canary Islands, these ancient people could have been a certain group of refugees from the lost civilization of Atlantis.

There are many mysteries considering the construction of these megalithic structures. Many were building using very large and very heavy stones. How could they have lifted them in ancient times without the aid of machines? Why did they go into the trouble of dealing with such heavy stones as they could use lighter and smaller stones? It makes no real sense unless they could do it with ease and/or for very specific reasons.

In Egypt, Peru (Cuzco, Machu Picchu, and Ollantaytambo) and Easter Island, there are certain walls which are consisting of very heavy interlocking stone blocks of various sizes, seamlessly pieced together like "Lego's", and without the use of composite building material.

These ancient mysteries are lined up in countries all over the world like Costa Rica, Central America, Malta, Easter Island and New Zealand with their gigantic stone balls and megaliths as evidence of Pre-Adamic peoples and their worlds.

We see these Pyramids and other building enigmas in Egypt and Americas and huge stone buildings in Peru, Mexico, Bolivia and Lebanon. In England we have Stonehenge and other megalithic structures playing with the best of us intellectually.

We can fill volumes looking at or trying to explain all these enigmas surrounding us today, most of which we have no logical explanation on how and why?

A lot can be said about this chapter, and I presume, a lot can be added as well, since I am not interested to rewrite all earths unexplained theory's into this book, it is my quest to bring home what is to follow in the coming chapters that really matters.

However it is important to have some of this information fresh in the mind in order to see through the smoke of information and to better understand.

After all this data the main question people tends to ask is:

> **Why so big, large, heavy and what for?**
> **What happened to the knowledge?**
> **Where did it come from?**
> **Why on earth?**

CHAPTER 3

Biblical and Scientific Fact

THE BIBLICAL CREATION

Jesus: is YAHSHUA

Christ: is MESSIAH

God: is ELOHIM

Lord: is YHWH

Lucifer: Is Satan / heylel

A remarkable difference between the modern Mesopotamian myths and the Bible is that in the Mesopotamian myths there is the mention of the word "gods" in place of the "LORD". This is because the word "Elohim", from the original ancient Hebrew text, had not been translated accurately.

In the modern Bible the ancient Hebrew word "Elohim" had been translated as the "LORD", and in more recent versions and revisions, it was even translated as "God". This translation is not accurate enough, because according to the original teachings the word "Elohim" literally translates to "Godly beings". According to the earlier mentioned Chronicle Project, the word translates to "the supreme ones". That the notion of "Elohim" on itself would refer to a hierarchy of spiritual beings involved with creation.

It is believed by some that when the word "Elohim" is used with other words or conjunctions such as "ha-", it refers to "the" one God, the highest authority. However, "Eloha" (or Eloah), which translates to "God", or seemingly more precise as "Godly being", is nothing more than the singular form of "Elohim". This word also does not specifically refer to a "male" being, because the form of this word is in fact both masculine and feminine.

We will use the following abbreviations to show what the different Bilbes have to say:

KJ is King James.

MS is Modern Standard.

LB is Living Bible.

RS is Revised Standard.

NIV is New International Version.

CREATION OR RENEWAL

The Pre-Adamic Age is the First Age in YHWH's Plan for All. It began at the creation of the heavens and the earth, and ended at the start of the six-day creation week, during which Adam and Eve were created.

The Pre-Adamic Age was the age when angels were the key focus of YHWH's dealings. The First Age is an important age in ELOHIM's Plan of the Ages.

The First Age, the Pre-Adamic Age.

Genesis 1:1

> *"In the beginning YHWH created the heavens and the earth."*

The heavens and the earth mean the whole, complete universe consisting of billions of galaxies with billions of stars and planets. Our minds cannot even begin to grasp the wonders and limitless power of YHWH, which the universe displays.

YHWH singles out the earth as the most important planet in the entire universe. This is because YHWH has a tremendous purpose to use the earth as the centre of the universe. It is on earth that YHWH will first establish His Millennial Kingdom, at the return of YAHSHUA MESSIAH. Then, after YHWH has refined and renewed the earth during the Lake of Fire Judgement Age, He will establish His Eternal Kingdom of the New Heaven and the New Earth.

So how did YHWH create the universe and the earth in the beginning? The Bible says that ELOHIM simply commanded and they were created.

Psalm 148:2-5

> 2 *"Praise Him, all His angels; Praise Him, all His hosts! 3 Praise Him, sun and moon; Praise Him, all you stars of light! 4 Praise Him, you heavens of heavens, and you waters above the heavens! 5 Let them praise the name of the YHWH, for* **He commanded and they were created.**"

When YHWH created the universe in the beginning, He also designed and created the Law of Gravity. YHWH introduced **the Law of Gravity** for the stability and continual existence of the universe. All bodies in the universe are held together and maintain their orbits because of gravitation. Smaller bodies are held in their orbits by bigger bodies. Moons orbit planets, planets orbit stars, stars orbit galactic centres, and galaxies orbit other galaxies in clusters.

The important point to understand is that it is impossible for the moon, as we know it, to exist without the earth; and it is impossible for the earth, as we know it, to exist without the sun; and for the sun to exist without our galaxy, the Milky Way; and for the Milky Way to exist without other galaxies. So, the whole universe must have been created instantaneously for it to exist, and this is exactly what YHWH did in the beginning, as Psalm 148:5 above confirms, '*He commanded and they were created*'.

Our present conception of time began when YHWH created the earth, the sun and the moon with the rest of the universe, in the beginning. This is when YHWH's Plan of the Ages began. How long ago was the beginning when YHWH commanded and instantaneously created the universe with the earth? The Bible does not say. However, star distances and many other modern scientific methods, all show us that the beginning was millions of years ago. It **cannot** have been around six thousand years ago.

However, we can be absolutely sure that earth is much older than six thousand years because the Bible clearly teaches us that there was a Pre-Adamic Age.

We were made to believe that the various scientific methods of calculating the age of the earth can be relied upon because all these methods and calculations are based on science.

These calculations can be considered to be legitimate assumptions in accordance with our understanding of the laws of physics operating in the universe, and their analysis of other scientific data. However, even if it turns out that these assumptions made by scientists, when calculating the age of the earth, are out by 99.9% in favour of a younger earth, then that would still make the age of the earth very old at 4.5 million years compared with only six thousand years.

Young Earth Creationists claim to interpret the Genesis account of creation literally to justify their belief in a young earth.

They say that anything other than about six thousand years is playing around with the literal translation of the creation account. In actuality, it is the Young Earth Creationists themselves who play around with the literal meaning of the Genesis account of creation.

THE BIBLE

We are misunderstanding the Genesis account of YHWH's creation when we misinterpret the very first verse of the Bible (Genesis 1:1) as being a summary statement of the six-day creation account, which is described in Genesis 1:3-31. This misunderstanding of the very first verse of the Bible has led us to believe that YHWH created the earth on the first day without the sun, and that it wasn't until the fourth day that YHWH created the sun, the moon and the stars. This is not only biblically untrue but also scientifically nonsensical. It is **impossible** for a 24-hour day comprising of both light and darkness, day and night with morning and evening to occur, without both the earth and the sun existing together. This is elementary physics and common sense. The Bible is extremely logical and it does not contradict true science, after all **YHWH Himself is the greatest scientist**. He does not want us to believe in something that is illogical and scientifically incorrect.

What was the state of the earth when YHWH created it along with the rest of the universe in the beginning? Let us see what the Bible says.

Job 38:4-7 (NIV)

> 4 *"Where were you when I laid the **earth's foundation**? Tell me, if you understand. 5 Who marked off its dimensions? Surely you know! Who stretched a measuring line across it? 6 on what were its footings set, or who laid its cornerstone—7 **while the morning stars sang together and all the angels shouted for joy?"***

Job Chapters 38 and 39 show YHWH humbling Job, who thought that he had a great fount of knowledge. In the verses above, He challenges Job about his knowledge of the creation of the earth. He did this to make Job acknowledge YHWH's greatness and to show Job that he knew absolutely nothing about how and when YHWH had created the earth.

Notice that **all the angels** sang and shouted for **joy** when YHWH laid the foundations of the earth. 'Morning stars' here also refers to angels.

The verses above reveal two important truths:

YHWH created angels **before** He created the earth and the universe.

When YHWH created the earth in the beginning, **He created it in such a beautiful and perfect condition** that the angels responded with joyful singing and shouting. I shall show you later using relevant scripture that this Pre-Adamic world was created as a beautiful Garden of Eden, teeming with plant and animal life.

However, shockingly, in the second verse of the Bible, Genesis 1:2, we read that the earth had changed from its beautiful and perfect Garden of Eden state, when it was first created in the beginning, to a totally different **ruined** state. It had **become** formless, empty, submerged under water, and dark.

Genesis 1:2 (NIV)

> *"Now the earth was (hayah) formless, and empty, darkness was over the surface of the deep, and the Spirit of YHWH was hovering over the waters."*

So before day one of the six day creation of earth, there was already an earth. In other words, all the elements on the periodic table, solids, liquids and gasses existed. Water was present so there must have been oxygen and hydrogen forming the water molecule. If there was an earth, the moon and the rest of the universe were also present . . . . all before day one of the creation! They call it the "Genesis gap" or the "Gap Theory".

Since YHWH did not create the earth in a formless, empty, flooded and dark state in the beginning, then it must have **become** that way at a later stage. This is exactly what happened to the earth, because an accurate translation of the Hebrew word *hayah* in Genesis 1:2 above is "**became**", as given in Strong's dictionary, and as confirmed by the NIV in their footnote. Strong's H1961 gives the meaning of *hayah* as: to be, become, come to pass, exist, happen and fall out. When you consider all of these possible meanings together, you get a more accurate meaning of *hayah* in Genesis1:2 as **became rather than was**.

We were made to believe that Genesis 1:2 is the description of **a stage** in the construction of the earth.

It is a misunderstanding and misinterpretation of this verse to believe that YHWH firstly had to create the earth in a formless, empty, dark state and totally submerged under water in order to proceed and complete the rest of His beautiful creation on earth. This is not how YHWH of the Bible operates.

The truth of the Bible is that Genesis 1:2 is the description of the earth resulting from YHWH's massive cataclysmic global judgement because of the sins of angels. It is not speaking about a stage in the construction of the earth.

YHWH'S JUDGEMENT

Genesis 1:2 (NIV)

> *"Now the earth was (hayah, meaning became) formless (tohuw), and empty (bohuw), darkness was over the surface of the deep, and the Spirit of YHWH was hovering over the waters."*

The Bible is abundantly clear that the inspired Hebrew words **tohuw** and **bohuw** in Genesis 1:2 above, **when used together**, are the descriptive words for YHWH's **global judgement.**

The Hebrew word *tohuw* occurs 20 times in the Old Testament and Strong's H8414 gives its meanings as: *formlessness, confusion, unreality, emptiness, wasteland, wilderness, place of chaos and vanity (worthlessness)*. Something that is in a state of formlessness, confusion, unreality, emptiness, wasteland, wilderness, place of chaos, and vanity (worthlessness) is obviously in a **chaotic** state. Therefore, the best meaning of tohuw in Genesis 1:2 is **chaotic.**

The Hebrew word *bohuw* occurs 3 times in the Old Testament and Strong's H922 gives its meanings as: *emptiness, void* and *waste*. God inspired the use of the Hebrew word *bohuw* in Genesis 1:2 to reinforce the meaning of *tohuw*, which we have just shown above means chaotic. Therefore, we believe that the best meaning of *bohuw* is wasted, meaning ruined.

The more accurate meaning of Genesis 1:2 is:

Now the earth became chaotic and wasted, darkness was over the surface of the deep, and the Spirit of YHWH was hovering over surface of the waters.

YHWH **did not** create the earth in the beginning (Genesis 1:1) in a chaotic, wasted, state submerged under water and in darkness. The earth **became** like that because a massive cataclysmic change took place in the earth between Genesis 1:1 and Genesis 1:2. The Bible specifically confirms in Isaiah 45:18 below that the earth was not created in the chaotic and wasted state that we see in Genesis 1:2.

Isaiah 45:18 (NKJV)

> *"For thus says YHWH, Who created the heavens, Who is HELOHIM, Who formed the earth and made it, Who has established it, Who **did not create it in vain** (tohuw), Who formed it to be inhabited: 'I am the HELOHIM, and there is no other'."*

Isaiah 45:18 (NAS)

> *"For thus says YHWH, who created the heavens (He is HELOHIM) who formed the earth and made it, He established it and **did not create it a waste place** (tohuw), but formed it to be inhabited), "I am the HELOHIM, and there is none else."*

Isaiah 45:18 (RSV)

> *"For thus says YHWH, who created the heavens (he is HELOHIM!), who formed the earth and made it (he established it; **he did not create it a chaos** (tohuw), he formed it to be inhabited!): "I am the HELOHIM, and there is no other."*

All versions of the Bible, like the NKJV, NAS and RSV given above, confirm what Isaiah 45:18 says that the earth was not created in a vain (worthless), wasted and chaotic state.

Let us believe what the Bible says that YHWH **did not create** the earth in a worthless, wasted, chaotic and uninhabitable state. As we have shown from Scripture, the earth was created in such a beautiful state that the angels sang and shouted for joy. Most certainly, the angels would not have sung and shouted for joy over the creation of a chaotic ruined earth.

Scripture show that there was **a gap of time** between the creation of the beautiful earth of Genesis 1:1 and the totally chaotic ruined earth of Genesis 1:2. This gap of time is **the Pre-Adamic Age**, which may have lasted for millions of years.

Why and how did the earth become chaotic and ruined as described in Genesis 1:2? In Genesis 1:2 In this verse we found the description of the earth resulting from YHWH**'s global judgement because of the sins of angels**.

2 Kings 19:25 KJ

> *"Hast thou not heard long ago how I have done it, and of **ancient times** that I have formed it? Now I brought it to pass, that thou should be to lay waste fenced cities into ruinous heaps."*

2 Peter 3:4-6 (Revised Standard)

> *4, "Where is the promise of His coming? For ever since the Fathers fell asleep, all things have continued as they were from the beginning of creation. 5, they **deliberately ignore the fact**, that by the word of ELOHIM heavens **existed long ago**, and an earth formed out of water and by means of water, 6, through which the world that then existed **was deluged with water and perished.**"*

> *5, (Living Bible) ". . . used the waters to form the earth and surround it . . . ."*

> *6, (Modern Standard)" . . . water by means of which the then existing world was destroyed . . ."*

6, (King James))" . . . Whereby the world that then was, being overflowed with water, perished."

Note that Peter is not talking about Noah's flood . . . . There is no ark or rain mentioned in this statement . . . . it is clear that he is talking about the formation of earth and heavens long before Noah's flood.

Using the correct translations and fact from the Bible, I think we can categorically state that the Bible states that there was a pre Adamic world before the Genesis creation.

These beings which we nowadays refer to as "angelic beings" were as the hands and feet of Creation. They were known under a number of different names in the past, in the Bible they were referred to as the "the sons of God" in the Book of Genesis and "the Watchers" in the Book of Daniel; In the Book of Enoch they are known as the "Grigori" (literary: "Watchers") and they are called the "Igigi" in the Sumerian myths.

The "Igigi" were known by the Sumerian scribes as the "gods of heaven", which could imply that those beings where usually residing in the heavens: the sky and possibly beyond, from where they had the possibility to watch the happenings on earth from above. The term "igi.gi" is a Sumerian term that describes "igi" as: "to see", and "gi" as: "to surround, besiege, or to lock up". In other words: those that are looking upon, and following something, thus the term "watchers" would be appropriate. The Sumerian and Acadian cultures are the oldest known cultures that mentioned and depicted winged beings, sometimes within a halo of light.

A number of books in the Bible including the "Book of Enoch", explaines and described those beings but were labelled as apocrypha and thus not included in the Bible. The story of the Anunnaki from the Sumerian clay tablets interconnects with the book of "Genesis" from the Bible and the "Book of Enoch"; here we find similar stories about a certain group of beings which we today would call the "fallen angels", which landed on Mount Hermon to choose and take wives for themselves from the "daughters of man". From the "Book of Enoch" and the Sumerian story it is clear that this was actually a forbidden act, the result of a rebellion within a certain group of angelic beings.

In the book Genesis, the Bible described that these "sons of God" mated with the "daughters of men" and that their offspring was referred to as the "Nephilim". (See Genesis 6:1-4) The word "Nephilim" derives from the Hebrew "to fall" which also includes "causing to fall" and "to kill, to ruin". It is therefore certainly not synonymous with "giants" which was often thought by translators in the past. It would mean something to the effect of "the Fallen Ones", or "those who had strayed from the path of righteousness". Therefore, it is possible that this was not only a reference that was limited to their offspring but to these "fallen" angels as well.

Emim means: "the fearful".

Rephaim means: "the dead ones".

Anakim means: "the long-necked ones."

Nephilim means: "the fallen ones".

The Book of Enoch, chapter 15:2, uses the word "Nephilim" in the context of "impious (not pious) offspring". This probably means that the use of the word "Nephilim" or "giant" in the scriptures is a word or name for the "evil" or "impure" mixed offspring from the "sons of God" and the daughters of men. Many caused a great disturbance upon the earth because of their gigantic size and force; they could do whatever they wanted without fear of punishment, because no ordinary man would be able to stop them.

THE SINS OF THE ANGELS

2 Peter 2:4-64

For if YHWH **did not spare the angels who sinned, but cast them down to hell** (*tartaroo*) and delivered them into chains of darkness, to be reserved for judgment;

> 5 *"and **did not spare the ancient world**, but saved Noah, one of eight people, a preacher of righteousness, bringing in the flood on the world of the ungodly";*

> 6 *"and **turning the cities of Sodom and Gomorrah into ashes**, condemned them to destruction, making them an example to those who afterward would live ungodly".*

Sin has consequences and it brings judgement from YHWH in the form of death and destruction. Please note that He **did not spare the angels who sinned**, and He did not spare the sinful world of Noah or the sinful cities of Sodom and Gomorrah.

In verse 4 above, the Greek word **tartaroo** is mistranslated as hell because all fallen angels are free to roam the earth as spirits of the air, and they are not in 'hell' but still awaiting their final judgement in the Lake of Fire. *Tartaroo* is used only once in the Bible. Now, let us clearly understand the significance of this Greek word *tartaroo*.

According to Strong's G5020, **tartaroo** is, "the name of the subterranean region, doleful and dark, regarded by the ancient Greeks as the abode of the wicked dead, where they suffer punishment for their evil deeds". Of course, this is the pagan ancient Greek belief in an underworld, but it does reflect to some extent the meaning of tartaroo.

The state of the earth described in Genesis 1:2 is in fact the *tartaroo* referred in 2 Peter 4:2 above. The Bible is clear that when Lucifer and his angels first rebelled, they were judged and **violently** cast back down to earth (Revelation 12:7-9). We can be sure that the chaotic, wasted, flooded and dark state of the earth as described in Genesis 1:2 was in fact the *tartaroo* judgement of Lucifer and his fallen angels. The beautiful Garden of Eden earth of Genesis 1:1 was violently thrown into the ruined and dark *tartaroo* state of Genesis 1:2 because of the sins of angels.

The Bible does not say for how long YHWH left the earth in this ruined flooded and dark *tartaroo* state, as a prison for **heylel** (Lucifer's new name after he rebelled and was cast down to earth) and his fallen angels. However, in accordance with YHWH's Plan for the Ages, the time came for YHWH to transform and renew the ruined earth of Genesis 1:2 into a Garden of Eden once again, at the beginning of the Adamic Age.

This is also why Adam was created and added to the new "revamped", re created earth, to manage and rule over it, give names and to keep order on earth as it mentions in Genesis 2:5 after the whole six day event of Biblical creation and after he rested on the seventh day that . . . . there was not a man to till the ground (KJ) . . . . so Adam was brought into the picture . . . all the creatures, early humans, hybrids, fallen angels and gods as we know them today, that was already present before the recreation and during it, was not fit for the job or unable to till the earth.

If we look at the word "till" we can reason the following:

Cultivate, farm, manage, and improve, this means to look after and use planet earth in its whole and to its maximum capability. To be able to qualify for this post a couple of traits must have been given to Adam by YHWH. It encompasses about every known science to man today.

His ability to manage and farm was obviously his main ability. He knew how to work the earth to maximum productivity and his total knowledge of the climate, earth, animals and nature was unsurpassed.

Wherever the Adamic seed went on earth a green organised creative environment followed immediately after they settled in any region.

The opposite is true for the **heylel** seed line through Cain, where they will not be successful no matter what they attempt, the opposite will follow, the earth will not bring forth or yield it's crop, emptiness, chaotic, wasted form, death and destruction will flourish.

Genesis 4:12 (Living Bible)

> *"No longer will the earth yield crops for you, even if you toil on it* ***forever!*** *From now on you will be a fugitive and a tramp upon the earth, wandering from place to place".*

We see that **heylel** was already present in the Garden of Eden when YHWH created man (Adam and Eve) for the very first time. Also, this is why YAHSHUA MESSIAH could say that **heylel** is a liar and a murderer from the beginning, meaning from the beginning of the Adamic Age and before in the Pre Adamic age (John 8:44).

We see that Cain was definitely not from the seed of Adam.

The name Cain means, "I have created"

Eve is recorded saying in Genesis 4:1 *"with the lord's help I have created a man"*

> *"With the lords help" "from the lord".* (Lord = Baal = heylel)

Who do we see have to enhance his gene pool on earth in order to get back the control? Who was obsessed to create on the same level as YHWH after Eve was misled believing Satan to be a god?

We also see that in Genesis 5 that Cain is not mentioned in the family tree "generations" of Adam confirming again that Cain was from Satan, and his direct seed line. He was not mentioned in Adams family tree because Cain was not Adams genetical son.

The Bible further reaffirms that **Genesis 1:2** is indeed speaking about the state of the earth, which resulted from YHWH's global judgement, and it is not a description of a stage in the construction of the earth.

The Hebrew words *tohuw* and *bohuw* occur together in the same verse **only twice** in the whole of the Bible. The first time is in Genesis 1:2 and the second time is in Jeremiah 4:23, which also describe YHWH's global judgement. However, the Jeremiah 4:23 global judgement of YHWH is yet to be carried out against this present sinful world of man, which remains deceived and inspired by **heylel** and his fallen angels. This judgement will occur at the Second Coming of YAHSHUA MESSIAH.

Genesis 1:2 (NIV)

> *"Now the earth **was** (hayah, meaning became) **formless** (tohuw), and **empty** (bohuw), **darkness** was over the surface of the deep, and the Spirit of ELOHIM was hovering over the waters."*

Jeremiah 4:23 (NIV)

> *"I looked at the earth, and it **was** formless (tohuw), and empty (bohuw); and at the heavens, and **their light was gone.**"*

Genesis 1:2 is a description of YHWH's global *tohuw* and *bohuw* judgement against sinful fallen angels carried out at some point in the Pre-Adamic Age millions of years ago, as previously discussed.

We know from the Bible that there was another global judgement when YHWH flooded the whole or part of the earth completely destroying Noah's world, approximately 4300 years ago, because of the wickedness of men who were deceived and inspired by Satan and his fallen angels. This global judgement of YHWH against Noah's world **was not** a *tohuw* and *bohuw* judgement, as Scripture does not describe it such.

However, at the Second Coming of YAHSHUA MESSIAH, there will be another global *tohuw* and *bohuw* judgement against this present sinful world of man, as described in Jeremiah 4:23 above.

Jeremiah was inspired to write about future events that will come to pass in this present age, during the final period of the Great Tribulation at the Second Coming of YAHSHUA MESSIAH. Jeremiah 4:5-28 is a prophecy of YHWH's horrific judgement against Israel and against the whole world.

Verses 6 and 7 say that YHWH will bring **disaster and destruction** from the north upon Israel. Israel will become **desolate,** and its cities will be laid **waste.** Verse 8 says that **the fierce anger of ELOHIM** will not be turned back. Verse 12 says that YHWH will speak **judgement** against the people of Jerusalem. Verse 13 speaks about **the return of YAHSHUA MESSIAH** on the clouds. Verses 14 to 18 speak about people's **wickedness.** Verse 20 says that YHWH will bring **destruction upon destruction**. We now come to the key verse Jeremiah 4:23.

Jeremiah 4:23 (NIV)

> *"I looked at the earth, and it was **formless** (tohuw), and empty (bohuw); and at the heavens, and their **light was gone"**.*

Notice that Jeremiah saw **the whole earth** in a state of *tohuw* and *bohuw*, which means a chaotic, wasted and empty state. Also, he saw that the heavens had no light, meaning that the earth was plunged into total darkness. The state of the earth, which Jeremiah saw, resembles the description of the earth as given in Genesis 1:2, except that there was no global flooding. This is because YHWH's promised never to flood the earth again following Noah's flood. Let us now read Jeremiah 4:24-28, in order to further understand what the future tohuw and bohuw judgement will involve.

Jeremiah 4:24-28

> *24 "I beheld **the mountains**, and indeed they **trembled**, and all **the hills moved back and forth**. 25 I beheld, and indeed there was **no man**, and all the birds of the heavens had fled. 26 I beheld, and indeed the fruitful land was a **wilderness**, and all its cities were broken down at the presence of ELOHIM, by **His fierce anger**. 27 For thus says YHWH "**The whole land shall be desolate; Yet I will not make a full end**. 28 For this shall the earth mourn, and **the heavens above are black**, because I have spoken. I have purposed and will not relent, nor will I turn back from it".*

Jeremiah is speaking about the future judgement against this present world, at the return of YAHSHUA MESSIAH. The future *tohuw* and *bohuw* judgement will not only involve **the sun being darkened** but also the mountains will shake and the hills and islands will be moved out of their place, and the earth will be reduced to a **wilderness**.

This *tohuw* and *bohuw* judgement against the whole earth at the Second Coming of YAHSHUA MESSIAH, as prophesied by the prophet Jeremiah, is also described and prophesied by Apostle John in Revelation 6:12-17, and by YAHSHUA MESSIAH Himself in Matthew 24:29-30. There are close similarities between these three prophecies, which mean that they are speaking of the same global tohuw and bohuw judgement.

Comparing Jeremiah 4:5-28, Revelation 6:12-17 and Matthew 24:29-30, we can clearly see that YHWH's future global tohuw and bohuw judgement at the end of this present age will be **absolutely cataclysmic**, involving the powers of the **heavens being shaken**, the **stars (meteorites) falling onto earth**, the sun and the moon being **darkened**, great **earthquakes** and upheavals causing every mountain and every island to **shake** and **moved out of its place**, great **global devastation** of the earth's surface causing **chaos** and **waste**, **massive destruction of all types of life**, and surviving unbelievers so terrified that they hide away from the face of the returning YAHSHUA MESSIAH and His wrath . . .

. . . And to put it mildly . . . I had heard of these events before . . . . somewhere way back in time . . . . somewhere a bell is ringing . . .

Unlike the previous global tohuw and bohuw judgement in the Pre-Adamic Age when all living plants and animals were killed, YHWH will not totally wipe out 'not make a full end' to all life on earth in the future global tohuw and bohuw judgement. There will be a proportion of earth's population who will survive it to enter YHWH's Millennial Kingdom, over whom ELOHIM and His resurrected Bride will reign.

It is significant that the Hebrew words *tohuw* and *bohuw* occur together in the same verse only twice in the Bible, the first time in Genesis 1:2 and the second time in Jeremiah 4:23. We have highlighted and described in detail the future global judgement against this present sinful world of man referred to in Jeremiah 4:23, to prove the point that Genesis 1:2 also speaks about ELOHIM's global judgement, and it is not a description of a stage in the construction of the earth.

There should now be no doubt in your mind that Genesis 1:2 is indeed a description of a horrific and cataclysmic global tohuw and bohuw judgement, which YHWH carried out during **the Pre-Adamic Age**, because of the sins of angels, and there is indeed **an age-gap** of perhaps millions of years between Genesis 1:1 and Genesis1:2.

The Pre-Adamic world was destroyed because of the sins of angels. However, YHWH understood right from the beginning, before He created the universe and the earth, that this would happen because YHWH is all knowing and He knows the end from the beginning.

Although YHWH destroyed the Pre-Adamic earth, it was always in His Plan to renew the earth and start a "New Age", the Adamic Age.

Man, who is the pinnacle and most important of all of YHWH's creation, was created for the very first time at the beginning of this Second Age. This was when YHWH renewed the earth and its atmosphere in the six-day creation week.

ANGELS OR MAN?

The fact that angels sinned **before** man cannot be disputed because **heylel** (Satan) was already a sinner and present in the Garden of Eden, before Adam and Eve sinned. This obvious truth that angels sinned before man is further confirmed by the historical sequence of the three judgements listed in the scripture 2 Peter 2:4-6 given previously, where the Bible places the sins of angels before the sins of man.

Let us now examine **Romans 5:12** in detail, as it is one of the three key 'proof texts' used by society to support the belief. Society or our early teachers misunderstands Romans 5:12 when it argues that sin and death first entered the world through man, and not through angels.

Romans 5:12

> "*Therefore, just as through* **one man sin entered the world***, and death through sin, and thus* **death spread to all men***, because all sinned*".

We used to **misinterpret** this scripture to believe that there was no death before Adam sinned; hence they say that there was no Pre-Adamic world of plants and animals that was destroyed.

Romans 5:12 above speaks only of **death spreading to all men** because of Adam's original sin, but it has absolutely **nothing** to say about death spreading to all plants and animals. Romans 5:12 simply does not address the question of whether or not there was any plant and animal death before Adam sinned. Therefore, this verse **cannot** be used to prove that there was no Pre-Adamic world. Yes, it is true that 'through one man sin entered the world', but which world does this scripture refer to? It obviously refers to sin entering the Adamic world, the world of man.

The truth of the Bible that **heylel** and his angels sinned, and were cast back down to earth out of heaven to undergo their *tartaroo* judgement, before Adam sinned cannot be disputed. This clearly proves the fact that there was a Pre-Adamic world when Lucifer, who became **heylel**, sinned before Adam was created.

Romans 5:12 is only concerned with sin and death spreading to all men because of Adam's original sin. In fact, Romans Chapter 5 is a beautiful chapter emphasising the truth of the Gospel of YAHSHUA MESSIAH, and His finished work on the cross. Through one man Adam, sin and death spread to all men. However, through One Man YAHSHUA MESSIAH, the gift of YHWH's righteousness and eternal life will be granted to all men.

There is absolutely nothing in the Bible to suggest that **heylel** was cast back down to earth from heaven **after** ELOHIM created Adam and Eve, during the Adamic Age. Also, if **heylel** sinned for the very first time during the Adamic Age, then how was it that **heylel** was not judged and he could still remain free to deceive Adam and Eve in the Garden of Eden, after his rebellion?

This view obviously contradicts 2 Peter 2:4, where it says that all fallen angels received their *tartaroo* judgement when they sinned.

Luke 10:18

*And He said to them, "I saw **heylel** fall like lightning from heaven".*

When did YAHSHUA MESSIAH see **heylel** fall like lighting from heaven? It can only have been during the Pre-Adamic Age, and not during the Adamic Age. When **heylel** fell from heaven, he together with his fallen angels had to go through their tartaroo judgement, before they became free to roam the earth and its atmosphere as 'spirits of the air during the Adamic Age.

How did sin first enter the Pre-Adamic world through **heylel** and his fallen angels, bringing death and destruction to the Pre-Adamic Garden of Eden earth?

Isaiah14:12-15

> 12 *"How you are fallen from heaven, O **heylel**, son of the morning! How you are cut down to the ground, you who weakened the nations! 13 **For you have said in your heart: 'I will ascend into heaven, I will exalt my throne above the stars of ELOHIM**; I will also sit on the mount of the congregation On the farthest sides of the north; 14 I will ascend above the heights of the clouds, I will be like the Most High.' 15 **Yet you shall be brought down to Sheol, to the lowest depths of the Pit**."*

This scripture confirms YAHSHUA MESSIAH's statement in Luke 10:18 above that He saw **heylel** fall from heaven. It was indeed **heylel** (previously the holy angel Lucifer), whom HE saw fall from heaven.

The Hebrew word **heylel (Satan)** is translated as Lucifer in the NKJV translation above. Lucifer is a Latin word meaning 'Light Bearer', which first appeared in the Latin Vulgate circa 400 A.D. This Latin word Lucifer has been retained by both the KJV and the NKJV, thus the Christian world has been familiar with the name Lucifer for over a thousand years. Modern versions of the Bible translate **heylel** to mean Morning Star, Bright Star, Shining One and Day Star, all of which are similar to the Latin word Lucifer, meaning Light Bearer.

Isaiah Chapter 14 refers to both the king of Babylon and **heylel.** However, it is important to note that Isaiah 14:12-15 above is specifically speaking about Lucifer who became **heylel (chaos)**.

This scripture is not referring to the king of Babylon. It is referring to a fallen angelic being and not a man, as no man is capable of ascending above the heights of the clouds. Notice that Lucifer coveted the throne of YHWH and he wanted to become like the Most High.

Isaiah 14:15 above says, "**Yet you shall be brought down to Sheol, to the lowest depths of the Pit**." *Sheol* in Hebrew means *grave, pit* or *underworld*. This verse confirms the *tartaroo* judgement, which **heylel** and his fallen angels received when they were cast back down to earth from heaven for their rebellion during the Pre-Adamic Age. They were imprisoned in the deep, frozen, watery, dark grave of the ruined and flooded earth until they became freed from their *tartaroo* prison. This was when ELOHIM renewed the surface of the earth in six-days.

When YAHSHUA MESSIAH returns, **heylel** will once again be imprisoned under the earth's surface, but this time in a 'bottomless pit' for the duration of ELOHIM's one thousand year Millennial Kingdom. After which, **heylel** will be released for a short time before his final judgement in the Lake of Fire.

Ezekiel 28:12-15

> 12 "*Son of man, take up a lamentation for the king of Tyre, and say to him, 'thus says the ELOHIM'*:
>
> "*You were the seal of perfection, Full of wisdom and perfect in beauty. 13 You were in Eden, the garden of ELOHIM; every precious stone was your covering: The sardius, topaz, and diamond, Beryl, onyx, and jasper, Sapphire, turquoise, and emerald with gold. The workmanship of your timbrels and pipes was prepared for you on the day you were created." 14 You were the anointed cherub who covers; I established you; you were on the holy mountain of ELOHIM; you walked back and forth in the midst of fiery stones. 15 You were perfect in your ways from the day you were created, till iniquity was found in you*".

Ezekiel Chapter 28 begins by describing the king of Tyre who became proud in his heart and thought of himself as YHWH. **The power and deceiver behind the king of Tyre** was **heylel** himself. The scripture Ezekiel 28:12-15 above takes us on from speaking about the king of Tyre to speaking about Lucifer who became **heylel**, as these verses can only fit the description of a fallen angelic being, and not a man. Lucifer was created perfect in his ways. He was the seal of perfection, full of wisdom, **the anointed cherub** and perfect in beauty before iniquity was found in him when he rebelled against YHWH. In contrast, the king of Tyre was born imperfect with a fallen, sinful Adamic nature, and he was not the anointed cherub. Therefore, these verses can only refer to YHWH speaking to **heylel**, who was the real influence and power behind the king of Tyre.

It was Lucifer and not the king of Tyre whom YHWH had placed in **Eden**, the Garden of ELOHIM. This Garden of Eden was not the same Garden of Eden of the Adamic Age, where **heylel** was present as a fallen angel who lied to and deceived Eve.

It is important to understand that the Bible speaks of at least **three Gardens of Eden in three different ages**. There was the first Garden of Eden in the Pre-Adamic Age, as given in Ezekiel 28:13 above. There was the second Garden of Eden during the Adamic Age, as given in Genesis 2:15. There will be yet another, the third Garden of Eden, in the coming Millennial Age of YAHSHUA MESSIAH, as given in Ezekiel 36:35.

A garden has both plant and animal life, thus YHWH created the Pre-Adamic world with plants and animals. The enormous deposits and reservoirs under the earth's surface of the fossil fuels; coal, oil and gas, and the abundant existence of fossils throughout the world bear witness to the fact that the Pre-Adamic earth was absolutely teeming with luxuriant plant and animal life. This Pre-Adamic earth was destroyed after 'war broke out in heaven' between the holy angels led by Michael and the, "tobe", fallen angels led by Lucifer.

So we need to determine the time frame of the first Eden on earth . . . . some time long before the second Eden when Adam was created.

Revelation 12:7-9

> *"And **war broke out in heaven**: Michael and his angels fought with the dragon; and the dragon and his angels fought, 8 but they did not prevail, nor was a place found for them in heaven any longer. 9 So the great dragon was cast out, that serpent of old, called **the Devil and Satan**, who deceives the whole world; **he was cast to the earth, and his angels were cast out with him**".*

These verses describe a war between armies of angels in heaven. We are speaking about an angelic war with massive destructive power at the angels' command. This angelic war started in heaven but was **finished on earth** when YHWH cast **heylel** (Lucifer became **heylel** after his fall) and his angels out of heaven back down to earth. As a result, the whole earth suffered cataclysmic violence of unimaginable proportions, and death, destruction, flooding, darkness and sin entered the world of the Pre-Adamic earth for the very first time.

Lucifer was the anointed cherub who governed the beautiful luxuriant Garden of Eden earth.

He was adorned with precious stones and gifted with musical instruments of worship. He had freedom of movement as a trusted holy angel of YHWH to move back and forth from earth to heaven. Lucifer became tempted and sinned when iniquity was found in his heart. He became jealous of YHWH and decided to lead a rebellion to try to usurp Him from His throne. Lucifer (a holy angel), became **heylel** (Satan a sinful angel) because of his sin of rebellion.

Lucifer ascended above the clouds from the earth to rebel against God in heaven. This is when war broke out in heaven between Lucifer and his angels and Michael and his angels. Lucifer and his angels were defeated and they were **violently** cast out of heaven back down to earth (Revelation

12:4) with global cataclysmic consequences for the earth, as previously described.

The beautiful Garden of Eden earth of Genesis 1:1, which YHWH created in the beginning and gave Lucifer dominion over, was transformed into a totally ruined chaotic earth in darkness and covered by deep frozen water (ice) by the time we come to Genesis 1:2. This ruined, ice covered and flooded dark earth became the tartaroo prison for Satan and his fallen angels until ELOHIM renewed the surface of the earth at the start of the Adamic Age. Satan and his fallen angels are now confined to earth and its atmosphere awaiting their final judgement in the Lake of Fire. However, Satan will once again be imprisoned, but this time to a 'bottomless pit' at the start of YAHSUA's Millennial Kingdom before he is released to receive his final Lake of Fire Judgement.

Young Earth Creationism confuses the beginning of the Pre-Adamic Age, which happened millions of years ago with the beginning of the Adamic Age, which happened only approximately six thousand years ago.

Genesis 1:1 refers to **the beginning of time**, millions of years ago, when YHWH created the heavens and the earth. This also marked the beginning of the First Age, the Pre-Adamic Age, in ELOHIM's Plan of the Ages.

Genesis 1:3-5 refers to the first 24-hour day in **the beginning of the Adamic Age**, the Second Age, after YHWH destroyed the Pre-Adamic world through His global tohuw and bohuw judgement because of the sins of angels. The Adamic Age started about six thousand years ago.

THE BEGINNING
OF THE ADAMIC AGE

As we have shown the original beautiful Garden of Eden earth of Genesis 1:1 was thrown into chaos and darkness (Genesis 1:2) when Satan and his fallen angels were cast back down to earth following their rebellion in heaven.

In Genesis 1:3-5, we find that YHWH reintroduced the light of the sun to shine onto the earth's surface at the dawn of the Second Age, the Adamic Age.

Genesis 1:3-53

> *"Then YHWH said, "Let there be light"; and there was light".*

> *"And YHWH saw the light that it was good; and YHWH divided the light from the darkness".*

> *"YHWH called the light Day, and the darkness He called Night. So the evening and the morning were the first day".*

It is clear that when YHWH said, 'Let there be light', it was the light of the sun, which YHWH had previously withheld, or caused by some other means to be blocked, from reaching the earth's surface in His global *tohuw* and *bohuw* judgement. We know for certain that the sun had already been created in the beginning (Genesis 1:1), and this was millions of years before YHWH reintroduced the light as described in the verses above.

There cannot be the first 24 hour day, evening and morning without the light of the sun, and it is impossible for the earth to hang and rotate by itself in the universe without the gravitational pull of the sun.

Young Earth Creationism (YEC) believes that it was not until the fourth day that YHWH created the sun, it becomes a huge problem for YEC to explain how there can be the first 24 hours of day and night without the sun. In order to get over this dilemma, YEC teaches that it was the light of the Holy Spirit which shone on the earth for the first three 24 hour days of creation. Of course, anything is possible with YHWH, but we find the YEC explanation unbiblical and illogical.

This viewpoint creates confusion and disbelief in the Word of YHWH from educational establishments and scientists, and it becomes a great stumbling block for young people to accept the Bible as the Word of ELOHIM.

The rest of the Genesis account of creation, Genesis 1:3-31, makes complete sense, once we understand that YHWH darkened the sun and withdrew its light in His Pre-Adamic *tohuw* and *bohuw* judgement against Satan and his fallen angels.

When YHWH began the Second Age, the Adamic Age, He reintroduced the light of the sun to the earth, and renewed the earth's surface and its atmosphere. Then, YHWH recreated or renewed plant and animal life, and finally He created mankind for the first time, as described in the six-day creation account of Genesis 1:3-31. This happened approximately six thousand years ago.

Whe have to understand that there is absolutely no contradiction whatsoever between Geneses 1:1, where it is says that YHWH created the heavens and the earth in the beginning, and Genesis 1:14-19 where it says that YHWH **made** the sun, the moon and the stars on the fourth day. Once we see and understand that the whole of the six-day creation account is written from man's earthly perspective rather than from a cosmic perspective, then the scriptures become clear and everything make sense.

Day One (Genesis 1:3-)

YHWH reintroduces the light of the sun to reach and shine onto the surface of the deep frozen waters of the flooded and ruined earth. The effect of this heat and sudden change in temperature resulted in a massive global melting of the ice.

The ice must have been so thick that the Spirit of ELOHIM first needed to shake, break and soften it, even before Day One when the light was reintroduced. This was in order to assist the melting process, which would occur on Day One. This is exactly what YHWH did because a correct meaning of the Hebrew word *rachaph*, where it says in Genesis 1:2

"And the Spirit of ELOHIM was **hovering** *(rachaph) over the face of the waters" (ice)* is to shake, break and soften. This meaning of *rachaph* is confirmed by Strong's H7363. So, the 'hovering' of the Spirit of ELOHIM over the face of the waters (ice) was not a gentle hovering movement of the Spirit of ELOHIM, but an **active** shaking and breaking of the deep ice. This was in preparation for the great melt that took place once the sunlight with its heat was reintroduced onto the earth's surface on Day One.

Day Two (Genesis 1:5-8)

YHWH forms the firmament by lifting the 'waters from the waters'. The firmament refers to the space or expanse within the earth's atmosphere between the earth's surface and the cloud strata, which YHWH formed using the process of evaporation, when the heat of the sunlight caused vast volumes of water vapour to rise up from the surface of the melt-waters to form dense dark clouds in the sky.

Day Three (Genesis 1:9-12)

YHWH forms the dry land by causing the melt-waters to recede from the flooded earth. This also causes plant life to start to grow again on the land.

Day Four (Genesis 1:14-19)

14 Then YHWH said, "Let there be lights in the firmament (the space between the earth's surface and the clouds) of the heavens (the earth's atmosphere) to divide the day from the night; and let them be for signs and seasons and for days and years,

15 "and let them be for lights in the firmament of the heavens to give light on the earth, and it was so".

16 "Then YHWH made (asah) two great lights: the greater light to rule the day, and the lesser light to rule the night. He made the stars also".

17 "God set them in the firmament of the heavens to give light on the earth",

18 "and to rule over the day and over the night and to divide the light from the darkness. And God saw that it was good".

19 "So the evening and the morning were the fourth day".

At the beginning of Day Four, YHWH said, *'Let there be lights in the firmament of the heaven'*. We can certainly conclude that by the end of Day Three the firmament of the heaven (the space between the earth's surface and the clouds) had become darkened again, but this time by the dense clouds of water vapour formed on Day Two.

These clouds would have blocked out light—sunlight, moonlight and starlight—from reaching the firmament and thus the earth's surface. So, on Day Four YHWH thinned and dispersed these dense dark clouds so that the sunlight, moonlight and starlight could shine through the firmament down onto the earth's surface.

From an earthly perspective, the sun, the moon and the stars were made (asah) on Day Four *'for signs and seasons, and for days and years'* for the benefit of mankind. Notice that verse 17 above, does not say that YHWH created these lights on Day Four, but that He **set** these lights in the firmament, meaning that He made them appear, be visible, in the firmament from man's earthly perspective. We know from the very first verse of the Bible, Genesis 1:1, that these lights (sunlight, moonlight and starlight) had already been created (bara) in the beginning, and not on Day Four.

Day Five (Genesis 1:20-23)

YHWH creates sea life and birdlife.

Day Six (Genesis 1:24-31)

YHWH re creates animal life. Adam is created in spiritual form to the image of YHWH. The pinnacle of YHWH's creation was the creation of man in ELOHIM's own image.

THE END OF TIME EVENTS

Revelation 6: 1-15, the four horsemen of the apocalypse

1: White horse—Conquering all.
2: Red horse—Take peace away from earth.
3: Black horse—Trade is being controlled and food rationed.
4: Pale horse—Quarter of world to be killed by war, hunger and pestilence.
5: Great Earthquake, the sun become dark and the moon turn red as blood.
6: Stars of heaven fell onto earth. (Meteorite storms)
7: **All** mountains and islands will move out of its place. (Tectonic plate movement.)

Revelation 7:1

No wind.

Revelation 8:1-13 the seven trumpets

5: Fire is casted onto earth, thunder, lightning and earthquakes. (Meteorites)
7: Hail and fire mixed with blood. One third devastation of plant life. (Hail and rain storms.)
8: Volcanic explosion in the sea. One third devastation of marine life.
10: Meteorite "Wormwood" strikes the earth. Third part of fresh water contaminated.
12: Heavens (sun, moon, stars) darkened by one third of its brightness.

Revelation 9:1-21

1-13: Meteorite leaves physical "Pit" or open crater in earth's crust. Great plaques roams, scorpions and locusts and strange new medical conditions prevail through humanity. One third of earth's human population devastated.

14-16: The fallen angels are released from the Euphrates river region with an army of 200 million.

18: One third of humanity devastated by fire, smoke and brimstone.

Revelation 12:4

"The great red dragon's tail swept down a third of the stars and cast them down to earth . . ."

13:7: *"And it was given to him to make war with the angels (again), and to overcome them . . ."*

It is important that we now look at what happens next and to magnify the era from after the K-T event 65 million years ago to Noah, to get a clear understanding about the scriptures, mythology and the sciences . . . . these guys have a lot to say . . . .

FALSE GODS, CREATURES AND IDOLS
IN THE BIBLE AND MYTHOLOGY

Amos 5:26

Sakkuth/Kewan Star god, Saturn, Satan

Six triangles . . . is the Egyptian hieroglyphic for the . . . Land of the Spirits. It is also the ancient Egyptian Seal of Solomon. In the Astro-Mythology of the Egyptians, we find belief in the first man-god (Horus I) . . . and his death and resurrection as Amsu.

This (6-pointed star) was the first sign or hieroglyphic of Amsu. Amsu—the risen Horus—was the first man-god raised in spiritual form.

I Kings 11:7

Kamos/Chemosh the god of the Moabites

Kamos was a Minotaur who is one of the two main mortal allies of Gargarensis, a Cyclops Hero. He is an old enemy of Arkantos; his wife was murdered by Kamos' pirates. At an early age, Kamos was kidnapped by an Egyptian fishing ship and raised by the goddess Bast.

Kamos is missing one hand, which he lost when attempting to hand-feed a Leviathan, later replaced with a khopesh. Kamos' first act against Arkantos is a raid on Atlantis in which he steals the trident held by the Poseidon statue in Atlantis' harbour. Arkantos pursues him to an island base where he recovers the trident, though Kamos escapes. Arkantos and Ajax later encounter and kill Kamos during a raid on one of his pirate bases.

Kamos is a hero unit whose special ability is a gore attack similar to that of the Minotaur unit, but is more powerful.

Chemosh was a god associated with the Semitic mother-goddess Ashtar, whose name he bears (Moabite Stone, line 17; compare Barton, "Semitic Origins," IV.).

Ashtar is more probably masculine here, as in South Arabia, and another name for Chemosh, the compound "Ashtar-Chemosh".

Whatever differences of conception may have attached to the god at different shrines, there is no adequate reason for doubting the substantial identity of the gods to whom these various names were applied.

At some period the impure cult of the Semitic goddess was practiced at Baal-peor Chemosh, therefore, was in general a deity of the same nature as Baal.

On critical occasions a human sacrifice was considered necessary to secure his favour (compare II Kings iii. 27), and when deliverance came, a sanctuary might be built to him (Moabite Stone, line 3). An ancient poem, twice quoted in the Old Testament (Num. xxi. 27-30; Jer. xlviii. 45, 46), regards the Moabites as the children of Chemosh, and also calls them "the people of Chemosh".

The name of the father of Mesha, Chemosh-melek ("Chemosh is Malik" or "Chemosh is king"; compare Moabite Stone, line 1), indicates the possibility that Chemosh and Malik or Moloch were one and the same deity.

Molog/Molag the god of the Ammonites (Egypt)

Molag Bal is the Daedric Prince whose sphere is the domination and enslavement of mortals. He is known as the King of Rape and the Harvester of Souls. His main desire is to harvest the souls of mortals and to bring them within his sway by spreading seeds of strife and discord in the mortal realms.

One legend claims that Molag Bal created the first vampire when he raped a Nedic virgin, who in turn slaughtered a group of nomads. He also made pacts with other mortals and turned them into vampires such as Lord Harkon and his family. Thus it is implied Lord Harkon and his family are the original Volkihar Clan of vampires being directly turned by the Daedric Prince himself.

He is a Daedric power of much importance in Morrowind, where he is always the archenemy of Boethiah, the Prince of Plots. Other enemies are Ebonarm and Mephala. His summoning day is Chil'a. In Aldmeris, his name means Fire Stone.

Num 21:29

Kewan = star god = Saturn

Acts 7:42-43

> *"Then YHWH turned, and gave them up to worship the host of heaven; as it is written in the book of the prophets, O ye house of Yisrayl, have ye offered to me slain beasts and sacrifices by the space of forty years in the wilderness?*
>
> *Yea, ye took up the tabernacle of Moloch, and the star of your god Remphan, figures which ye made to worship them: and I will carry you away beyond Babylon".*

Remphan

(Acts 7:43; R.V., "Rephan"). In Amos 5:26 the Heb. Chiun (q.v.) is rendered by the LXX. "Rephan," and this name are adopted by Luke in his narrative of the Acts. These names represent the star-god Saturn or Moloch.

The Star of David is nowhere Mentioned in Biblical Scriptures as a Sign or Symbol for The Hebrews. It is from pagan origins.

The so-called" star of David" is actually the six pointed star of the god Remphan and it is associated, with the worship of the system of Baal and Ashtoreth or Moloch. The 6-pointed star is not a Hebrew symbol

2 kings 23:10-13

Astarte, Serimanus, goddess of the Sidoniers Diana

Astarte is also known as Astarat and Astoreth. She is an incarnation of Ishtar and Inanna. This Semitic Goddess was worshipped by the Syrians, Canaanites (today called Palestinians), Phoenicians, Egyptians and other Semitic Tribes. King Solomon built a Temple to Her as Astoreth, near Jerusalem.

Astarte was worshipped as many things, to the Egyptians, She was honoured as a Goddess of War and tenacity, to the Semites; She was a Goddess of Love and Fertility. Among the Greeks she was transposed into the Goddess of Love Aphrodite. In the Bible, she is referred to as "the abomination". Considering her widespread devotion in Biblical times.

Baal Num 25:3

Baal is a title meaning "lord" that was applied to a number of West Semitic gods Baal Hadad, probably the most widely worshiped Baal, was worshiped by Arameans who brought his worship to other parts of the Mediterranean. Early demonologists, unaware of Hadad or that the instances of the term "Baal" in the Bible referred to any number of local deities, few to none of them referring to Hadad, came to regard the term as referring to but one personage. Until archaeological digs at Ras Shamra and Ebla uncovered texts explaining the Syrian pantheon, the Baal Zebûb was frequently confused with various Semitic deities named Baal, and in the New Testament might refer to a high-ranking devil or to Satan himself.

The Biblical and historical evidence shows that the Moabites worshiped a Baal. The pre-Islamic and Muslim sources show that the Meccans took over the idol Hubal from the Moabites. It is also this word "Lord" translated wrongly on purpose into the Bible in order to create chaos in the Christian believe system and to hide the true name of God namely YHWH Elohim.

Baal is a Christian demon. According to Christian demonology, Baal was ranked as the first and principal king in Hell, ruling over the East. According to some authors Baal is a Duke, with sixty-six legions of demons under his command. The term "Baal" is used in various ways in the Old Testament, with the usual meaning of master, or owner. It came to sometimes mean the local pagan god of a particular people and at the same time all of the idols of the land. It is also found in several places in the plural Baalim, or Baals (Judges 2:11, Judges 10:10). There were many variations, such as the sun god, the god of fertility, and Beelzebub, or the "lord of flies".

During the English Puritan period, Baal was either compared to Satan or considered his main assistant. According to Francis Barrett, he has the power to make those who invoke him invisible, and to some other demonologists his power is stronger in October. According to some sources, he can make people wise, speaks hoarsely, and carries ashes in his pocket.

While his Semitic predecessor was depicted as a man or a bull, the demon Baal was in grimoire tradition said to appear in the forms of a man, cat, toad, or combinations thereof. An illustration in Collin de Plancy's 1818 book "Dictionnaire Infernal" rather curiously placed the heads of the three creatures onto a set of spider legs.

Nabu/Nebo Jesaja 46:1

Nebu is the Assyrian and Babylonian god of wisdom and writing, worshipped by Babylonians as the son of Marduk and his consort, Sarpanitum, and as the grandson of Ea. Nabu's consort was Tashmetum.

Originally, Nabu was a West Semitic deity introduced by the Amorites into Mesopotamia, probably at the same time as Marduk shortly after 2000 BC. While Marduk became Babylon's main deity, Nabu resided in nearby Borsippa in his temple E-zida. He was first called the "scribe and minister of Marduk", later assimilated as Marduk's beloved son from Sarpanitum. During the Babylonian New Year Festival, the cult statue of Nabu was transported from Borsippa to Babylon in order to commune with his father Marduk.

Nabu later became one of the principal gods in Assyria and Assyrians addressed many prayers and inscriptions to Nabu and named children after him. Nabu was the god of writing and scribes and was the keeper of the Tablets of Destiny, in which the fate of humankind was recorded. He was also sometimes worshiped as a fertility god and as a god of water.

Nabu is accorded the office of patron of the scribes, taking over from the Sumerian goddess Nisaba. His symbols are the clay writing tablet with the writing stylus. He wears a horned cap, and stands with hands clasped, in the ancient gesture of priesthood. He rides on a winged dragon (mušhuššu, also known as Sirrush) that is initially Marduk's

Marduk

According to The Encyclopaedia of Religion, the name Marduk was probably pronounced Marutuk. The etymology of the name Marduk is conjectured as derived from amar-Utu ("bull calf of the sun god Utu"). The origin of Marduk's name may reflect an earlier genealogy, or have had cultural ties to the ancient city of Sippar (whose god was Utu, the sun god), dating back to the third millennium BCE.

In the perfected system of astrology, the planet Jupiter was associated with Marduk by the Hammurabi period.

The Leviathan Job 41:1 to 34 (KJ)

> *"Can you pull in the leviathan with a fishhook or tie down his tongue with a rope?*
>
> *Can you put a cord through his nose or pierce his jaw with a hook?*
>
> *Will he keep begging you for mercy? Will he speak to you with gentle words?*
>
> *Will he make an agreement with you for you to take him as your slave for life?*
>
> *Can you make a pet of him like a bird or put him on a leash for your girls?*
>
> *Will traders barter for him? Will they divide him up among the merchants?*
>
> *Can you fill his hide with harpoons or his head with fishing spears?*
>
> *If you lay a hand on him, you will remember the struggle and never do it again!*
>
> *Any hope of subduing him is false; the mere sight of him is overpowering.*

No-one is fierce enough to rouse him. Who then is able to stand against me?

Who has a claim against me that I must pay? Everything under heaven belongs to me.

I will not fail to speak of his limbs, his strength and his graceful form.

Who can strip off his outer coat? Who would approach him with a <u>bridle</u>?

Who dares open the doors of his mouth, ringed about with his fearsome teeth?

His back has rows of shields tightly sealed together; each is so close to the next that no air can pass between.

They are joined fast to one another; they cling together and cannot be parted.

His snorting throws out flashes of light; his eyes are like the rays of dawn.

Firebrands stream from his mouth; sparks of fire shoot out.

Smoke pours from his nostrils as from a boiling pot over a fire of reeds.

His breath sets coals ablaze, and flames dart from his mouth.

Strength resides in his neck; dismay goes before him.

The folds of his flesh are tightly joined; they are firm and immovable.

His chest is hard as rock, hard as a lower millstone.

When he rises up, the mighty are terrified; they retreat before his thrashing.

The sword that reaches him has no effect, nor does the spear or the dart or the javelin.

Iron he treats like straw and bronze like rotten wood.

Arrows do not make him flee; sling stones are like chaff to him.

A club seems to him but a piece of straw, he laughs at the rattling of the lance.

His undersides are jagged potsherds, leaving a trail in the mud like a threshing-sledge.

He makes the depths churn like a boiling cauldron and stirs up the sea like a pot of ointment.

Behind him he leaves a glistening wake; one would think the deep had white hair.

Nothing on earth is his equal—a creature without fear.

He looks down on all that are haughty; he is king over all that are proud".

Amazing to think that this creature could reason and speak to people?

APE TO MAN AND ADAM

(Sciences point of view)

The field of science which studies the human fossil record is known as paleoanthropology.

It is the intersection of the disciplines of palaeontology (the study of ancient life forms) and anthropology (the study of humans).

Homo sapiens

The Upper Palaeolithic (or Upper Palaeolithic, Late Stone Age) is the third and last subdivision of the Palaeolithic or Old Stone Age as it is understood in Europe, Africa and Asia. Very broadly, it dates to between 50,000 and 10,000 years ago, roughly coinciding with the appearance of behavioural modernity and before the advent of agriculture. The terms "Late Stone Age" and "Upper Palaeolithic" refer to the same periods. For historical reasons, "Stone Age" usually refers to the period in Africa, whereas "Upper Palaeolithic" is generally used when referring to the period in Europe.

The Palaeolithic Age, Era or Period, is a prehistoric period of human history distinguished by the development of the most primitive stone tools discovered, and covers roughly 99% of human technological prehistory. It extends from the earliest known use of stone tools, probably by Hominines such as Australopithecines, 2.6 million years ago, to the end of the Pleistocene around 10,000 BP. The Palaeolithic era is followed by the Mesolithic. The date of the Palaeolithic-Mesolithic boundary may vary by locality as much as several thousand years.

During the Palaeolithic, humans grouped together in small societies such as bands, and subsisted by gathering plants and hunting or scavenging wild animals. The Palaeolithic is characterized by the use of knapped stone tools, although at the time humans also used wood and bone tools. Other organic commodities were adapted for use as tools, including leather and vegetable fibres; however, due to their nature, these have not been preserved to any great degree. Surviving artefacts of the Palaeolithic era are known as paleoliths. Humankind gradually evolved from early members of the genus Homo such as Homo habillis —who used simple stone tools —into fully behaviourally and anatomically modern humans during the Palaeolithic era.

During the end of the Palaeolithic, specifically the Middle and or Upper Palaeolithic, humans began to produce the earliest works of art and engage in religious and spiritual behaviour such as burial and ritual. The climate during the Palaeolithic consisted of a set of glacial and interglacial periods in which the climate periodically fluctuated between warm and cool temperatures.

The term "Palaeolithic" was coined by archaeologist John Lubbock in 1865. It derives from Greek: palaios, "old"; and lithos, "stone", literally meaning "old age of the stone" or "Old Stone Age."

The average cranial capacity is, on average, 1350 cc. At about 40,000 years ago, with Cro-Magnon culture first appearing, we use our first diversified tool kits.

Such technological breakthroughs would lead to others, allowing Homo sapiens to take over and inhabit nearly every ecological niche on the planet.

Artwork, in the form of decorated tools, beads, ivory carvings of humans and animals, clay figurines, musical instruments, and spectacular cave paintings appeared over the next 20,000 years. (34 000 before Adam) (Leakey 1994)

Compared to the Neanderthals and other late archaic humans, modern humans generally have more delicate skeletons. Their skulls are more rounded and their brow ridges generally protrude much less. They rarely have the occipital buns found on the back of Neanderthal skulls. They also have relatively high foreheads and pointed chins.

Homo sapiens began migrating into the lower latitudes of East Asia by 70,000 years ago. Along the way, some of them interbred with archaic humans, including both Neanderthals and Denisovans. Genetic markers from these archaic human populations are found in the gene pool of some Southern Chinese, New Guinean, and other Micronesian Island populations today.

Homo sapiens from Southeast Asia travelled to Australia by 46,000 years ago and possibly as early as 60,000 years ago. Because Australia was not connected to Southeast Asia by land, it is probable that these first Australian Aborigines arrived by simple boats or rafts.

Modern humans reached the Japanese Islands by 30,000 years ago or somewhat earlier. Around 30,000 years ago, Homo sapiens big game hunters moved into North-eastern Siberia. Some of them migrated into North America via the Bering Plain, or Beringia, by 20,000-15,000 years ago.

Some Homo sapiens may have reached the Americas a bit earlier than this, but the evidence is still considered questionable by most paleoanthropologists. The Bering Plain intercontinental land connection appeared between Siberia and Alaska as a result of sea levels dropping up to 450 feet (137 m.) during the final major cold period of the last ice age. Until that time, all human evolution had occurred in the Old World.

A consequence of human migrations into new regions of the world has been the extinction of many animal species indigenous to those areas. By 11,000 years ago (5000 before Adam), human hunters in the New World apparently had played a part in the extermination of 135 species of mammals, including 75% of the larger ones (mammoths, mastodons, giant sloths, etc.).

Most of these extinctions apparently occurred within a few hundred years. It is likely that the rapidly changing climate at the end of the last ice age was a contributing factor. However, the addition of human hunters with spears to the existing top predators (mostly saber-toothed cats, lions, and dire-wolves) very likely disrupted the equilibrium between large herbivores and their predators.

As a consequence there was a major ecosystem disruption resulting in the rapid decline of both non-human carnivores and their prey. "Humans" were very likely the trigger that set off this "tropic cascade".

Following the arrival of aboriginal people in Australia and Polynesians in New Zealand there were similar dramatic animal extinctions. In both of these cases humans apparently were directly responsible for wiping out easily hunted species. Large vulnerable marsupials were the main victims in Australia.

Within 5,000 years following the arrival of these "humans", approximately 90% of the marsupial species larger than a domesticated cat had become extinct there. In New Zealand, it was mostly large flightless birds that were driven to extinction by modern hunters following their arrival in the 10th-13th centuries A.D.

The rate of animal and plant extinction has once again accelerated dramatically. During the last century and a half, the explosion in our global human population and our rapid technological development has allowed us to move into and over-exploit most areas of our planet including the oceans. That exploitation has usually involved cutting down forests, changing the courses of rivers, pushing wild animals and plants out of farm and urban areas, polluting wetlands with pesticides and other man-made chemicals, and industrial-scale hunting of large land animals, whales, and fish.

During the early 19th century, there were at least 40 million bison roaming the Great Plains of North America. By the end of that century, there were only a few hundred remaining. They had been hunted to near extinction with guns. The same fate came to the African elephant and rhinoceros during the 20th century. Likewise, commercial fishermen have depleted one species of fish after another during the last half century. Governments have had to step in to try to stem the tide of these human population effects on other species. However, they have been only marginally successful.

The World Conservation Union conservatively estimates that 7,266 animal species and 8,323 plant and lichen species are now at risk of extinction primarily due to human caused habitat degradation. The endangered list includes 30% of all amphibian species, nearly 50% of the turtles and tortoises, 25% of the mammals, 20% of the sharks and rays, and 12.5% of the birds. This list does not include the many millions of species that are still unknown to science. It is likely that most of them will become extinct before they can be described and studied.

There is no reliable evidence of modern humans elsewhere in the Old World until 60,000-40,000 years ago, during a short temperate period in the midst of the last ice age.

It would seem from these dates that the location of initial modern Homo sapiens evolution and the direction of their dispersion from that area are obvious. That is not the case. Since the early 1980's, there have been two leading contradictory models that attempt to explain modern human evolution, the replacement model and the regional continuity model.

The replacement model of Christopher Stringer and Peter Andrews proposes that modern humans evolved from archaic "humans" 200,000-150,000 years ago only in Africa and then some of them migrated into the rest of the Old World replacing all of the Neanderthals and other late archaic "humans" beginning around 60,000-40,000 years ago. If this interpretation of the fossil record is correct, all people today share a relatively modern African ancestry.

All other lines of "humans" that had descended from Homo erectus presumably became extinct. From this view, the regional anatomical differences that we now see among humans are recent developments evolving mostly in the last 40,000 years. This hypothesis is also referred to as the "out of Africa", "Noah's ark", and "African replacement" model.

The regional continuity model (or multiregional evolution model) advocated by Milford Wolpoff proposes that modern humans evolved more or less simultaneously in all major regions of the Old World from local archaic humans. For example, modern Chinese are seen as having evolved from Chinese archaic humans and ultimately from Chinese Homo erectus. This would mean that the Chinese and some other peoples in the Old World have great antiquity in place. Supporters of this model believe that the ultimate common ancestor of all modern people was an early Homo erectus in Africa who lived at least 1.8 million years ago. It is further suggested that since then there was sufficient gene flow between Europe, Africa, and Asia to prevent long-term reproductive isolation and the subsequent evolution of distinct regional species. It is argued that intermittent contact between people of these distant areas would have kept the human line a single species at any one time. However, regional varieties, or subspecies, of humans are expected to have existed.

REPLACEMENT MODEL ARGUMENTS

There are two sources of evidence supporting the replacement model—the fossil record and DNA. So far, the earliest finds of modern *Homo sapiens* skeletons come from Africa. They date to nearly 200,000 years ago on that continent. They appear in Southwest Asia around 100,000 years ago and elsewhere in the Old World by 60,000-40,000 years ago. Unless modern human remains dating to 200,000 years ago or earlier are found in Europe or East Asia, it would seem that the replacement model better explains the fossil data for those regions. However, the DNA data supporting a replacement are more problematical.

Through comparisons of mitochondrial DNA sequences from living people throughout the world, it is concluded that Africa has the greatest genetic diversity and, therefore, must be the homeland of all modern humans. Assuming a specific, constant rate of mutation, they further concluded that the common ancestor of modern people was a woman living about 200,000 years ago in Africa. This supposed predecessor was dubbed "mitochondrial Eve".

More recent genetic research at the University of Chicago and Yale University lends support to the replacement model. It has shown that variations in the DNA of the Y chromosome and chromosome 12 also have the greatest diversity among Africans today. John Relethford and other critics of the replacement model have pointed out that Africa could have had the greatest diversity in DNA simply because there were more people living there during the last several hundred thousand years. This would leave open the possibility that Africa was not necessarily the only homeland of modern humans.

Critics of the genetic argument for the replacement model also point out that the rate of mutation used for the "molecular clock" is not necessarily constant, which makes the 200,000 year date for "mitochondrial Eve" unreliable. The rate of inheritable mutations for a species or a population can vary due to a number of factors including generation time, the efficiency of DNA repair within cells, ambient temperature, and varying amounts of natural environmental mutagens. In addition, some kinds of DNA molecules are known to be more subject to mutation than others, resulting in faster mutation rates. This seems to be the case with the Y chromosome in human males.

Further criticism of the genetic argument for the replacement model has come from geneticists at Oxford University. They found that the human beta globin gene is widely distributed in Asia but not in Africa.

Since this gene is thought to have originated more than 200,000 years ago, it undercuts the claim that an African population of modern *Homo sapiens* replaced East Asian archaic humans less than 60,000 years ago.

REGIONAL CONTINUITY
MODEL ARGUMENTS

Fossil evidence also is used to support the regional continuity model. Its advocates claim that there has been a continuity of some anatomical traits from archaic humans to modern humans in Europe and Asia. In other words, the Asian and European physical characteristics have antiquity in these regions going back over 100,000 years.

They point to the fact that many Europeans have relatively heavy brow ridges and a high angle of their noses reminiscent of Neanderthals. Similarly, it is claimed that some Chinese facial characteristics can be seen in an Asian archaic human fossil from Jinniushan dating to 200,000 years ago. Like *Homo erectus*, East Asians today commonly have shovel-shaped incisors while Africans and Europeans rarely do. This supports the contention of direct genetic links between Asian *Homo erectus* and modern Asians.

Alan Thorne of the Australian National University believes that Australian aborigines share key skeletal and dental traits with pre-modern people who inhabited Indonesia at least 100,000 years ago. The implication is that there was no replacement by modern humans from Africa 60,000-40,000 years ago. However, the evidence does not rule out gene flow from African populations to Europe and Asia at that time and before.

David Frayer, of the University of Kansas, believes that a number of European fossils from the last 50,000 years have characteristics that are the result of archaic and modern humans interbreeding.

ASSIMILATION MODEL

It is apparent that both the complete replacement and the regional continuity models have difficulty accounting for all of the fossil and genetic data. What has emerged is a new hypothesis known as the assimilation (or partial replacement) model. It takes a middle ground and incorporates both of the old models.

Guenter Braour, of the University of Hamburg in Germany, proposes that the first modern humans did evolve in Africa, but when they migrated into other regions they did not simply replace existing human populations. Rather, they interbred to a limited degree with late archaic humans resulting in hybrid populations.

In Europe, for instance, the first modern humans appear in the archaeological record rather suddenly around 45-40,000 years ago.

The abruptness of the appearance of these Cro-Magnon people could be explained by their migrating into the region from Africa via an eastern Mediterranean coastal route.

They apparently shared Europe with Neanderthals for another 12,000 years or more. **During this long time period, it is argued that interbreeding occurred and that the partially hybridized predominantly Cro-Magnon population ultimately became modern Europeans.**

In 2003, a discovery was made in a Romanian cave named Peştera cu Oase that supports this hypothesis. It was a partial skeleton of a 15-16 year old male *Homo sapiens* who lived about 30,000 years ago or a bit earlier. He had a mix of old and new anatomical features. The skull had characteristics of both modern and archaic humans. This could be explained as the result of interbreeding with Neanderthals according to Erik Trinkaus of Washington University in St. Louis.

Alan Templeton, also of Washington University, reported that a computer-based analysis of 10 different human DNA sequences indicate that there has been interbreeding between people living in Asia, Europe, and Africa for at least 600,000 years.

This is consistent with the hypothesis that humans expanded again and again out of Africa and that these emigrants interbred with existing populations in Asia and Europe. It is also possible that migrations were not only in one direction—people could have migrated into Africa as well. If interbreeding occurred, it may have been a rare event. This is supported by the fact that most skeletons of Neanderthals and Cro-Magnon people do not show hybrid characteristics.

Europe's biggest ever volcanic eruption, a catastrophic event around 40,000 years ago, may have sent temperatures plummeting as clouds of ash blocked out the sun.

This "volcanic winter" caused by the Campanian Ignimbrite eruption in Italy, coming on top of a cold climate episode, marked the beginning of the end for the Neanderthals. Volcanic deposits from the CI eruption, consisting of tiny glass particles, were found in Greece, Libya and Central Europe.

Humans are uniquely adept at utilizing systems of symbolic communication such as language for self-expression, the exchange of ideas, and organization. Humans create complex social structures composed of many cooperating and competing groups, from families and kinship networks to states.

Social interactions between humans have established an extremely wide variety of values, social norms, and rituals, which together form the basis of human society. Humans are noted for their desire to understand and influence their environment, seeking to explain and manipulate phenomena through science, philosophy, mythology, and religion.

FLOODS OF SATAN AND NOAH

(DIFFERENCES)

The flood of Noah's day was an act of judgment passed upon men because of sin. Those of us who understand the Genesis 8 account as a literal event do not doubt the extent of the destruction described by Moses. Scripture is clear that except for Noah and his family, all men and animals were destroyed as a result of God's judgment.

There are those who claim the flood narrative is a fable, but no one doubts the existence of men prior to Noah's flood. Why then doubt the existence of a pre-Adamite world which was destroyed by the flood of Genesis 1:2? That this was a greater flood than the one of Noah's time, and an act of greater judgment in punishment of more horrible sins is clear from the following contrasts:

The flood of Noah's day lasted over a year, yet vegetation was not destroyed. But as a result of the flood sent in judgment upon heylel, the fruitful places became a wilderness (Jer. 4:23-26). New vegetation had to be planted during the six days of re-creation, for the earth was totally desolate (Gen. 1:11-12; Gen 2:5, 8-17).

This indicates that **Satan** flood was of a much longer duration than Noah's and, without doubt, was a judgment for a more serious rebellion-a complete rebellion of the pre-Admit world.

SATAN'S FLOOD

Earth made waste (Gen. 1:2; Jer. 4:23)

Earth made empty (Gen. 1:2; Jer. 4:23)

Earth made totally dark (Gen. 1:2; Jer. Evolutionary Timeline 4:23)

No light from heaven (Gen. 1:2; Jer. 4:23)

No days (Gen. 1:2-5)

All vegetation destroyed (Jer. 4:23-26)

No continual abating waters off earth (Gen. 1:6-12)

Waters taken off earth in one day (Gen. 1:10)

Supernatural work of taking waters off earth(Gen. 1:6-12)

God rebuked the waters (Gen. 1:6-12; Ps. 104:7)

Waters hasted away (Ps. 104:7)

God set bounds for waters (Ps. 104:9)

All fish destroyed because sun withheld from earth
(Gen. 1:2, 20-23; Jer. 4:23-26)

No fowls left (Gen. 1:20; Jer. 4:25)

No animals left (Gen. 1:24-25; Gen 2:19)

No man left (Gen. 1:26-28; Jer. 4:25)

No social system left (2 Peter. 3:6; Jer. 4:23-26)

No ark made to save life (Jer. 4:23-26; 2 Peter. 3:6-7)

Cause: fall of Satan (Isa. 14:12-14; Jer. 4:23-26; Ezek. 28:11-17)

Result: necessary to make new fish, fowl animals, man, vegetation,
(Gen. 1:3-Gen 2:25)

NOAH'S FLOOD

Not made waste Gen. 8:11-12, 22)

Not made empty (Gen. 6:17-22; Gen 8:16)

Not made totally dark (Gen. 8:6-22)

Light from heaven (Gen. 8:6-22)

Days (Gen. 8:1-22)

Vegetation left (Gen. 8:11-12, 22)

Continual abating of waters off the earth
(Gen. 8:1-14)

Months abating off earth (Gen. 8:1-14)

Natural work of taking waters off the earth
(Gen. 8:1-14)

No rebuke of the waters (Gen. 8:1-14)

Waters gradually receded (Gen. 8:1-14)

Bounds already set (Gen. 1:6-12; Gen 8:2)

No fish destroyed, only the land animals
(Gen. 6:18-Gen 8:22)

Fowls preserved (Gen. 6:20; Gen 8:17)

Animals preserved (Gen. 6:20; Gen 8:17)

Eight men and women saved (Gen. 6:18)

A social system left (Gen. 6:18; Gen 8:22; 2 Peter. 2:5)

An ark made to save life (Gen. 6:14-22; 1 Peter. 3:20)

Cause: wickedness of man and fallen angels (Gen. 6:1-13)

Result: no new creations were made, for all things were preserved (Gen. 6:18-Gen 8:22)

RESULTS OF THE FLOOD

Evidence for a great catastrophe that resulted in the destruction of the Pre-Adamite world can be found in Scripture, as we have seen, but we can look to the sciences as well for further verification. Most scientists assert that the earth went through at least one great catastrophe at an unknown period in the past.

Many animal remains have been discovered that indicate a sudden environmental calamity befalling large populations. Speaking of the flood of Noah, but more accurately describing the results of the flood which destroyed the Pre-Admit world, Douglas B. Sharp states that the flood explains the geologic column, which is the order of the strata and the fossils found in them:

Hydrodynamic sorting action of the water, habitats, the ability of an animal to escape the flood and ecological zones are all factors which would have produced fossil layers. This explanation handles the problem of out-of-order strata and fossils, which is a nasty problem for evolutionists . . . . In many places, large fossils such as trees extend through several strata.

Rapid burial is also necessary for coal and oil formation and for fossilization; otherwise the normal process of decay would completely disintegrate the organisms, even the bones.

We've mentioned briefly that many fossils have been found which was evidently the result of a great catastrophe, being entombed in the strata instead of being slowly buried by sedimentation over millions of years. During Lucifer's flood God turned the earth upside down by earthquakes.

In Peleg's time, we read of a great division of the earth. It is interesting that while we have only a brief mention of this catastrophic event, it was significant enough to define an entire generation in the genealogical record:

> "And unto Eber were born two sons: the name of one was Peleg; for in his days was the earth divided; and his brother's name was Joktan" (Gen. 10:25).

It's at least possible that this short account of a division of the earth is a reference to a shifting of the continents and a great division of land masses. Lucifer's flood and the division of the earth in Peleg's day may well account for much of the fossil record and help to explain many questions which otherwise remain unanswered by other creationist theories.

As we've seen, the other creationist theories struggle to account for scientific evidence which points to an old earth. Part of the difficulty is that these theories are attempting to force the scientific data into a mould that is simply not large enough to contain it. Most creationist theories cannot account for an old earth because they have not factored into the equation the existence of the pre-Adamite world.

Only an understanding of an original creation of the earth that preceded the destruction of Genesis 1:2 can shed light on the questions posed by the scientific evidence. The existence and overthrow of the pre-Adamite world resolves the following questions:

Why are we finding remains of animals that never existed in Adam's day? Quite simply, these animals were a part of the original creation of the earth and were destroyed and buried with the destruction of the earth following Lucifer's rebellion. The Bible doesn't tell us how long Lucifer was allowed to remain in rebellion against God before he was cast back down to the earth in judgment. The earth could have existed in a sinful state as a result of Lucifer's sin, with animals living and dying for centuries before God judged Lucifer and his rebellious followers.

How did the remains of animals get thousands of feet in the earth underneath many layers of solid rock if there was no catastrophe as described in Gen. 1:2; Jer. 4:23-26; and 2 Peter. 3:5-6?

Noah's flood, however, could not have resulted in the extensive deposits found deep beneath the earth on a worldwide scale, and no other global cataclysm has happened since Adam.

Why do we find geological evidence pointing to an earth that is much older than Adam's creation about 6,000 years ago? This is easily explained when we understand that the earth was created in the dateless past, underwent cataclysmic changes during the judgment brought about by Lucifer's rebellion, and was re-created about 6,000 years ago.

There is literally hundreds of "Flood" stories in about every culture around the world . . . but all originated after Noah's flood in the time line of the recorded history.

For example, the story of Noah's ark from the Book of Genesis is quite similar to the Akkadian Epic of Atrahasis, and part of the story about Utnapistim in the Babylonian Epic of Gilgamesh (which is essentially the same story from the Epic of Atrahasis with some minor differences).

Even the texts side by side are similar:

> "The gods smelled the savour"—Atrahasis III, v, 34
> "The gods smelled the sweet savour"—Gilgamesh XI, 160
> "And the Lord smelled the sweet savour . . ."—Genesis 8:21

There also was another flood myth called: the tale of Ziusudra, who was the ruler of Shuruppak, which was written in Sumerian. The single fragmentary tablet containing the story was dated to the 17th century BCE (Old Babylonian Empire), which makes it older than the Epic of Gilgamesh which was dated to c. 1,100 BCE.

Here follows a couple of these flood myths for they are too numerous to show them all.

DIFFERENT FLOOD STORIES

Europe

Zeus sent a flood to destroy the men of the Bronze Age. Prometheus advised his son Deucalion to build a chest. All other men perished except for a few who escaped to high mountains. The mountains in Thessaly were parted, and the entire world beyond the Isthmus and Peloponnese was overwhelmed. Deucalion and his wife Pyrrha (daughter of Epimetheus and Pandora), after floating in the chest for nine days and nights, landed on Parnassus. When the rains ceased, he sacrificed to Zeus, the God of Escape. At the bidding of Zeus, he threw stones over his head; they became men, and the stones which Pyrrha threw became women.

The first race of people was completely destroyed because they were exceedingly wicked. The fountains of the deep opened, the rain fell in torrents, and the rivers and seas rose to cover the earth, killing all of them. Deucalion survived due to his prudence and piety and linked the first and second race of men. Onto a great ark he loaded his wives and children and all animals. The animals came to him, and by God's help, remained friendly for the duration of the flood. The flood waters escaped down a chasm opened in Hierapolis. (Frazer, pp. 153-154)

An older version of the story told by Hellanicus has Deucalion's ark landing on Mount Othrys in Thessaly. Another account has him landing on a peak, probably Phouka, in Argolis, later called Nemea. (Gaster, p. 85)

The Megarians told that Megarus, son of Zeus, escaped Deucalion's flood by swimming to the top of Mount Gerania, guided by the cries of cranes. (Gaster, p. 85-86)

An earlier flood was reported to have occurred in the time of Ogyges, founder and king of Thebes. The flood covered the whole world and was so devastating that the country remained without kings until the reign of Cecrops. (Gaster, p. 87)

Nannacus, king of Phrygia, lived before the time of Deucalion and foresaw that he and all people would perish in a coming flood. He and the Phrygians lamented bitterly, hence the old proverb about "weeping like (or for) Nannacus." After the deluge had destroyed all humanity, Zeus commanded Prometheus and Athena to fashion mud images, and Zeus summoned winds to breathe life into them. The place where they were made is called Iconium after these images. (Frazer, p. 155)

"Many great deluges have taken place during the nine thousand years" since Athens and Atlantis were preeminent. Destruction by fire and other catastrophes was also common. In these floods, water rose from below, destroying city dwellers but not mountain people. The floods, especially the third great flood before Deucalion, washed away most of Athens' fertile soil. (Plato, "Timaeus" 22, "Critias" 111-112)

Arcadian:

Dardanus, first king of Arcadia, was driven from his land by a great flood which submerged the lowlands, rendering them unfit for cultivation. The people retreated to the mountains, but they soon decided that the land left was not enough to support them all. Some stayed with Dimas, son of Dardanus, as their king; Dardanus led the rest to the island of Samothrace. (Frazer, p. 163)

Samothrace:

The sea rose when the barriers dividing the Black Sea from the Mediterranean burst, releasing waters from the Black Sea in a great torrent that washed over part of the coast of Asia and the lowlands of Samothrace. The survivors on Samothrace retreated to the mountains and prayed for deliverance. On being saved, they set up monuments to the event and built alters on which to continue sacrifices through the ages. Fishermen still occasionally draw up parts of stone columns in their nets, signs of cities drowned in the sea. (Frazer, pp. 167-168)

Roman:

Jupiter, angered at the evil ways of humanity, resolved to destroy it. He was about to set the earth to burning, but considered that that might set heaven itself afire, so he decided to flood the earth instead. With Neptune's help, he caused storm and earthquake to flood everything but the summit of Parnassus, where Deucalion and his wife Pyrrha came by boat and found refuge. Recognizing their piety, Jupiter let them live and withdrew the flood. Deucalion and Pyrrha, at the advice of an oracle, repopulated the world by throwing "your mother's bones" (stones) behind them; each stone became a person. (Ovid, book 1)

Jupiter and Mercury, travelling incognito in Phrygia, begged for food and shelter, but found all doors closed to them until they received hospitality from Philemon and Baucis. The gods revealed their identity, led the couple up the mountains, and showed them the whole valley flooded, destroying all homes but the couple's, which was transformed into a marble temple. Given a wish, the couple asked to be priest and priestess of the temple, and to die together. In their extreme old age, they changed into an oak and lime tree. (Ovid, book 8)

One of the kings of Alba (named Romulus, Remulus, or Amulius Silvius), set himself up as a god equal to or superior to Jupiter. He made machines to mimic thunder and lightning, and he ordered his soldiers to drown out real thunder by beating on their shields. For his impiety, he and his house were destroyed by a thunderbolt in a fierce storm. The Alban lake rose and drowned his palace. You may still see the ruins when the lake is clear and calm. (Frazer 1993, p. 149)

Scandinavian:

Oden, Vili, and Ve fought and slew the great ice giant Ymir, and icy water from his wounds drowned most of the Rime Giants. The giant Bergelmir escaped, with his wife and children, on a boat made from a hollowed tree trunk. From them rose the race of frost ogres. Ymir's body became the world we live on. His blood became the oceans. (Sturluson, p. 35)

German:

A louse and a flea were brewing beer in an eggshell. The louse fell in and burnt herself. This made the flea weep, which made the door creak, which made the broom sweep, which made the cart run, which made the ash-heap burn, which made the tree shake itself, which made the girl break her water-pitcher, which made the spring begin to flow. And in the spring's water everything was drowned. (Grimm 30)

Celtic:

Heaven and Earth were great giants, and Heaven lay upon the Earth so that their children were crowded between them, and the children and their mother were unhappy in the darkness. The boldest of the sons led his brothers in cutting up Heaven into many pieces. From his skull they made the firmament. His spilling blood caused a great flood which killed all humans except a single pair, who were saved in a ship made by a beneficent Titan. The waters settled in hollows to become the oceans. The son who led in the mutilation of Heaven was a Titan and became their king, but the Titans and gods hated each other, and the king titan was driven from his throne by his son, who was born a god. That Titan at last went to the land of the departed. The Titan who built the ship, whom some consider to be the same as the king Titan, went there also. (Sproul, pp. 172-173)

CHAPTER 4

Archaeology and Mythology

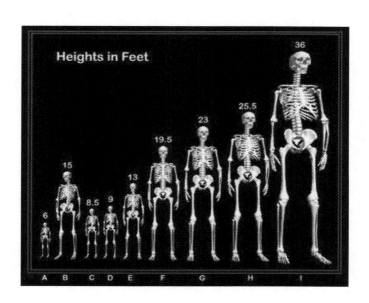

ARCHAEOLOGY AND MYTHOLOGY

Now, if you thought there was confusion in previous chapters you were wrong, for this part is where we will need every single brain cell to synchronies and work as a team to keep it together.

Let us start with the Bible.

In Genesis 5 we have the descendants of Adam and then in Genesis 6 we have Noah building the ark. Not much is said Biblically in this small part but a lot happened that shaped our thinking and the way the world operates today.

First of all it tends to look like a short period of time from Adam to Noah, just half a page in the Bible . . . but in reality we are talking about 1900 years . . . . That is 112 years less than from the Crucifixion to now . . . . 2012.

Genesis 6:1 Living Bible

> *"Now a population explosion took place upon the earth. It was at this time that beings from* **the spirit world** *looked upon the beautiful earth women and took* **any they desired** *to be their wives.* (**Without consent means raped**) *Then God said, My Spirit must not forever be disgraced in man, wholly evil as he is. I will give him 120 years to mend his ways. In those days, and even afterwards, when the* **evil beings from the spirit world** *were sexually involved with human woman, their children became giants of whom so* **many legends are told**. (**Birth of Mythological beings and legends**) *When the Lord God saw the*

extent of human wickedness and that the trend and direction of
men's lives were only towards evil . . . ."

Genesis 6:1-9 King James Version (KJV)

*"And it came to pass, when men began to multiply on the face of
the earth, and daughters were born unto them, that the sons of God
saw the daughters of men that they were fair; and they took them
wives of all which they chose. And the* LORD *said my spirit shall
not always strive with man, for that he also is flesh: yet his days
shall be an hundred and twenty years. There were giants in the
earth in those days; and also after that, when the sons of God came
in unto the daughters of men, and they bear children to them, the
same became* **mighty men which were of old, men of renown.**
And God saw that the **wickedness** *of man was great in the earth
and that every imagination of the thoughts of his heart was only
evil continually. And it repented the* LORD *that he had made man
on the earth, and it grieved him at his heart. And the* LORD *said,
I will destroy man whom I have created from the face of the earth;
both man, and beast, and the creeping thing, and the fowls of the
air; for it repented me that I have made them. But Noah found
grace in the eyes of the* LORD*".*

***"These are the generations of Noah: Noah was a just man and <u>perfect
in his generations</u>,*** (genetically pure) ***and Noah walked with God".***

Why was YHWH sorry that he created the animal's birds and reptiles,
why did HE decide to wipe them from the earth as well as the giants and
their horrific offspring?

We can see that the "**main sin**" or problem leading to YHWH's decision
to send a flood over the earth was that the pure genetic line of YHWH via
Seth became corrupt with different races and evil beings from the spirit
world and the rest of nature. These different gene pools were corrupted
with each other, in other words they interbred widely with each other and
the animals, birds and reptiles.

They disobeyed one of the biggest and most important rules of YHWH and nature not to mix the gene pool. They literally mix every gene possible in nature trying to create something better, something superior to Adam after the Biblical recreation, and are still in process today.

Heylel and his fallen angels kept on trying to be creators like YHWH by trying every mix possible. To create at the same level as YHWH will mean to be equal to Him. By mixing the gene pool they are trying to eradicate the pure seed line of Adam wiping YHWH's creation from planet earth establishing only one corrupt gene pool on it, that of Satan.

Even in the Pre Adamic world they created beings trying to equal YHWH and to be like him to create something perfect. Out of these attempts we saw the "creatures" and "myths" born into mythology from the Mesozoic era before Adam up to Noah's flood after Adam.

Their creations and experiments led to all the creation of the following creatures where they ended up in Mythology today.

Dragon's—Snake like reptile with wings and long tale.

Mermaids—half fish half woman (fish body with human upper torso)

Centaur—Half man half horse (horse body human upper torso)

Minotaur—Half man half bull (bull's head on human body)

Dwarf—Unaturally small, ugly and shy male human that dwells in mountains.

Unicorn—Highly intellagent Horse with single horn on head.

Harpy—Bird woman (bird with woman head)

Satyr—Half goat male companions (lower extremities goat and top human)

Griffin—Lions body with woman's head and wings. Sometimes claws of
the eagle,

Sphinx—Lion body with human or cats head.

We find these hybrids painted on cave walls in the upper stone age from
about 50 000 to 10 000 before Adam. We also found them carved and
created from clay to service as gods . . . . men of renown even before
Adam, and afterwards.

All of a sudden we get more answers for the archaeologist and
palaeontologists that needs to deliberately hide or ignore some finds
because of the lack of intellectual evidence for what is not in line with
the mainstream of thought within their own science, scared to be labelled
idiot of the month by their peers.

All of a sudden we can start puzzling together strange and indescribable
human remains that does not fit the creation or evolution theory but are
truly and physically different from other skeletal remains.

We know that the fallen one, **heylel** is the power behind the Mystery of
Iniquity, which is working to bring about the advent of the Anti Christ.
We also are told that when he comes on the scene, he will come with all
signs and lying wonders.

There is a debate amongst Christian UFO researchers that falls along these
lines. Those that believe that UFOs, implants, hybrids, modern Nephilim
are all a demonic illusion, and others who think that the phenomena is
real, i.e. the abductions, breeding program and hybrids all mirror the
events of Genesis 6, and are happening in real-time today.

All of a sudden we don't need to try to push every piece of evidence into a
box in our existing theory's that doesn't make sense.

Noah was the only man with a perfectly pure genetic seed line left . . . .
He was not chosen because he went to church every Sunday, but because

he carried the pure seed from Adam via Seth . . . . not the seed of the Cain line.

This is exactly what happened with Eve and **heylel** in the Garden of Eden . . . . a sexual act leading to the birth of Cain . . . so nothing new about the modus operandi of **heylel** and his evil fallen angels.

1 John 3:12 RS *"and not be like Cain of the evil one and murdered his brother . . . ."* KJ *"Not as Cain, who was of that wicked one and slew his brother."*

These fallen angels, together with their hybrid offspring and some other mongrel races survived the cataclysmic events that occurred before Adam.

These are the mixed generations where Cain found a place in humanity to flee to and to be the first Nephilim after the Biblical recreation containing corrupt Godly DNA he received from his mother Eve. (Canaanites)

So we also have a better understanding on why Adam was created . . . and debate the following:

After the Cambrian explosion, the first creation of life on earth by Elohim, where all life spontaneously occurred simultaneously as proven in the geology . . . Lucifer and his angels were placed in charge of earth in its most perfect condition. This could have been during the Perm entering the Mesozoic but we can't be sure exacately when.

Perfect conditions prevailed in nature. There were no sickness and the climate was clean and perfect. Nature flourished and plants and animals grew out of proportionally large and plentiful. Some animals and different phyla adapted and changed minutely were necessary as climate forced it upon them. The natural rules applied to all and the rule of nature "eat or been eaten" applied as today.

When exactly this happened we cannot say but we do know that it reached its climax in the Mesozoic era during the Triassic and coming to an end with the Jurassic period with the K-T event. It could also have been in the Cenozoic during the Quatenary. Theire is just not enougth evidence at this stage to put a precise date stamp on this but evidence should be forthcoming to solve this in near future.

Lucifer and his angels were able to metamorphose or "shape shift" into equal proportions as needed by nature, combined with super powers and the ability to have super natural abilities and knowledge they build for themselves strange and abnormally huge homes, cities and monuments as time went by.

Something had to give. Lucifer and his band rebelled and after a great war in heaven **Heylel** and his angels were cast down to earth because they sinned and interbred and corrupted with nature, causing or coinciding with the K-T Event.

The earth was reformed in time and eventually mammals start roaming the earth during the Cenozoic era in the Tertiary and Quaternary periods, now *heylel*, cloned and interbred with the whole of nature and especially with some species out of the ape-like phylum leading to the later homo erectus and Neanderthal man . . . . what we would call evolution or the quick jump from species to species called mutation.

Another theory, enjoying some credence, is that early man was created in full and that DNA manipulation and experimentation led to the ape like species mutating to the species of ape-like phyla that whe have today, mutating from normal Pre-Adamic man, and for that reason we do have these large gaps in the archaeological evidence concerning early man, just the other way around.

This theory carries a lot of water if you consider the fact that it is impossible to better an existing gene, it can only stay the same or degenerate in time to other less perfect genes than the original gene. You can go from good to bad, but not from bad to good, impossible.

Heylel was the ruler of the earth because it is said that he had a throne and subjects. This must have been before Adam since after Adam he was not sitting on any throne. Since he was cast down and lost his kingship and got it back after misleading Eve, so it is also indicates to be happening before the Genesis creation.

He wanted to climb up *"above the clouds"* also indicating that he was living on the physical earth below the clouds . . . . If this is so then the earth, clouds and stars where already in existence before Genesis . . .

The extinction of earth before Adam was decided by YHWH because of the sins of **heylel** and his angels towards YHWH and the fact that the interbreeding and genetic mixing led to malformed, DNA manipulated creatures, mongrels and hybrids.

It reached a point (in wickedness and mismanagement) where nearly all mammals and various ecosystems collapsed to extinction, leading to the earth becoming *"without form and void"*.

According to science we had a mass extinction 5000 before Adam where we lost most mammals like the Mammoths and sable tooth tiger type of animal's roaming the earth at that stage.

The six day recreation of earth was planned by YHWH to put someone else in charge with a Godly spirit resembling YHWH to rule the earth from then on . . . . With the creation of Adam, Lucifer lost control of the kingship of earth just to get it back almost immediately after Lucifer misled Eve trying to corrupt YHWH seed line and to better his own via Cain with Godly DNA tapped from Eve.

We can also debate that because Adam and Eve had superior DNA to anything else Satan had on earth at that stage, he saw a great opportunity to steel DNA from Eve to improve his own existing gene pool on earth. He used Eve to see if he could create something better than Elohims creation of Adam, reclaiming his position of master and ruler on earth and made them sin and disobey Elohim at the same time.

Heylel had offspring from Eve named Cain and therefore established his own living seed line on earth to be in eternal fight against the direct seed line of YHWH through Adam and Seth. These two seed lines are alive and well today living on earth, and it is not identified by believers or non believers at first, but by race and genealogy, as Noah was chosen by genetic purity.

This corrupt gene pool is still at work daily trying to corrupt the pure Godly seed. If he can't create it, he will corrupt it instead.

THE ANCIENT BOOK OF GIANTS

This book is one of the books from the New Testament apocrypha which concerned the Old Testament. The text relates how before the great flood, there was a giant named Ogias.

Ogias the Giant is thought to have been based on the *Book of Enoch*, a pseudepigraphical work from the 3rd century, itself based on a passage from Genesis (6:1-4) concerning the Nephilim, which, in the Enoch version, are the offspring of fallen angels; they saw the beauty of the daughters of men, married them, and thus fathered Giants in the land. The book concerns itself with filling in the details about the giants and their offspring that the *Book of Enoch* is lacking.

Aramaic fragments, along with other fragments of the *Book of Enoch*, were found among the Dead Sea Scrolls at Qumran:

The Book of Giants (Dead Sea Scrolls) includes 4Q203, 1Q23, 2Q26, 4Q530-532, 6Q8.

In the version of the *Book of Giants* which was spread by the Manichaean religion, the book became well travelled and exists in Syriac, Greek, Persian, Sogdian, Uyghur, and Arabic, although each version is somewhat distorted, incorporating more local myths. In 1904, German expeditions to Central Asia (Turpan in present northwest China) brought back many fragments of Manichaean holy texts, some of which were identified as belonging to *The Book of Giants*.

The text relates how before the Biblical Deluge (flood), a giant named Ogias fought a great dragon. A brief mention of this giant, "Ohia", is found in the Babylonian Talmud (Nidah, Ch 9), where it is said "Sihon and Og were brothers, as they were the sons of Ohia the son of Samhazai (one of the leaders of the fallen angels in the *Book of Enoch*).

The version found at Qumran also describes the hero Gilgamesh and the monster Humbaba as two of the giants accompanying Ogias.

Before you question the validity of the non-canonical books I mention, keep in mind that not only was they part of the original Old Testament, but many of them—particularly Enoch—were quoted from by the Apostles in the New Testament.

Quotes from the book of Enoch can be found in the books of Jude, Revelation, and several other places.

The Nephilim angels set themselves up as pagan "gods" to be worshipped, and their hybrid, genetically monstrous sons as "demigod" kings over the rest of humanity. These offspring were also called Nephilim; they were brutal, cruel, occultist and cannibalistic giants who treated ordinary human beings with contempt.

There were 300 original "Watchers" above the Earth, who rebelled and became the Nephilim. Their leader was named Semyaza (azazel). Through corrupt angelic knowledge (gene manipulation and cloning), the pre-flood world was corrupted.

The book of Enoch says that the Nephilim and their children "sinned against all flesh," creating hybrid creatures which were part human, part beast, part fowl (or bird). Sound familiar? The 300 fallen "watchers," whose original job had been to protect humanity and the Earth, were utterly depraved.

They taught mankind the arts of witchcraft, sorcery, drug abuse, and war. As mentioned earlier the gene-pool of the human race was tainted as well, almost beyond recovery. When you read the story of Noah and his family, it should be understood that he was not only selected to survive because of the quality of his character;

Genesis states that, unlike the majority of the rest of humanity, Noah was *"found perfect in all his generations."* In other words, he and his family were not tainted by the fallen angelic bloodline, which God had cursed to eternal damnation, in the Hebrew Old Testament, the word "rapha" means "the damned," the "eternally dead," "demon," "ghost," and GIANT, i.e., the spirit of one of the offspring of the Nephilim, the word Giant/Gigantic meaning "created on earth".

After the flood, when MOST but not all of the Nephilim offspring and hybrid mutations were destroyed, the 300 former "watchers" were confined inside the Earth, in a prison from which they cannot escape. These are those who are referred to by Paul in Ephesians chapter 6 as *"the rulers of the spiritual darkness of this world."*

Although imprisoned, they are still VERY powerful and can influence world events, particularly through their offspring and creations. Jude refers to them, quoting directly from the book of Enoch, when he says *"the angels who are chained in eternal darkness, awaiting the judgement of the great day."*

The issue of technology, based on advanced scientific (fallen angelic) knowledge, comes into play in all of this as well. UFOs and all different types of advanced technology are described in both the Old and New Testament.

The oldest extant written story, tradition, or text that has been translated is the Epic of Gilgamesh, a half-human demigod who lamented his mortality, and who went on a journey (part of it below the ground, in the underworld) in search of immortality (like that of his father).

In the "Book of Giants" (4Q203, 1Q23, 2Q26, 4Q530-532, 6Q8), a Hebrew text, several giants, and their Nephilim fathers, are mentioned by name. One of them is Gilgamesh, the same Gilgamesh from the Sumerian tradition, a "mighty man" who is lamented his own impending death and damnation:

Now keep in mind that these guys' are the direct incarnation, children of Satan and his fallen comrades i.e. demons. We tend to idolise these tales as harmless folklore, but we are wrong. They are part of the enemy.

Additionally, there's an entire related tradition of the pre-Adamic world, which was populated by humanoid beings of various types, along with other strange beings.

These may be some of the same hominids that are represented in the fossil record; and some of these forms, as survivors and anachronisms, may explain some sightings of anomalous beings.

"Lilith" of the recreation story and first wife to Adam according to Jewish religion, may well have been of one of these races, and she fled into the wilderness, where she mated with subterranean "demons" and other beings, swearing that she and her children (the "Lilim") (Nephilim) would always prey on human children, and seduce human beings into hybrid-producing sexual encounters.

Again, this is paralleled in nearly EVERY ancient tradition, from the Lamias of Greece, to the Huldre-folk and seductresses of Scandinavia and the Dragon-kings, queens, princes and princesses of China and Japan.

We also see in the book of giants how Biblical Enoch tried to reason and warn these entities, to no avail. He failed miserably to establish peace and harmony between them.

In the 5th Century 3 Enoch, Azazel is one of the three angels (Azza [Shemhazai] and Uzza [Ouza] are the other two) who opposed Enoch's high rank when he became the angel Metatron. Whilst they were fallen at this time they were still in Heaven, but Metatron held a dislike for them, and had them cast out.

They were henceforth known as the 'three who got the most blame' for their involvement in the fall of the angels marrying women. It should be remembered that Azazel and Shemhazai were said to be the leaders of the 200 fallen.

Everywhere we look we see the trail of these strangely connected tales and fables stringing along time with name changes and genealogy between them. The family tree of these Nephilim does exist and if it was not for the name changes in every culture we would understand it with more depth and clarity.

NAMES OF THE GIANTS

In the book of Enoch and in the Qur'an we find the names of these fallen angels . . . they are the fathers of the giants . . . you will see the correlation between them and the mythological Titans with their children in chapter 5.

Virogdad, Shahmizad, Samhazai, Sham-Ohya, Pat-Sham, Mahawai, Hobabis, Taxtag, Nariman, Vistasp, Ogias/Og/Ohia, Waizan, Khudos, Nimrod, Goliath, Arba, E/Anak/x, Sheshai, Ahiman, Talmai, Sihon, Horim, Doeg, Gilgamesh, Humbaba,

With detailed study, remnants of their names can be found today as they are still been worshipped willingly and unwillingly, but mostly unknowingly.

We see them in the Bible as the children of Anak and Rephaim.

Numbers 13:31 to 34:

> *"And all the people that we saw in it are men of great stature. And there we saw the giants, the sons of Anak, which come of the Nephilim: and we were in our own sight as grasshoppers, and so we were in there sight."*

The Egyptian Execration texts of the Middle Kingdom (2055-1650 BC) mention a list of political enemies in Canaan, and among this list are a group called the "ly Anaq" or people of Anaq. The three rulers of ly Anaq were Erum, Abiyamimu, and Akirum. Anak could be related to the Sumerian god Enki, considering the relationship between the Anakites and Philistia (Joshua 11:21, Jeremiah 47:5), identifies the Anakim with Anax, the giant ruler of the Anactorians in Greek mythology.

The book of Enoch also tells the tale of these "Watchers" (fallen angels) that descended on mount Hermon. They called it mount Hermon because they had sworn and bound themselves by mutual imprecations upon it.

These are the names of the chiefs of tens:

Samiazaz the leader, Arakiba, Rameel, Kokabiel, Tamiel, Ramiel, Danel, Ezegeel, Baraqijal, Asael, Armaros, Batarel, Ananel, Zaqiel, Samsapeel, Satarel, Turel, Jomjael, Sariel

> *"And all the others with them took unto themselves wives, and each chose for himself one, and they began to go in unto them and to defile themselves with them, and they taught them charms and enchantments (the first witches) and the cutting of roots (witch doctors), and made them acquainted with plants".*

> *"And they became pregnant, and they bare great giants, who consumed all the acquisitions of men". "And when men could no longer sustain them, the giants turned against them and devoured mankind".*

There are numerous myths from around the world which speak about "giants", which usually refers to humans of gigantic size. In certain ancient Mesopotamian myths, these giants where often discriminated and blamed for things like the exhaustion of food supplies. Because of this, many of them eventually turned against the "ordinary" people, and caused havoc upon the earth, because no ordinary man could stand up against them to punish their unlawful deeds.

Because of this happening the Elohim became more and more convinced that His creation of modern man was a serious error and created, or allowed to happen, a great flood to wash the "world" clean of its disease.

For 10,000 years or more, early modern man known as "Cro-Magnon man" did co-exist together with the much shorter Neanderthals in Europe which averaged from 5.3 to 5.5 feet. The earliest Cro-Magnon men were in comparison quite large in stature, averaging from 6.1 to 6.7 feet (male), which is somewhat taller than the average height of current modern man.

These giants from biblical texts including Genesis were the offspring of "the sons of God" and the "daughters of man". It makes sense that these "sons of God" could possibly have been these quite large Cro-Magnon men. Could this also mean that the daughters of man" were the shorter Neanderthal man, and could it possibly be that their offspring was even much larger? The giant known as "Goliath the Philistine", from the story of David and Goliath (1 Samuel, chapter 17), had been described as "six cubits and one span" in height, which is approximately 10 feet and 6 inches.

There are other references to humans of gigantic height to be found in the Bible, like in the book Numbers, 13:32-33:

In the original Old Hebrew text "Anak" is read as: "Anakim", which means "the long-necked." It is stated that the Anakim are related to the Nephilim. Both stories took place in the times after Noah's flood, and these giants were probably remnants which survived, or were born after the Deluge.

The book Deuteronomy 3:11 mentions the king Og of Basan as the last of the Rephaim and his bed, or coffin, was described as nine cubits long and four cubits wide, or thirteen and a half feet long and six feet wide.

We have on record that some of these giants reached from 11 feet up to 39 feet in hight.

"And they began to sin (procreate, DNA cloning, experimenting etc.) ***against birds, beasts, reptiles, fish*** *and to devour one another's flesh, and drink the blood." (Gen 6)*

It is getting clearer, we are becoming more aware, as we read and understand this theory that we are in some serious trouble right now. Our lives are entwined with these gods, unknowingly their holy days and feasts names of months and days, stars, heavenly bodies and galaxies, willingly or unwillingly, floods our existence.

DNA manipulation and cloning the human genome is on our doorstep and probably because of secrecy already into the living room.

Lucifer became Satan (heylel) because he wanted to be like YHWH. If he can successfully create at the same level as YHWH he will be like YHWH. If he can copy or manage to create to the top level of genetic engineering namely the Adamic gene, he will be successful in his quest. It goes without saying that we are technologically and spiritually perilously close to the point where the earth was before Noah's flood.

WAR AGAINST THE GIANTS

From an article dated from September 3th, 2011, giant human remains were found in Georgia. The scientists are telling that the height of these human giants could range from 2.5 to 3 metres (8.2 feet to 9.8 feet (decimal)). From the article at Trend.Az:

"Georgia, Tbilisi, Sept. 3/Trend N. Kirtskhalia/

"The bones of giant people aged over 25,000 years were found in the mountains of the Borjomi Gorge (South Georgia). This is a sensational discovery, academician of the Georgian Science Academy Abesalom Vekua told media."

(Source: pda.trend.az/en/1926150.html)

Prof. Dr. Abesalom Vekua, a leading scientific researcher of the Georgian National Museum, further explained:

"Pay attention to the lumbar bone, it differs from the bones of modern man in size and thickness. The skull is also much larger. These people have lived and evolved in isolation from the rest of civilization, they are so different in features and growth. In the literature they were referred to as giants, but evidence supporting this hypothesis does not exist. Thus, we are on the threshold of a sensation. But a confirmation will have to be preceded by hard work."

(Source: www.sydhav.no/giants)

This finding probably could turn this myth into a scientific fact: that there indeed once lived a race of giants in the ancient past.

Before the Israelites renamed the area Hebron in the Palestine area, the Anakim called it Kiriath Arba, or City of Arba, in honour of their forefather, Arba. He was a great hero of the Anakim. In time, Arba's overgrown children grew so numerous that they were able to possess much of southern Canaan. These giants divided into three clans. They were ruled from Hebron by Ahiman, Sheshai, and Talmai, descendants of Arba, but Hebron also had its own king (Joshua 10:37).

Joshua viewed Hebron's capture as having both a strategic and a morale-breaking importance; strategic because it was the most southerly road-crossing centre of the highland system; and morale-breaking because, as the principal mountain stronghold of the Anakim, its downfall would further demoralize the natives. At Joshua's command, the Israelites stormed Hebron, drove out Ahiman, Sheshai, and Talmai, slew its king, and put all its huge occupants who could not escape to the sword.

Following the battle at Hebron, the invaders struck out across the Negeb toward Debir (modern Dhaheriyeh). It stood as a frontier town between the hill country and the Negeb, some eleven miles southwest of Hebron.

In Joshua's day, however, many Anakim giants occupied the city. Here no trees grew, so Debir, being located on a higher elevation than the surrounding bald hills, became visible to Israel's marching legions from a long way off.

Archaeologist also found clear evidence of a time when Debir thrived as a centre for culture and learning—until its overthrow by the Hyksos from Egypt about 1550 B.C. But when the city was rebuilt, he writes, it "showed indications of relative poverty: the houses were poorly built and departed by open spaces containing grain pits. In this period the derelict fortifications of the earlier period were restored, and the east gate was entirely rebuilt, on the same general plan."

When this fortress-city of the giants fell to them, the Israelites slew its king and all who were unable to escape. After this great slaughter, the Israelites marched on Anab. In earlier times, another people occupied this city. But the Anakim giants assailed it, wiped out its inhabitants, and made it their possession. Anab, the name of which still survives today as Khirbet Anab, stood amid the Judean hills, only a short distance from Debir.

After breaching its walls, Israel's legions totally demolished the city and put to death all its giants. After this, the Israelites likely cleared a number of giants out of the "Valley of the Rephaim" southwest of Jerusalem. Also about this time they probably slaughtered the remnant of the monstrous Awim, who lived at nearby Avvim. Then they captured Jerusalem, or at least that part of it that was known as the "lower city." Despite their greatest efforts, however, they were unable to dislodge the Jebusites from the "upper city."

These few but determined people occupied the narrow plateau of Mt. Ophel, just southeast of Jerusalem. Bounded by the Kidron, Tyropoeon, and Zedek Valleys, Jebus encompassed no more than eleven or twelve acres. But because of its bold rock escarpments, the small city stood as an impregnable bastion, and "not to be taken without great difficulty, through the strength of its walls, and the nature of the place." And, indeed, it was not taken until some four centuries later, in the time of David. When Joshua attacked it, some Horim giants supposedly lived among the Jebusites.

Except for several pockets of resistance, like this one at Jebus, much of southern Canaan now belonged to the Israelites. So Joshua ordered his legions to invade the north country. We have no way of knowing how many giants the Israelites fought in these latter campaigns, for Joshua, who kept careful records of his battles against the Anakim in the south, now devoted much less time to the chores of journal-keeping. Concerning the northern giants, he penned the briefest summary, noting only that the Anakim occupied "all the hill country of Israel," meaning all the territory later allotted to the ten northern tribes. He also barely mentions the

Rephaim—and then only in connection with a complaint by Ephraim and the half-tribe of Manasseh.

That complaint came after the tribes had received their land allotments. Feeling that they had not gotten a fair shake, the sons of Joseph grumbled that their allotment was not sufficient for their great numbers. So Joshua told them: "If you are so numerous, and if the hill country of Ephraim is too small for you, go up into the forest and clear land for yourself there in the land of the Perizzites and of Rephaites." The Perizzites, whom some scholars also identify with the giant Horim, lived in the vicinity of Shechem. A large clan of the Rephaim occupied a territory just north of them, with their settlements extending perhaps as far as the Valley of Jezreel. The children of Joseph apparently took Moses' advice and destroyed or drove out all these giants, for afterward they occupied that land.

Against the northern cities Joshua waged war a long time. But while they were thus occupied with the conquest of upper Canaan, and bent upon cleansing it of the giants, the Anakim who had escaped the Israelites' swords during their earlier sieges in the south later returned and reoccupied Hebron and Debir, cities that were assigned to Caleb. Consequently, after the land was divided by lot among Israel's twelve tribes, some men of Judah, with Caleb at their head, returned to the south country and again came against these places.

An account of Caleb's renewed campaign against the giants who reoccupied Hebron appears in Josephus histories. After telling what great difficulty the people of Judah faced in their long siege against Jebus, or upper Jerusalem, he relates that they removed their camp to Hebron to assist Caleb against the Gibborim there.

"And when they had taken it," he adds, "they slew all the inhabitants. There were till then left races of giants, who had bodies so large, and countenance so entirely different from other men, that they were surprising to the sight, and terrible to the hearing. The bones of these

men are still shown to this very day, unlike to any credible relations of other men."

After retaking Hebron, Caleb proceeded southward to the re-occupied Debir (i.e., Kiriath Sepher). Upon reaching that place, he said to his chief men: "I will give my daughter Acsah in marriage to the man who attacks and captures Kiriath Sepher." Quick to volunteer, Othniel, a son of Caleb's younger brother, advanced with his men into the city, slew all its defiant giants, and retook it. So Caleb gave his daughter Acsah to him in marriage.

With Caleb's recapture of Hebron and Debir, Israel's seven-year campaign against the giants and Canaan's other inhabitants came to an end. Their many victories put the Hebrews in control of much of the country and broke the once awesome military power of its people. But the legions of Israel failed to exterminate or drive all the other pagan trespassers off God's land, as they had been commanded. Even a few cities remained untaken.

Had they done as well in dispossessing all the other Canaanites as they had the giants, later Hebrew history may have followed a much different and less tragic course. But after seven long years of intense fighting and much gore, the Hebrews grew weary of war. So, assenting to their plea, Joshua gave them rest from war.

Even though these few places of resistance remained throughout the country, Israel's men of war had at least accomplished their major objective—to cleanse God's land of the Gibborim. That this cleansing was complete we learn from our chronicler. In his final summary of the campaign, he wrote:

"Then Joshua came at that time and cut off the Anakim from the hill country, from Hebron, from Debir, from Anab and from all the hill country of Judah and from all the hill country of Israel". Joshua utterly destroyed them with their cities.

There were no Anakim left in the land of the sons of Israel; only in Gaza, in Gath, and in Ashdod some remained." But these giants who survived Joshua's campaigns and fled to the Philistines on the coast, or to Africa and other countries, were so few that they never again posed a serious threat to the children of Israel.

SATANIC GAMES

War is one of the great levellers on earth.

When we look at the impact it has on nations, on all levels thinkable things can, and do change overnight in the chaotic atmosphere of war. Some areas in life came to a standstill while others accelerate to unimaginable heights and speed. One of the most visible effects of war is the loss of the "top" or "superior" genes in the average population concerned.

War is a means by Satan to kill of these "superior, none corrupted" genes and weaken the gene pool that is left of the warring parties or people (Adamites) in order to attack the nations of earth even more successfully with his lesser quality of gene and promoting race mixing.

It is simple . . . if you take a pure gene and mix it with an already corrupt gene, you will down grade to an even more corrupt gene . . . The mixing or experimentation of any pure gene with that of a mixed gene will always deliver weaker offspring.

So the question stands, who benefits from gene mixing or DNA manipulation?

The minute you corrupt a specific gene pool you generate inferior offspring in all living creatures . . . . scientific fact.

The strongest and best gene's is in the frontlines of war, while the weakest of the gene pool cannot go to war, they stay at home . . . . The effect is obvious, the genes left to repopulate this group of people after the war, are inferior and weak.

These "lesser" genes then also has to compete with other superior genes brought in by the war from other countries (mixed genes) that have now settled in that area.

A good example of this is when you compare the German nations average IQ and physique before and after the second world war . . . . there is actually no comparison.

As you consider that after the fall of Germany all the top German scientist were divided by Russia and the USA leading to the development of the space and atomic bomb projects directly after their capture, brilliant gene pool.

War also helps to move large numbers of people to areas on earth where they shouldn't be. The wars are always stretched out to the maximum time frame in order for the aggressor to make money, but also to help Satan in his quest in order and hope that these soldiers will start putting up house in that particular area . . . . if it doesn't happen naturally the forces of Satan will force it to manifest.

It is astonishing to think that even today 67 years after the second world war, the USA still have soldiers and huge military camps in Japan to insure that Japan comply to their surrendering agreement signed in 1945!

Several other countries also sit with similar forced issues like Italy and France.

In Africa the situation is even worse where masses of captured peoples in modern wars is captured for slavery and moved internally across Africa to make sure the gene pool gets so mixed up that any effort to rectify or rebuild nations are almost impossible, suddenly we understand why the slave trade in earth's history with the Western world occurred at all.

Thousands of Russian and Cuban soldiers was shipped to Angola in the seventies and eighties during the wars between Swapo and South

Africa . . . . Again more than half of them stayed and settled in their newfound country years after the war ended.

Children are been born out of wed lock by adultery and rape on both sides of the war. At home where all the woman are left behind the same happens than in the war torn country, so Satan gets a double shot into the pure seed of Adam.

War dissolves families, relationships and believe systems in rapid succession. War is one of the most successful tools that Lucifer use in order to succeed in his fight against YHWH and the pure Adamic seed.

We are sitting with a global threat of different nations and their traditions coming to an abrupt end, forming a new one world nation, mixed and mongrelised exactly as the Bible warns us will happen in the end of days.

Nations and parents across the world experience the same global problem, old views and believe systems are thrown out of the window, the word "conservative" became a joke and society has replace it with "liberal" and "enlightenment", the effect is shocking and people doesn't understand why their children would not cope with the normal ups and downs of life.

Alcohol, cigarettes and other "light" drug addictions are so numerous that it is legalised in a lot of states and countries. Billions of people across the world are totally addicted to some sort of psychotropic drug in medical or drug related form.

95% of the pure Adamic genetic pool on earth is corrupt and sick. It has altered and lost its ability to heal and the first signs are obviously visible in our IQ levels and dramatic psychotic fallouts worldwide.

The DSM or (Diagnostic and Statistical Manual of Mental Disorders) that psychiatrists use to label your mental disorder, had grown from a volume of 130 pages in 1966 to a book of over the 800 pages today. They added new disorders from 44 confirmed illnesses, or disorders,

in 1974 to 174 disorders in 2000, and still growing, relating to a 400% growth in the last 26 years.

A yearly growth of 7% in new different types of psychotic disorders, reaping trillions, boxing the population into jelly type, backboneless hybrids?

Ever wondered why, that even today, no member of any royal family gets to wed just anybody. It is "law" in the royal circles. The prospecting person gets "checked out" genetically and later politically and all the other important factors, but most importantly, genetically.

If the person does not fit the bill in his or hers family tree "genetics" the wedding is off. It is imperative and important to them, why is not important to the masses? It was in the days where the word "conservative" was still in use and accepted socially.

The world population is totally powerless and they follow these dark forces almost hypnotically, they don't realise the enormity of the global problem facing us.

What disables the people on earth to fail to realise the problem, are they genetically so impaired by this time that they are unable to use their common sense or is it a shortage of knowledge or global brainwashing.

Now if it is knowledge, I am pleading with you to pass this information on or inspire someone with this knowledge and warn them in order to stop the total disappearance, extinction, of intellectual Adamic man on earth?

CHAPTER 5

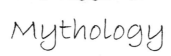

Mythology

MYTHOLOGY

To understand the mythology it is important for you to understand that we are working with four main groups.

The Titans which was the fathers of the Gods. (heylel and his leaders of fallen angels)

The God's (children of Titans . . . . men of renown)

The Hero's (hundreds of semi gods and legends born out of the nations legends)

The Creatures (Hybrids half man/beast)

By comparing the texts of the book of Genesis, like the stories of the sons of God, the Deluge and the confusion of tongues (the Tower of Babel story), with the Mesopotamian myths, one should note these stories are not only very similar but also that there is the mention of multiple gods instead of one. The ancient Mesopotamian people knew, like the old Greeks, a whole pantheon of various deities where each of one had his/her own place within the hierarchy.

Like the Greek gods, the Mesopotamian deities were not seen as the creators of the world but as the almighty rulers of a world which was already in existence. The Mesopotamian gods existed from gods of the earth which were known as "Anunnaki in Sumerian and "Anunna" in Akkadian cultures, which were also called the "fifty great gods and the gods of the sky or the heavens: the "Iggi", the so-called "lesser gods".

Where the God with the highest authority was known as the "LORD" (God in modern translations of the Bible) in the Biblical scriptures and the book of Enoch, we find instead the name "Enki" (known as "Ea" by the Akkadians") like in the story of the Deluge, or the name of another god who was known as "Enlil" as in other stories. "En.ki" translates to "Lord of the Earth" and "En.lil" means: "Lord of the Storm".

Enlil was the local chief god who shares similarities with YHWH, the Biblical God of Abraham and Moses, also called the "God of Israel". Enlil was a stern but righteous god but when he was pushed to his limits he was merciless for anyone who opposed him. So when he saw the creation of modern man as a total failure he did send out the great flood. His half brother Enki was an alchemist, advisor and a god of fertility and wisdom. He would have been involved with the creation of modern man and was the one who saved the pius man known as: Atrahasis (Akkadian), Utnapishtim (Sumerian) and Noah (by the later Babylonian and Hebrews), and his family from the flood. Because Yahweh insisted that he did not want any other (false) gods besides Him.

Like the Romans borrowed most of their gods from the old Greeks, so may it be possible that the Greek gods were based upon the ancient Mesopotamian gods from, or even before, the age of the civilization of Atlantis. Enki and Enlil actually share similarities with the Greek gods Poseidon and Zeus; They also were brothers with leading roles, whereof Enlil, like Zeus, was the chief god, and like Enki had the watery abyss (the "abzu") as his domain, was Poseidon the god of the sea. The Book of Enoch (ch. 14:8-23) describes the temple of the "LORD" with an interior made out of crystal stones which could make one think of Plato's description of the richly decorated temple of Poseidon in his work "Critias". If one already was known with the god Poseidon during the Atlantean times, this would mean that the origins of Greek mythology were much older than the Greek civilization and possibly could be traced back to the golden age of the civilization of Atlantis.

Zeus and YHWH alike would dwell in high mountains; Zeus would have liked on mount Olympus (the highest mountain in Greece) while Moses spoke with Yahweh on mount Sinai (in the Sinai mountains in Egypt), also known as tm. Horeb ("mountain of God"). Long was assumed that the name YHWH would have been derived from the Old Hebrew word "hayah", which means "he who he is" or "I am who I am", some Bible scholars from today think it could have derived from the word "hawah", which means "blow" or "fall" and may thus indicate a "storm god" like Zeus and Enlil. Storm, thunder and lightning were often associated with the display of power and the fury of the deity.

YHWH, Zeus and Enlil are also likewise depicted on many artistic interpretations as a powerful manly figure with a long (gray or white) beard.

Above Enlil and Enki stood the great Anu, the god of the heaven (firmament) and the supreme head of the gods. His kingdom was in the expansion of the heavens and is like the Greek god Ouranos (latinized: Uranus)—whose name is similar to the name Anu—known as a personification of the heavens/sky. Possibly, Anu never descended to the earthly material world and maybe he was the so-called "oversoul" of these gods. According to the stories all other gods of the Anunnaki would be his descendants. His leadership was followed up by the god Enlil, what eventually lead to a conflict with his half brother Enki about who would be the righteous leader. Also the Sumerian goddess Inanna, granddaughter of Enlil and great-granddaughter of Anu, and known by the Akkadians as "Ishtar", has similarities with the Greek goddess Aphrodite, known by the Romans as Venus.

Many ancient Mesopotamian wall reliefs are depicting mixed creatures including humans with animal-like features.

The "Ishtar Gate", which among known depictions of numerous creatures such as: lions, bulls, horses and the now extinct aurochs, also include numerous depictions of this "Mushhushshu" creature. Walls of the Ishtar Gate have been transported to Berlin where they now reside at the Pergamum Museum.

The "Mushhushshu", loosely translated as "splendour serpent" in Akkadian, had been depicted mostly unchanged in ancient Babylonian art for centuries, which lead German archaeologist and architect Robert Koldewey (also the discoverer of the Ishtar Gate between 1899 and 1914) to the belief this creature really could have existed in the past. Popular interpretations view the mushhushshu as a dragon.

This beast looks a lot like the so-called "Questing Beast" ("questing as in "barking") or "Beast Glatisant" (French) from the King Arthur legends, in which it is described having the head of a serpent, the body of a leopard, and the backside of a lion and the front paws of a reindeer or a rabbit. From his belly would have sounded a sound like thirty yelping dogs?

Some of these mixed creatures are now believed to be possibly some kind of guardian spirits. There is for example the "Lammasu": a human-headed lion with eagle's wings and the "Sedu": the human-headed winged bulls. The Lammassu could be a symbolical reference to the astrological age of Leo (the lion), while the bull could have been a reference to the age of Taurus (the bull), which began in 4,300 BCE according to Neil Mann's interpretation, which actually is within the timeframe when the Mesopotamian culture flourished.

In the Biblical scriptures, there is also mention of what we today could see as mixed creatures which are called "cherubim" (singular: "cherub") which were seen as servants of the "Lord". The term "cherubim" is cognate with the Assyrian "karabu" (meaning "great", "mighty"), and the Akkadian and Babylonian term "kuribu" (meaning: "propitious", "blessed".)

The "unicorn", is also mentioned in several books of the Bible: See Job 39:9-10, Numbers 23:22 and 24:8, Deuteronomy 33:17, Psalm 22:21, 29:6, 92:10 and Isaiah 34:7. In fact, unicorns were still depicted on 15th and 16th century European tapestries and renaissance man Leonardo da Vinci wrote about the unicorn in one of his notebooks, making it plausible that this animal wasn't a fantasy animal but did probably exist in the past.

These Creatures are probably our best reference to these gods and times since names change but the picture or hybrid stayed the same in his/hers appearance. It is for us the most recognisable way to identify these gods.

Dragon—Snake like reptile with wings and long tale

Mermaid—Half fish half woman (fish body with human upper torso)

Centaur—Half man half horse (horse body human upper torso)

Minotaur—Half man half bull (bulls head on human body)

Dwarf—Unnaturally small, ugly and shy male human that dwells in mountains.

Unicorn—Highly intelligent Horse with single horn on head.

Harpy—Bird woman (bird with woman head)

Satyr—Half goat male companions (lower extremities goat and top human)

Griffin—Lions body with woman's head and wings of an eagle. Sometimes claws of the eagle

Sphinx—Lion body with human or cats head.

Now looking at cave paintings and idol worship from up to 50 000 years before Adam where some of these above mentioned hybrids features on the cave walls, we can contemplate the facts.

So why did these early humans paint these hybrids on their cave walls?

Was this the big sin, did angels mix or cloned with humans and animals before Adam as we know that they did after as stated in Genesis and other writings?

Were these monsters and hybrids the offspring of these ungodly creations?

Is this trend happening again today like the time of Noah?

Is there any archaeological evidence?

BIRD HEADED BEINGS
IN MYTHOLOGY

Bird Headed Gods or Entities in Mythology always represent rebirth and resurrection. Pictographs on stone walls depict God type entities, or extraterrestrial beings, that have bird heads. Most are masks worn by the priests of Egypt depicting their Creator Gods to symbolize something connected to that God and ascension of soul—the evolution of human consciousness. The most common birds are—white pigeons or doves, eagles, hawks, thunderbirds, ibis, hummingbird, among endless others native to the area in which a myth was created. Human and semi human forms of some of the chief Egyptian deities:

Horus, son of Osiris, a sky god closely connected with the king.

Set, enemy of Horus and Osiris, god of storms and disorder.

Thoth, a moon deity and god of writing, counting and wisdom.

Khnum, a ram god who shapes men and their *kas* on his potter's wheel.

Hathor, goddess of love birth and death.

Sobek, the crocodile god, Lord of the Faiyum.

Ra, the sun god in his many forms.

Amon, a creator god often linked with Ra.

Ptah, another creator god and the patron of craftsmen.

Anubis, god of mummification.

Osiris, god of agriculture and ruler of the dead.

Isis, wife of Osiris, mother of Horus and Mistress of Magic. Most depicted with bird heads and others with a range of different animals.

THE PHOENIX

"She Who Rises From the Ashes to Recreate"

The phoenix is a mythical sacred firebird that can be found in the mythologies of the Egyptians, Arabian, Persians, Greeks, Romans, Chinese, Hindu, Phoenicians, Mesoamericans, Native Americans, and more.

A proponent of Ancient Astronaut Theory we can see a connection between what is described as the phoenix—a flaming bird who created—to ancient space ships that visited the planet leaving their imprint in the sacred landscape of our reality, that one day would be understood and interpreted to mean the end of this consciousness and the beginning of another

In Egyptian mythology and in myths derived from it, the Phoenix is a female mythical sacred firebird with beautiful gold and red plumage. Said to live for 500 or 1461 years (depending on the source), at the end of its life-cycle the phoenix builds itself a nest of cinnamon twigs that it then ignites; both nest and bird burn fiercely and are reduced to ashes, from which a new, young phoenix arises.

The phoenix embalms the ashes of the old phoenix in an egg made of myrrh and deposits it in Heliopolis ("the city of the sun" in Greek), located in Egypt. The bird was also said to regenerate when hurt or wounded by a foe, thus being almost immortal and invincible—a symbol of fire and divinity.

The phoenix was identified by the Egyptians as a stork or heron-like bird called a bennu, known from the Book of the Dead and other Egyptian texts as one of the sacred symbols of worship at Heliopolis, closely associated with the rising sun and the Egyptian sun-god Ra.

GREEK MYTHOLOGY

In the Greek Mythology the Titans appeared after Gaia, Mother Earth, lay with her son Uranus and through the union, 18 children were born:

(18 + 2, mother and father = 20 watchers) Of the 18 the following were born:

3 Giants—Cottus, Briareus and Gyges. Each of them had 50 heads and 100 arms.

They became the mightiest of Gaia's children where even the Titans and Olympians fear them.

3 Cyclopes—Brontes, Sterops and Arges. Each had only one large eye in the middle of the forehead, but their enormous size and strong limbs more than made up for it. More recently you can see them as cute and cuddly toys as the official 2012 Olympic mascot in the UK for our children to play with and keep as toys in their rooms.

12 Titans—There were 6 sons and 6 daughters. The daughters are:

Theia, the early goddess of light.
Rhea, an earth goddess who would become the mother of the Olympian gods.
Themis, another earth goddess.
Mnemosyne, personification of memory.
Phoebe, an early moon goddess.
Tethys, personification of the fertile ocean.

The sons were named:

Oceanus, the eldest of the Titans and god of the primordial river and river itself.
Coeus, who would become the father of Leto.
Crius, who would become the father Astraeus.
Hyperion, an early god of the sun.
Iapetus, who would become the father of Prometheus.
Cronus, the youngest and most daring of the twelve Titans, who would revolt against Uranus.

After the birth of his children, Uranus became fearful of their strength and power. He did not want to give up his power. So, as soon as Gaia had given birth to one of these children, Uranus would throw the baby back into Gaia's womb. Gaia was very uncomfortable with all her already-born children still stuck in her womb. When she couldn't endure it anymore, she hatched a plan to end the passions of Uranus so that no more children could be produced.

Gaia needed the help of one of her children, but only one responded, it was Cronus, her youngest child Titan. She gave Cronus a sharp adamantine sickle. Cronus hid and waited for his father to arrive. When Uranus came at night to lay with Gaia, Cronus struck by surprise. Seizing his father's genitals in his left hand, he sliced it off with the sickle on this right hand. He then tossed the organ into the sea.

The organ covered with blood splattered over Gaia. From the blood, more children were born:

Enrinyes (Furies)—Alecto, Tisiphone, and Megara. The avengers of wrong, who avenge perjury and crimes against one's own family
Giants—Born in full armour and with spears in their arms. Also known as Gig antes (monstrous giants).
Meliae—The "Ash Tree Nymphs" who would inhabit the forest of Greece.

According to Hesiod, the organs bobbing in the sea gave rise to white foam. From the foam, Aphrodite (means "out of white foam"), the goddess of love, beauty and sexual rapture arise. Naked and riding on a scallop shell, the sea carried her to Cythera island or Cyprus.

Naturally, Uranus was furious at Cronus and all his children. He cursed them with the name "Titans" which means "Overreaches".

After the Titans were freed, they made Cronus the king (golden age) and also freed the Cyclopes and Giants brothers from Tartarus. However, Cronus wasn't as kind a ruler either, before long he once again threw the Cyclopes and Giants back to dungeons in Tartarus.

THE TITANS

The 12 Titans were still free and eight of them married and had children:

Theia and Hyperion—Gave birth to the sun (Helius) and two daughters Selene (the moon) and Eos (the dawn)

Phoebe and Coues—Had two daughters—Let and Astoria

Oceans and Tethys—Associated with the seas. Their offspring include 3,000 rivers and 3,000 female Oceanside

Cronus also spelled Crones and Rhea—The father and mother of the gods produced six children. Three daughters—Hestia, Demeter, and Hera and three sons—Hades, Poseidon and Zeus, who would soon be gods on Mount Olympus.

As Crones ruled the immortals, he was even more a tyrant than Uranus. He feared that the Gaia and Uranus' prophecy that he would one day be overthrown by his own son. To prevent this, he swallowed his entire newborn whole as soon as they were born, so that they could do no harm.

Rhea, grieving for the lost of her children, pleaded with her parents Gaia and Uranus when she conceived her sixth child, Zeus. They sent Rhea to Lycos in Crete and when she gave birth to Zeus, she gave him to Gaia who hid him in a cave in Mount Dice and nourished him. Meanwhile, Rhea returned to Crones giving him a large stone wrapped in swaddling clothes. Crones thinking that it was the newborn swallowed the stone.

ZEUS BATTLE AGAINST THE TITANS

When Zeus grew up into a young man, he travelled to the oceans and sought the help of Métis, a wise Ocean dweller. Métis gave him an emetic potion. Zeus returned and disguised as Crones' cupbearer he gave Crones the drink. After Cronus drank the potion, he threw up all his children, including the stone he swallowed.

Once Zeus was in control, he battled the nearly invincible Titans with the help of his siblings. The combat continued for 10 years but a stalemate resulted.

Gaia foretold that Zeus can only win if they had the help of their uncles, the Cyclopes and Giants still imprisoned in Tartarus, the Underworld. Zeus raced down to Tartarus, killed the jailer (Campe) and freed his six uncles. The Cyclopes showed their gratitude by forging new weapons for their rescuers:

For Zeus, thunder and lightning

For Hades, the helmet of darkness, which made its' wearer invisible

For Poseidon, a trident, which would become the emblem for the future god of the sea

The Titans are now led by a new Titan Atlas who was hand-picked by the fellow Titans to replace Cronus. However, they could not overcome Zeus with the new weapons and the help of the Giants and Cyclopes. Zeus finally overthrew the Titans and locked them deep in the depths of Tartarus, with the three Giants keeping watch.

Only one of the Titans, who had opposed Zeus avoided eternal imprisonment. For the Titan Atlas, Zeus ordered him to lift up the sky and bear the weight of the heavens forever on his head and shoulders.

As for his supporters, unlike his father and grandfather, Zeus rewarded them handsomely. This ensured his reign as lord of the gods would last forever.

It is clear that these were not your average day to day "Gods" they had enormous powers.

Their daily routine includes incest, child abuse, deceit, cannibalism, murder, adultery and rape with no remorse or mercy.

There are literally hundreds of these "gods" and "semi gods" it will be too tedious to name them all here, but we will have a look at the main deities just to explain the structure of importance.

NAMES AND MEANINGS

Chaos—in one ancient Greek myth of creation, the dark, silent abyss from which all things came into existence. According to the Theology of Hesiod, Chaos generated the solid mass of Earth, from which arose the starry, cloud-filled Heaven. Mother Earth and Father Heaven, personified respectively as Gaea and her offspring Uranus, were the parents of the Titans. In a later theory, Chaos is the formless matter from which the cosmos, or harmonious order, was created.

Gaea—She was the mother and wife of Father Heaven, Uranus. They were the parents of the first creatures, the Titans, the Cyclopes, and the Giants—the Hecatoncheires (Hundred-Headed Ones). Uranus hated the monsters, and, even though they were his children, locked them in a secret place in the earth. Gaea was enraged at this favouritism and persuaded their son Cronos to overthrow his father. He emasculated Uranus, and from his blood Gaea brought forth the Giants, and the three avenging goddesses the Erinyes. Her last and most terrifying offspring was Typhon, a 100-headed monster, who, although conquered by the god Zeus, was believed to spew forth the molten lava flows of Mount Etna.

Tartarus—The lowest region of the underworld. Hesiod claimed that a brazen anvil would take nine days and nights to fall from heaven to earth, and nine days and nights to fall from earth to Tartarus. Tartarus rose out of Chaos and was the destination of wicked souls. Uranus banished his children the Cyclopes and the Hecatoncheires to Tartarus, as Zeus also did to the Titans. Other famous inhabitants of Tartarus include Sisyphus, Ixion, Tantalus, Salmoneus, Tityus, Ophion, and the daughters of Danaus.

Eros—The god of love. He was thought of as a handsome and intense young man, attended by Photos ("longing") or Himeros ("desire"). Later mythology made him the constant attendant of his mother, Aphrodite, goddess of love.

Erebus—Personification of the darkness of the Underworld and the offspring of Chaos. In later myth, Erebus was the dark region beneath the earth through which the shades must pass to the realm of Hades below. He is often used metaphorically for Hades itself.

Uranus—Gaea—The personification of the sky; the god of the heavens and husband of Gaea, the goddess of the earth. Their children are the Hecatonchires, the Cyclopes and the Titans.

Pontus—The sea god.

Cyclopes—Three sons: Arges, Brontes, and Steropes of Uranus and Gaea. The Cyclops was giant beings with a single, round eye in the middle of their foreheads. They helped Zeus defeat their brother, Cronus, by forging lightning bolts. They also made Poseidon's trident and Hades invisibility cap.

Hecatonchires—Three sons of Uranus and Gaia. There were three of them: Briareus also called Aegaeon, Cottus, and Gyges also called Gyes. They were gigantic and had fifty heads and one hundred arms each of great strength. They had 100 hands and helped Zeus in his war against the Titans.

Cronus—Rhea—Cronus was a ruler of the universe during the Golden Age. He was one of the 12 Titans and the youngest son of Uranus and Gaea, Cronus and his sister-queen, Rhea, became the parents of 6 of the 12 gods and goddesses known as the Olympians. Cronus had been warned that he would be overthrown by one of his own children. To prevent this, he swallowed his first five children as soon as they were born. Rhea did not like this. She substituted a stone wrapped in swaddling clothes for their sixth child, Zeus. He was hidden in Crete, and when he was older, he returned and forced Cronos to disgorge all the other children, who had grown inside of him. Zeus and his siblings fought a war against Cronos and the Titans. Zeus won, and the Titans were confined in Tartarus, a cave in the deepest part of the underworld.

Coeus—Phoebe—Coeus was a titan of Intelligence, the father of Leto, husband of Phoebe.

Oceanus—Tethys—The personification of the vast ocean. Together with his wife Tethys, they produced the rivers and six thousand offspring's called the Oceanids. He ruled over Ocean, a great river encircling the earth, which was believed to be a flat circle. The nymphs of this great river, the Oceanids, were their daughters, and the gods of all the streams on earth were their sons.

Hestia—Virgin goddess of the earth. She was the symbol of the house, around which a new born child was carried before it was received into the family. Although she appears in very few myths, most cities had a common hearth where her sacred fire burned. I

Hades—He was made lord of the underworld, ruling over the dead. He is a greedy god who is greatly concerned with increasing his subjects. Those who are calling increase the number of dead were seen favourably by him. He was also the god of wealth, due to the precious metals mined from the earth. His wife was Persephone whom Hades abducted.

The underworld itself was often called Hades. It was divided into two regions: Erebus, where the dead pass as soon as they die, and Tartarus, the deeper region, where the Titans had been imprisoned. It was a dim and unhappy place, inhabited by vague forms and shadows and guarded by Cerberus, the three-headed, dragon-tailed dog. Sinister rivers separated the underworld from the world above, and the aged boatman Charon ferried the souls of the dead across these waters.

Poseidon—God of the sea. His weapon was a trident, which could shake the earth, and shatter any object. He was second only to Zeus in power amongst the gods. Under the ocean, he had a marvellous golden palace. Poseidon was the husband of Amphitrite, one of the Nereids, by whom he had a son, Triton. Poseidon had numerous other love affairs. At one point he desired Demeter. To put him off Demeter asked him to make the most beautiful animal that the world had ever seen. To impress her Poseidon created the first horse. In some accounts his first attempts were unsuccessful and created a variety of other animals in his quest. By the time the horse was created his passion for Demeter had cooled.

Zeus—Hera—The god of the sky and ruler of the gods of Mount Olympus. He displaced his father and assumed the leadership of the gods of Olympus. Zeus was considered the father of the gods and of mortals. He did not create either gods or mortals; he was their father in the sense of being the protector and ruler both of the Olympian family and of the human race. His weapon was a thunderbolt. His breastplate was the aegis, his bird the eagle, his tree the oak. He was married to Hera but, is famous for his many affairs, which resulted in many known children and probably many more that were not known to be his. Athena was his favourite child. He bore her alone from his head. One of the greatest feasts for Zeus was the Olympic games. They were taking place every four years in Olympia. Even if there was a war between the city-states of Greece they were stopping the war to take part on those games.

Hera's marriage was founded in strife with Zeus and continued in strife. Writers represented Hera as constantly being jealous of Zeus's various amorous affairs. She punished her rivals and their children, among both goddesses and mortals, with implacable fury. The peacock (the symbol of pride; her wagon was pulled by peacocks) and the cow (she was also known as Bopis, meaning "cow-eyed", which was later translated as "with big eyes") were her sacred animals. Her favourite city was Argos.

Demeter—Zeus—Goddess of corn and the harvest. She taught mankind the art of sowing and ploughing so they could end their nomadic existence. She was of a severe, a beauty scarcely relieved by her hair. Which was as fair as ripened grain? Poseidon coveted her, but Demeter refused herself to him. To escape him she fled to Arkadia where, assuming the shape of a mare, she mingled with the herds of King **Oncus. Poseidon**, however, succeeded in finding her, changed himself into a stallion and made her the mother of the horse Arion.

When her daughter Persephone was abducted by Hades, god of the underworld, Demeter's grief was so great that she neglected the land; no plants grew, and famine devastated the earth. Dismayed at this situation, Zeus demanded that his brother Hades return Persephone to her mother. Hades agreed, but before he released the girl, he made her eat some pomegranate seeds that would force her to return to him for four months each year. In her joy at being reunited with her daughter, Demeter caused the earth to bring forth bright spring flowers and abundant fruit and grain for the harvest.

However, her sorrow returned each autumn when Persephone had to return to the underworld. The desolation of the winter season and the death of vegetation were regarded as the yearly manifestation of Demeter's grief when her daughter was taken from her. Demeter and Persephone were worshipped in the rites of the Eleusinian Mysteries.

Persephone—Persephone was the Queen of the Underworld and the daughter of Demeter. Persephone is the goddess of the underworld in Greek mythology. She is the daughter of Zeus and Demeter, goddess of the harvest. Persephone was such a beautiful girl that everyone loved her; even Hades wanted her for himself. Although Zeus gave his consent, Demeter was unwilling. Hades, therefore, seized the maiden as she was gathering flowers and carried her off to his realm. Persephone was a personification of the revival of nature in spring. Her attributes in iconography can include a torch, a crown, a sceptre, and stalks of grain.

Leto—Zeus—The mother of Artemis, goddess of the bow and of hunting. She was loved by the god Zeus, who, fearing the jealousy of his wife, Hera, banished Leto when she was about to bear his child. All countries and islands were also afraid of Hera's wrath and refused the desperate Leto a home where her child could be born. Finally, in her wanderings, she set foot on a small island floating in the Aegean Sea, which was called Delos.

Iapetus—The son Uranus and Gaea. Iapetus' wife was Clymene.

Athena—or Pallas-Athene, is one of the most important goddesses in Greek mythology. Goddess of wisdom, war, the arts, industry, justice and skill. Athena sprang full-grown and armoured from the forehead of the god Zeus and was his favourite child. She was fierce and brave in battle but, only fights to protect the state and home from outside enemies. She was the goddess of the city, handicrafts, and agriculture. She invented the bridle, which permitted man to tame horses, the trumpet, the flute, the pot, the rake, the plough, the yoke, the ship, and the chariot. Her attributes in iconography include the aegis (a fringed cloak, sometimes decorated with a Gorgon's head), the helmet, and the spear.

Ares—God of war. He was very aggressive. He was unpopular with both gods and humans. Ares was not invincible, even against mortals. He personified the brutal nature of war. He was immortal but whenever he would get hurt he would run back to his father, Zeus and was healed. Ares was mainly worshipped in Thracia.

Hebe—The goddess of youth. She, along with Ganymede was the cupbearers to the gods, serving them their nectar and ambrosia. She also prepared Ares' bath, and helped Hera to her chariot. Hebe was Hercules' wife.

Hephaestus—God of fire and metalwork. He was born lame and weak, and shortly after his birth, he was cast out of Olympus. In most legends, however, he was soon honoured again on Olympus and was married to Aphrodite, goddess of love, or to Aglaia, one of the three Graces. His workshop was believed to lie under Mount Etna, a volcano in Sicily. He made many wonderful artefacts for the gods, including the twelve golden thrones of the Olympians, their weapons and treasures.

Apollo—Apollo was primarily a god of prophecy. He sometimes gave the gift of prophecy to mortals whom he loved, such as the Trojan princess Cassandra. As a prophet and magician, he is the patron of medicine and healing. He was a gifted musician, who delighted the gods with his performance on the lyre. He was also a master archer and a fleet-footed athlete, credited with having been the first victor in the Olympic games. His twin sister was Artemis. He was famous for his oracle at Delphi. People travelled to it from all over the Greek world to divine the future. He was also the god of agriculture and cattle, and of light and truth.

Artemis—Artemis was the goddess of the hunt and animals, as well as of childbirth. Her twin brother was Apollo. As the moon goddess, she was sometimes identified with the goddesses Selene and Hecate. Her attributes are the bow and arrow, while dogs, deer and goose are her sacred animals. Her most elaborate temple was in Ephesus.

Atlas—Son of the Titan Iapetus and the nymph Clymene, and brother of Prometheus. Atlas fought with the Titans in the war against the deities of Mount Olympus. Atlas stormed the heavens and Zeus punished him for this deed by condemning him to forever bear the heavens upon his shoulders. He was the father of the Hesperidins, the nymphs who guarded the tree of golden apples, and Heracles (Hercules).

Prometheus—Prometheus was the wisest Titan, known as the friend and benefactor of humanity. He stole the sacred fire from Zeus and the gods. He also tricked the gods so that they should get the worst parts of any animal sacrificed to them, and human beings the best. Zeus commanded that Prometheus be chained for eternity in the Caucasus. There, an eagle would eat at his liver and each day, the liver would be renewed. So the punishment was endless, until <u>Heracles</u> finally killed the bird.

Epimetheus—Epimetheus was a Titan, whose name meant "afterthought". In some accounts, he was delegated, along with his brother Prometheus by Zeus to create mankind. He foolishly ignored his brother Prometheus' warnings to beware of any gifts from Zeus. He accepted Pandora as his wife, thereby bringing ills and sorrows to the world.

Maia—Zeus—Maia was a daughter of Atlas. She was one of Zeus' lovers. She, along with Zeus was the mother of Hermes.

Dione—Zeus—The goddess Dione became by Zeus the mother of Aphrodite.

Hermes—Hermes' main role was as a messenger. As the special servant and courier of Zeus, Hermes had winged sandals and a winged hat and bore a golden caduceus, or magic wand, entwined with snakes and surmounted by wings. He conducted the souls of the dead to the underworld and was believed to possess magical powers over sleep and dreams. Five minutes after he was born, he stole a herd of cows from Apollo. He invented the lyre from a cow's internal fibbers. Hermes was the patron of trickster and thieves because of his actions early in life. His attributes in iconography include the kerykeion (messenger's staff), winged boots, and petassos (cap).

Aphrodite—The goddess of love and beauty. Aphrodite loved and was loved by many gods and mortals. Among her mortal lovers, the most famous was perhaps Adonis. Some of her sons are Eros, Anteros, Hymenaios and Aeneas (with her Trojan lover Anchises). Perhaps the most famous legend about Aphrodite concerns the cause of the Trojan War. She was the wife of Hephaestus. The myrtle was her tree. The dove, the swan, and the sparrow were her birds.

Zeus—Before the pantheon of Greek gods we are familiar with ruled atop Olympus, an earlier generation of deities, known as Titans, held power. The ruler of these divine beings was Cronus, son of Gaia (Mother Earth). Cronus' mother had informed him that he would be usurped by one of his offspring who would be tremendously powerful. Therefore, whenever Cronus' wife Rhea bore a child he would swallow the newborn god to prevent them from overturning his power.

IDENTIFYING THE
MYTHOLOGICAL GODS

When they are not in disguise, each of them can be recognized by their body features or their special emblems. These emblems may be weapons or they may be animals and birds that are always associated with them.

Zeus (Jupiter) for example, wields the thunderbolt as his weapon, and his bird is the eagle.

Athene (Minerva) is associated with the owl.

Aphrodite (Venus) is associated with the dove.

Hera (Juno) with the peacock.

Hermes (Mercury) has small wings at each ankle and a winged cap. He carries the caduceus, a staff whose handle is made up of intertwined snakes, and so we can go on . . .

There is no all-powerful, all wise, and totally good father god in Greek myth. Instead, the story of the gods of Olympus is a complicated tale of crime, conspiracy, mutilation and murder. One after the other claimed sovereign power, but their hold on kingship was shaky.

Zeus fathered a lot of children out of wed log. He was married to Hera. If these children's mothers were goddesses they also would then be gods, all children of Zeus. He became the king of the gods, it was then prophesied by Gaia that he would be overthrown by a son.

Zeus found a way to avoid this prophecy by promptly swallowing the pregnant Métis, as his father Crones had swallowed his children. From this act Athena (Minerva) was born by jumping out of his forehead dressed for battle in full battledress.

Zeus was even credited to destroyed the world with a flood in the age of Deucalion because Lyceum's disrespect for Zeus's status and standing.

TRAITS OF THE GODS

Cronus . . . . Devouring his own children.

Cronus sometimes spelled Cronos envied the power of his father, the ruler of the universe, Uranus. Uranus drew the enmity of Cronus' mother, Gaia, when he hid the gigantic youngest children of Gaia, the hundred-armed Hecatonchires and one-eyed Cyclopes, in Tartarus, so that they would not see the light. Gaia created a great stone sickle and gathered together Cronus and his brothers to persuade them to castrate Uranus.

Only Cronus was willing to do the deed, so Gaia gave him the sickle and placed him in ambush. When Uranus met with Gaia, Cronus attacked him with the sickle castrating him and casting his testicles into the sea.

From the blood (or, by a few accounts, semen) that spilled out from Uranus and fell upon the earth, the Gigantes, Erinyes, and Meliae were produced. The testicles produced white foam from which Aphrodite emerged. For this, Uranus threatened vengeance and called his sons Titenes (according to Hesiod meaning "straining ones," the source of the word "titan", but this etymology is disputed) for overstepping their boundaries and daring to commit such an act

Aphrodite . . . . born from foam because of the castration of Cronus.

Aphrodite is usually said to have been born near Paphos, on the island of Cyprus, for which reason she is called "Cyprian", especially in the poetic works of Sappho. Her chief centre of worship was at Paphos, where the goddess of desire had been worshipped from the early Iron Age in the form of Ishtar and Astarte.

However, other versions of her myth have her born near the island of Kythira (Cythera), for which reason she is called "Cytherea". Kythira was a stopping place for trade and culture between Crete and the Peloponnesus, so these stories may preserve traces of the migration of Aphrodite's cult from the Middle East to mainland Greece.

In the most famous version of her myth, her birth was the consequence of a castration: Cronus severed Uranus' genitals and threw them behind him into the sea. The foam from his genitals gave rise to Aphrodite (for which reason she is called "foam-arisen"), while the Erinyes (furies) emerged from the drops of blood. Hesiod states that the genitals "were carried over the sea a long time and white foam arose from the immortal flesh; with it a girl grew." This girl became Aphrodite. She floated ashore on a scallop shell.

Pandora . . . . released disasters on human kind.

Pandora was allegedly the first woman, who was made out of clay. As Hesiod related it, each god helped create her by giving her unique gifts. Zeus ordered Hephaestus to mould her out of earth as part of the punishment of mankind for Prometheus' theft of the secret of fire, and all the gods joined in offering her "seductive gifts".

Her other name, inscribed against her figure on a white-ground kylix in the British Museum, is Anesidora, "she who sends up gifts," up implying "from below" within the earth. According to the myth, Pandora opened a jar pithos, in modern accounts sometimes mistranslated as "Pandora's box", releasing all the evils of mankind—although the particular evils, aside from plagues and diseases, are not specified in detail by Hesiod—leaving only Hope inside once she had closed it again.[5] She opened the jar out of simple curiosity and not as a malicious act

Lycaon . . . . changed into a wolf at full moon and display preference for human flesh.

Baby's flesh was his preference. He was a king of Arcadia, son of Pelasgus and Meliboea, who in the most popular version of the myth tested Zeus by serving him a dish of his slaughtered and dismembered son in order to see whether Zeus was truly omniscient. In return for these gruesome deeds Zeus transformed Lycaon into the form of a wolf, and killed Lycaon's fifty sons by lightning bolts, except possibly Nyctimus, who was the slaughtered child, and instead became restored to life.

Poseidon . . . . With his "trident" he causes tidal waves, storms and earthquakes.

Poseidon was a son of Cronus and Rhea. In most accounts he is swallowed by Cronus at birth but later saved, with his other brothers and sisters, by Zeus. However in some versions of the story, he, like his brother Zeus, did not share the fate of his other brother and sisters who were eaten by Cronus. He was saved by his mother Rhea, who concealed him among a flock of lambs and pretended to have given birth to a colt, which she gave to Cronus to devour.

Vulcan . . . His mother (Juno) discarded him as a baby and through him of a mountain.

The nature of the god is connected to religious ideas concerning fire. The Roman concept of the god seems to be connected both to the destructive and fertilizing powers of fire.

In the first aspect he is worshipped to avert its potential danger to harvested wheat in the Volcanalia and his cult is located outside the boundaries of the original city to avoid its causing fires in the city itself.

This power is however considered useful if directed against enemies and such a choice for the location of the god's cult could be interpreted in this way too. The same idea underlies the dedication of the arms of the defeated enemies, as well as those of the survived general in a devotion ritual to the god. Through comparative interpretation this aspect has been connected to the third (or defensive) fire in the Vedic theory of the three sacrificial fires. Another meaning of Vulcan is related to male fertilizing power.

Apollo . . . . Sun god . . . . **Amon—Ra**

The ideal of the kouros (a beardless, athletic youth), Apollo has been variously recognized as a god of light and the sun, truth and prophecy, healing, plague, music, poetry, and more. Apollo is the son of Zeus and Leto, and has a twin sister, the chaste huntress Artemis

As sun-god and god of light, Apollo was also known by the epithets Aegletes Helius Phanaeus and Lyceus; (Λύκειος, Lukeios, from Proto-Greek *λύκη, "light").

The meaning of the epithet "Lyceus" later became associated Apollo's mother Leto, who was the patron goddess of Lycia (Λυκία) and who was identified with the wolf (λύκος), earning him the epithets Lycegenes.

Apollo is the healer under the gods, but he is also the bringer of disease and death with his arrows, similar to the function of the terrible Vedic god of disease Rudra. He sends a terrible plague (λοιμός) to the Achaeans. The god who sends a disease can also prevent from it, therefore when it stops they make a purifying ceremony and offer him a "hecatomb" to ward off evil. When the oath of his priest appeases, they pray and with a song they call their own god, the beautiful Paean.

Amon was Zeus, Osiris was Dionysus, Ptah was Hephaestus

Zeus

In the ancient Greek religion, Zeus is the "Father of Gods and men" who rules the Olympians of Mount Olympus as a father rules the family. He is the god of sky and thunder in Greek mythology. His Roman counterpart is Jupiter and Etruscan counterpart is Tinia. His Hindu equivalent is Indra.

Zeus is the child of Cronus and Rhea, and the youngest of his siblings. In most traditions he is married to Hera, although, at the oracle of Dodona, his consort is Dione: according to the Iliad, he is the father of Aphrodite by Dione. He is known for his erotic escapades.

These resulted in many godly and heroic offspring, including Athena, Apollo and Artemis, Hermes, Persephone (by Demeter), Dionysus, Perseus, Heracles, Helen of Troy, Minos, and the Muses (by Mnemosyne); by Hera, he is usually said to have fathered Ares, Hebe and Hephaestus.

Even the gods who are not his natural children address him as Father, and all the gods rise in his presence. For the Greeks, he was the King of the Gods, who oversaw the universe. As Pausanias observed, "That Zeus is king in heaven is a saying common to all men". In the Homeric Hymns he is referred to as the chieftain of the gods.

His symbols are the thunderbolt, eagle, bull, and oak. In addition to his Indo-European inheritance, the classical "cloud-gatherer" also derives certain iconographic traits from the cultures of the Ancient Near East, such as the sceptre. Zeus is frequently depicted by Greek artists in one of two poses: standing, striding forward, with a thunderbolt levelled in his raised right hand, or seated in majesty.

Some pairs of Greek and Roman gods, such as Zeus and Jupiter, are thought to derive from a common Indo-European archetype (Dyeus as the supreme sky god), and thus exhibit shared functions by nature. Others required more expansive theological and poetic efforts: though both Ares and Mars are war gods, Ares was a relatively minor figure in Greek religious practice and deprecated by the poets, while Mars was a father of the Roman people and a central figure of archaic Roman religion.

Some deities dating to Rome's oldest religious stratum, such as Janus and Terminus, had no Greek equivalent. Other Greek divine figures, most notably Apollo, were adopted directly into Roman culture, but underwent a distinctly Roman development, as when Augustus made Apollo one of his patron deities. In the early period, Etruscan culture played an intermediary role in transmitting Greek myth and religion to the Romans.

Atlas

Atlas and his brother Menoetius sided with the Titans in their war against the Olympians, the Titanomachy. His brothers Prometheus and Epimetheus weighed the odds and betrayed the other Titans by forming an alliance with the Olympians. When the Titans were defeated, many of them (including Menoetius) were confined to Tartarus, but Zeus condemned Atlas to stand at the western edge of Gaia (the Earth) and hold up Uranus (the Sky) on his shoulders, to prevent the two from resuming their primordial embrace.

Thus, he was Atlas Telamon, "enduring Atlas," and became a doublet of Koios, the embodiment of the celestial axis around which the heavens revolve. A lot of people wrongly believe that it is the earth he is holding on his shoulders but it is in fact the heavens. Why should he hold up the heavens?

This is because these gods didn't want heaven close to them. The myth states that the lower the heavens moved down to earth the more the people and the gods have to kneel in the lesser "head space" between earth and heaven and they felt that that the farther they can keep the heavens away from earth the lesser the people will kneel and by that way they will move away from the act of kneeling to pray to YHWH.

It is also symbolic that they want to place as much as possible distance between people and YHWH by keeping them apart.

In the book Mythology, Myths, Legends and fantasies by Grange Books they state the following:

"The gods took many other nonhuman forms, especially when they came to earth in search of desirable human beings to rape or take as

lovers, and they also took the form of ideas, inspirations and moments of particular clarity or confusion."

Was Biblical Eve the first human woman to be deceived by a fallen angel (Satan) that metamorphose "shape shift" himself into a desirable being creating confusion in Eves mind for a moment? Was Cain the first to be born out of the Adamite human for the Anak (heylel, nephilim, giant) seed line in the Adamic age?

HIDDEN FESTIVALS
AND CELEBRATION'S

We know that the Satan and his fallen angels ended up in the mythology of the world. It found a true home where it lives today in the Pagan Babylonian believe systems and traditions. Today's nations and Christian holidays are interwoven with Pagan Traditions without the people ever realizing who or what is being honoured.

Easter History

The history of Easter reveals rich associations between the Christian faith and the seemingly unrelated practices of the early pagan religions. Easter history and traditions that we practice today evolved from pagan symbols, from the ancient goddess Ishtar to Easter eggs and the Easter bunny.

Easter, perhaps the most important of the Christian holidays, celebrates the Christ's resurrection from the dead following his death on Good Friday, a rebirth that is commemorated around the vernal equinox, historically a time of pagan celebration that coincides with the arrival of spring and symbolizes the arrival of light and the awakening of life around us.

Ostara, Goddess of Spring

Easter is named for a Saxon goddess who was known by the names of Oestre or Eastre, and in Germany by the name of Ostara. She is a goddess of the dawn and the spring, and her name derives from words for dawn, the shining light arising from the east. Our word for the "female hormone" estrogens derives from her name.

Ostara was, of course, a fertility goddess. Bringing in the end of winter, with the days brighter and growing longer after the vernal equinox, Ostara had a passion for new life. Her presence was felt in the flowering of plants and the birth of babies, both animal and human. The rabbit (well known for its propensity for rapid reproduction) was her sacred animal.

Easter eggs and the Easter Bunny both featured in the spring festivals of Ostara, which were initially held during the feasts of the goddess Ishtar (Inanna). Eggs are an obvious symbols of fertility and the newborn chicks an adorable representation of new growth. Brightly collared eggs, chicks, and bunnies were all used at festival time to express appreciation for Ostara's gift of abundance.

EASTER EGGS

The history of Easter Eggs as a symbol of new life should come as no surprise. The notion that the Earth itself was hatched from an egg was once widespread and appears in creation stories ranging from Asian to Ireland.

Eggs, in ancient times in Northern Europe, were a potent symbol of fertility and often used in rituals to guarantee a woman's ability to bear children. To this day rural "granny women" (lay midwives/healers in the Appalachian mountains) still use eggs to predict, with uncanny accuracy, the sex of an unborn child by watching the rotation of an egg as it is suspended by a string over the abdomen of a pregnant woman.

Dyed eggs are given as gifts in many cultures. Decorated eggs bring with them a wish for the prosperity of the abundance during the coming year.

Folklore suggests that Easter egg hunts arose in Europe during "the Burning Times", when the rise of Christianity led to the shunning (and persecution) of the followers of the "Old Religion". Instead of giving the eggs as gifts the adults made a game of hiding them, gathering the children together and encouraging them to find the eggs. Some believe that the authorities seeking to find the "heathens" would follow or bribe the children to reveal where they found the eggs so that the property owner could be brought to justice.

The meat that is traditionally associated with Easter is ham. Though some might argue that ham is served at Easter since it is a "Christian" meat, (prohibited for others by the religious laws of Judaism and Islam) the origin probably lies in the early practices of the pagans of Northern Europe.

Having slaughtered and preserved the meat of their agricultural animals during the Blood Moon celebrations the previous autumn so they would have food throughout the winter months, they would celebrate the occasion by using up the last of the remaining cured meats. In anticipation that the arrival of spring with its emerging plants and wildlife would provide them with fresh food in abundance, it was customary for many pagans to begin fasting at the time of the vernal equinox, clearing the "poisons" (and excess weight) produced by the heavier winter meals that had been stored in their bodies over the winter.

Some have suggested that the purpose of this fasting may have been to create a sought-after state of "altered consciousness" in time for the spring festivals. One cannot but wonder if this practice of fasting might have been a forerunner of "giving up" foods during the Lenten season.

Chocolate Easter bunnies and eggs, marshmallow chicks in pastel colours, and candy of all sorts have pagan origins as well! To understand their association with religion we need to examine the meaning of food as a symbol. The ancient belief that, by eating something we take on its characteristics formed the basis for the earliest "blessings" before meals (a way to honour the life that had been sacrificed so that we as humans could enjoy life) and, presumably, for the more recent Christian sacrament of communion as well.

Shaping candy Easter eggs and bunnies out of candy to celebrate the spring festival was, simply put, a way to celebrate the symbols of the goddess and the season, while laying claim to their strengths (vitality, growth, and fertility) for ourselves.

THE EASTER BUNNY

Feeling guilty about arriving late one spring, the Goddess Ostara saved the life of a poor bird whose wings had been frozen by the snow. She made him her pet or, as some versions have it, her lover. Filled with compassion for him since he could no longer fly (in some versions, it was because she wished to amuse a group of young children), Ostara turned him into a snow hare and gave him the gift of being able to run with incredible speed so he could protect himself from hunters.

In remembrance of his earlier form as a bird, she also gave him the ability to lay eggs (in all the colours of the rainbow), but only on one day out of each year. Eventually the hare managed to anger the goddess Ostara, and she cast him into the skies where he would remain as the constellation Lupus (The Hare) forever positioned under the feet of the constellation Orion (the Hunter). He was allowed to return to earth once each year, but only to give away his eggs to the children attending the Ostara festivals that were held each spring. The tradition of the Easter Bunny had begun.

The Hare was sacred in many ancient traditions and was associated with the moon goddesses and the various deities of the hunt. In ancient times eating the Hare was prohibited except at Beltane (Celts) and the festival of Ostara (Anglo-Saxons), when a ritual hare-hunt would take place.

In many cultures rabbits, like eggs, were considered to be potent remedies for fertility problems. The ancient philosopher-physician Pliny the Elder prescribed rabbit meat as a cure for female sterility and in some cultures the genitals of a hare was carried to avert barrenness.

Medieval Christians considered the hare to bring bad fortune, saying witches changed into rabbits in order to suck the cows dry. It was claimed that a witch could only be killed by a silver crucifix or a bullet when she appeared as a hare. Given their "mad" leaping and boxing displays during mating season as well as their ability to produce up to 42 offspring each spring, it is understandable that they came to represent lust, sexuality, and excess in general. Medieval Christians considered the hare to be an evil omen, believing that witches changed into rabbits in order to suck the cows dry. It was claimed that a witch could only be killed by a silver crucifix or a bullet when she appeared as a hare. In later Christian tradition the white Hare, when depicted at the Virgin Mary's feet, represents triumph over lust or the flesh. The rabbit's vigilance and speed came to represent the need to flee from sin and temptation and a reminder of the swift passage of life.

And, finally, there is a sweet Christian legend about a young rabbit that, for three days, waited anxiously for his friend, Jesus, to return to the Garden of Gethsemane, not knowing what had become of him. Early on Easter morning, Jesus returned to His favourite garden and was welcomed the little rabbit. That evening when the disciples came into the garden to pray, still unaware of the resurrection, they found a clump of beautiful larkspurs, each blossom bearing the image of a rabbit in its centre as a remembrance of the little creature's hope and faith.

ISHTAR, GODDESS OF LOVE

Ishtar, goddess of romance, procreation, and war in ancient Babylon, was also worshipped as the Sumerian goddess Inanna. One of the great goddesses, or "mother goddesses", the stories of her descent to the Underworld and the resurrection that follows are contained in the oldest writings that have ever been discovered . . . the Babylonian creation myth Enuma Elish and the story of Gilgamesh. Scholars believed that they were based on the oral mythology of the region and were recorded about 2,100 B.C.E.

The most famous of the myths of Ishtar tell of her descent into the realm of the dead to rescue her young lover, Tammuz, a Vegetation god forced to live half the year in the Underworld. Ishtar approached the gates of the Underworld, which was ruled by her twin sister Eresh-kigel, the goddess of death and infertility.

She was refused admission. Similar to the Greek myths of Demeter and Persephone that came later, during Ishtar's absence the earth grew barren since all acts of procreation ceased while she was away. Ishtar screamed and ranted that she would break down the gates and releases all of the dead to overwhelm the world and compete with the living for the remaining food unless she was allowed to enter and plead her case with her twin. Needless to say, she won admission. But the guard, following standard protocol, refused to let her pass through the first gate unless she removed her crown. At the next gate, she had to remove her earrings, then her necklace at the next, removing her garments and proud finery until she stood humbled and naked after passing through the seventh (and last) gate.

In one version, she was held captive and died but was brought back to life when her servant sprinkled her with the "water of life". In the more widely known version of the myth, Ishtar's request was granted and she regained all of her attire and possessions as she slowly re-emerged through the gates of darkness.

Upon her return, Tammuz and the earth returned to life. Annual celebrations of this "Day of Joy" was held each year around the time of the vernal equinox. These celebrations became the forerunners of the Ostara festivals that welcomed Oestre and the arrival of spring.

A section on the Goddess Inanna (the Sumerian version of the Goddess Ishtar), her myths and symbols, is included with the myths of the goddesses at this website. Easter eggs, the Easter Bunny, the dawn that arrives with resurrection of life and the celebration of spring all serve to remind us of the cycle of rebirth and the need for renewal in our lives. In the history of Easter, Christian and pagan traditions are gracefully interwoven.

In these days of excess entertainment and consumption, it is easy to get caught up in the so-called "holiday season", rarely stopping to consider its significance. I say so-called, because the very word *holiday* is derived from the two words *holy* and *day*. However, under closer scrutiny from the Judeo-Christian and Islamic perspectives, these days are anything but holy. Celebrations such as Easter, Christmas, All Saints Day and Halloween all find their roots in pagan traditions, alien to the prophets. Proof of this lies in the lack of historical evidence that the prophets ever celebrated their birthdays, decorated eggs, placed ornaments on trees, or dressed up in costumes.

CHRISTMAS

Christ Mass, or Christmas, is one of many Christian celebrations which find its origins in pagan ritual. To understand its origins one must examine the cult of the sun god. Be it Roman, Persian, Babylonian, or Egyptian worship of the sun god, there are common features. In general, the festivals of sun god worship occurred throughout the year and were based on the path of the sun and the relative hours of day and night. Therefore, the most significant pagan rites occurred during transition periods such as the vernal equinox, autumnal equinox, summer solstice, and winter solstice.

As autumn progresses to winter, the days get shorter and shorter until the winter solstice. At that point, the daylight hours begin to increase again. With respect to sun god worship, then, this represented the birth of the sun. In Rome and northern Europe, it was celebrated as the birth of Mithras, the sun god. These celebrations were ultimately merged with Christian teachings, perhaps to make Christianity palatable to the pagan masses.

By adopting [seasonal] festivals as Christian, the early Church sought both to win the allegiance of the populace as well as to harness the vitality of such festivals. While there is nothing to indicate the actual time of Jesus' birth, such an event most easily correlated to winter solstice festivals. The Roman celebration of the birth of the sun god, Mithras, for instance, had also been observed on December 25th . . . . the Church adopted the winter solstice as Christmas. The birth of God's sun at the solstice easily correlated to the birth of God's son.

The birth of Osiris in Egyptian pagan worship also correlated with the winter solstice.

An Egyptian winter solstice celebration of the birth of Osiris, the divine representation of masculine fertility, on January 6th became the Christian Epiphany. The Church declared that it signified the manifestation of Jesus' divinity. Yet, the spirit of both Christmas and the Christian Epiphany embodied timeless celebrations of the winter solstice. The difference between them was due more to a difference in calendars than a difference in meaning; the Egyptian calendar was twelve days behind the Julian calendar.

Evergreens were important symbols of life to pagan northern Europe. The fact that they stood the test of winter by remaining green was quite significant to pagan worship. Words attributed to Jeremiah in the Old Testament warn against following the way of the pagans. Specifically, the warning pertains to the decorating of trees with silver and gold after cutting them down from the forest.

(Jeremiah 10:2-5)

> *2 "Do not learn the way of the pagans (people who make horoscopes); do not be dismayed at the signs of heaven; for the pagans are dismayed at them".*
>
> *3 "For the customs of the people are futile; for one cuts a tree from the forest, the work of the hands of the workman, with the axe".*
>
> *4 "They decorate it with silver and gold; they fasten it with nails and hammers so that it will not topple".*
>
> *5 "They are upright, like a palm tree, and they cannot speak; they must be carried, because they cannot go by themselves. Do not be afraid of them, for they cannot do evil, nor can they do any good."*

Whether or not this was directed at winter festivals surrounding evergreens is not known. But regardless, there is a general warning against following traditions which are alien to the prophetic tradition.

And there are certainly no records of prophets cutting down and erecting Christmas trees. And what of Santa Claus? Is this simply another innocent custom? Just something benign for the kids? Certainly not. The dangers in Santa Claus lie less in the realm of *bid'ah*, or religious innovation, and more in the realm of *shirk*, or associating others with God. Attributes are given to Santa, which apply to God Alone.

Answering children's prayers and requests for toys, knowing whether they have been naughty or nice, and the ability to reach every home in the world in a single night are things which apply only to God. God, Alone, is Omniscient, and He alone knows the behaviour of the children. God, Alone, is Omnipotent and able to answer everyone's request without decreasing His Dominion. To apply attributes of God to other than God is to have gods beside the One True God.

Time of Year	Pagan Traditions	Christian Synthesis
Winter Solstice	The birth of the sun. The birth of Mithras on December 25th. Often celebrated with Yule fires, processions of light, and tree decorating.	Christmas & the Epiphany
Winter Season	A time of nurturing and honouring inspiration and creativity. Common practices involving festivals of light, wearing animal masks and skins in hopes of augmenting the coming year's supply.	Candle mass
Spring Equinox	The sun is resurrected and gains prominence over the night. Fertility celebrations involving symbols such as the egg and the prolific hare.	Easter

Spring Season	The mating of the earth and the sky from which will come the year's harvest. Often celebrated with maypole dancing, decorating with new foliage.	Pentecost & the Feast of the Ascension
Summer Solstice	The peak of the sun's light. Celebrated with large bonfires, burning fragrant herbs, decorating with flowers.	Feast of St. John
Summer Season	The sun's energy transfers to the crops. Ritual blessings of the harvest, herbs, fields, mountains, and ocean.	Assumption Day
Autumnal Equinox	A time of gratitude for the harvest. Feasts and decorating with fall fruits, grains, and vegetables.	Michaela's & the Nativity of Mary
Fall Season	Acknowledgement of the year's completion. Honouring the dead, honouring and releasing the past.	All Soul's Day & All Saints Day, Halloween

EASTER, FERTILITY, &
THE ORIGIN OF THE CROSS

While holidays like Christmas, New Year's Day, and Valentine's Day have names which indicate either the holiday's origin or its significance, Easter stands out. Most people have no idea what the name *Easter* means. It turns out that *Easter* is a corruption of *Austre*, the name of the ancient pagan Scandinavian goddess of life and fertility.

As noted above, many holidays celebrated today represent a synthesis between Christian doctrine and pagan ritual. The basis for most of these "holy" days revolves around natural phenomena such as the autumnal equinox, vernal equinox, summer solstice, and winter solstice. With regards to the spring season and the vernal equinox, pagans, especially the pagans of cold, northern Europe, celebrated the renewal of life, as was demonstrated by the budding of the leaves, blooming of the flowers, return of the birds, and the re-emergence of many mammals previously in hibernation. These celebrations often utilized symbols of fertility and life such as the egg, the baby chick, and the rabbit.

The use of these same symbols in present day celebrations of Easter is quite obvious. Decorating eggs, Easter egg hunts and the Easter bunny are all familiar icons. These things have carried over from pagan traditions via a synthesis with Christian doctrine. In particular, the worship of the sun god has been incorporated into the once monotheistic Christian teachings. The vernal equinox represents a time in which the hours of daylight equal the hours of night. The days following the vernal equinox mark an increase in the number of hours of daylight over the night. This time, then became viewed as the time of *sol invictus* or the unconquerable sun, demonstrating its supremacy by conquering the night.

The synthesis with Christian ideas was simple. Just as the sun conquered the night, the son conquered death. Thus, the pagan holidays of fertility and life were replaced with the Christian concept of the resurrection of YAHSHUA.

The Church adopted spring equinox celebrations as Easter. As this time had already been one of celebrating the sun's resurrection and return to prominence, celebrating the resurrection of the son of God required no great change in understanding. In fact, the Easter celebrations were so similar to earlier celebrations—particularly those which recognized the resurrection of the Babylonian Adonis, the Greek Apollo, and the Roman Attis—that a bitter controversy arose with pagans claiming that the Christian Easter celebration was a spurious imitation of the ancient traditions. Vernal equinox bonfires, originally prohibited by the Catholic Church, found their way as Easter fires into the official liturgy of Rome by the ninth century. Fertility symbols associated with spring, such as the egg and the incredibly prolific rabbit, survived as well. (Ellerbe p. 148)

In fact, the very symbol of the cross is derived from pagan fertility practices. It is known by many that the symbol of the cross was utilized by many civilizations prior to the emergence of Christianity. The ancient Egyptian symbol of the *ankh*, then, deserves mentioning for its connection to fertility. The ankh is a symbol which resembles the Christian cross, except that it has a loop at the top. Some sources indicate that this symbol derives its shape from ancient Egyptian studies of human anatomy. The loop, it is said, represents the gravid (pregnant) uterus, while the arms of the cross represent the Fallopian tubes. And the base of the cross serves as the vaginal canal. The ankh, then, serves as the ultimate fertility symbol. In support of this theory of the derivation of the ankh, the fertility dolls of many African peoples, in particular the Ashanti are shaped like the ankh.

The pagan roots of holidays celebrated in the name of Christianity testify to its having been altered. Christianity, as it exists today, does not represent the message of YAHSHUA MESSIAH.

VALENTINE'S DAY

For those who don't know about cupid, it's often said that he has become the very symbol of love. Especially when it comes to Valentine's Day. Yet why is that? How did a naked baby, with a bow and arrow, become a symbol for Valentine's Day?

According to Greek mythology, Eros was the son of Venus, goddess of love. Hence, how the word erotic became into fruition as Eros was quite a sex symbol back in those days. Plus, he wasn't always portrayed as a baby. In fact, according to Greek mythology he was allegedly portrayed as a very handsome and charismatic man. A man that was so charming, that he could easily make both gods and humans fall in love. Even his trademark arrows have been around forever, as it's said according to legend, which the gold arrows could cause anyone to fall in love with the first person they saw. Whereas his lead ones, could easily make the person hate the first person they saw.

In one famous story, Eros was cited shooting a gold arrow at the sun god, Apollo, whom fell in love with a nymph named Daphne. However, as part of a cruel joke, he shot Daphne with a lead arrow that made her detest Apollo severely; despite his affections. Indeed, Cupid has been portrayed as mischievous over the years. Often being depicted wearing a blindfold in later illustrations, to coin the term, "love is blind."

In another legend, Eros became victim to his own arrow as his mother, Venus, grew jealous of a mortal named Psyche. Therefore, she sends her son out to make Psyche fall in love with a hideously disfigured creature, but he gets pricked by his own arrow. Thus, falling madly in love with her. However, this is just one of the many legends foretold about cupid over the years.

The ancient Romans were the first to rename Eros, to Cupid. It wasn't until around the Renaissance era, those artists starting to give Cupid a more child like appearance with images they phrased as "putty." By the time, valentine greeting cards started to use the pictures of baby cupid, the image became stuck in the minds of modern mythology as society now associates him with the Valentine holiday.

Indeed, cupid has now been used as the symbol to represent love in today's modern culture. Not only to display how love can come in all shapes and sizes, but you can even see him portrayed with a blindfold, as many like to say love is blind.

Love is in the air, and spring is here. It has been known for many centuries that Valentine's Day is considered to be the most romantic time of the year. However, why is that so? What's so special about it? I mean it's only one day, so why should it be any more special than any other day? Over the years, February 14 has become the one day of the year, where romance springs around all over the globe. To uncover this mystery, I feel it's important to look at our earlier history to examine why this holiday so prestigious to our modern culture today.

According to one legend, in third century Rome, Emperor Claudius II came to the theory that single men made better soldiers than married ones. Therefore, he outlawed marriages for young men, that were deemed to make potentially good soldiers, and only allowed elderly men to marry. Seeing the unfair and injustice of this new law, St. Valentine defied this law and continued performing marital rituals for young lovers in secret. Needless to say, this angered Emperor Claudius II once he found out, and ordered to have St. Valentine put to death.

Although other historians believe, that St. Valentine might have been killed while aiding Christians from escaping the torture and harsh treatments of Roman prisons.

While some historians have often debated this theory as to how St. Valentine died, what is certain that the mystique and romance behind the holiday continues to intensify the world to this day?

In another legend, it's said that St. Valentine actually conjured and sent the first "valentine" greeting card, while he was in prison. During his stay in prison, he met a young girl, whom would often visit him during his sentence. Some historians believe she may have been the jailor's daughter. Before he was sentenced to be executed, he allegedly sent her a farewell letter with the final words being, "from your valentine." Since then the name Valentine has become the word most often associated with various forms of eroticism and romance over the years. Each culture giving their own unique tastes on the legend, as the mystery of St. Valentine still continues to inspire the hearts of many lovers even to this day.

To answer why February 14 be deemed under his name? There have been many historians whom have debated that as well. Some widely believe that it's celebrated in mid-February to honour his death or burial, which is estimated to have occurred around 270 A.D. Other historians believe that it might have been an attempt to Christianize the pagan Lupercalia festival.

In ancient Rome, spring time marked the beginning of purification. Houses were thoroughly swept, as the Romans would sprinkle salt and spelt, a special type of wheat, throughout their interiors. The Lupercalia festival was held on February 15, which was considered a fertility festival dedicated to Faunas, the Roman God of Agriculture, and the Roman founders, Romulus and Remus.

Members of Luperci, an order of Roman priests, would begin the festival by gathering at a sacred cave where it's believed Romulus and Remus were cared for by a she-wolf or lupa. Priests would then sacrifice a goat, for fertility, and a dog, for purification.

Then they would slice the goat's hide into strips, and dipped them into sacrificial blood as they took to the streets. Gently slapping women and fields of crops with goat hide strips. As repulsive and vile as this may sound, women back then welcomed being slapped with bloody goat hides as it was believed that it would make them more fertile during the coming year. It's then said that women would put their names in a big urn, later on in the day. The men would then pick a name out of the urn, and would become paired with the chosen woman for a year; often ending in marriage.

It wasn't until later around 498 A.D., that Pope Gelasius declared February 14, Valentine's Day. The Roman lottery system was then deemed unchristian and outlawed, as Christianity began to take over as the dominant religion, in Rome. In other countries such as England and France, February 14 was also the first day of the birds mating season, which added to the idea of romance during the holiday.

According to history, the oldest Valentine letter was in the form of a poem by Charles, Duke of Orleans. He wrote a letter to his wife during his imprisonment, in the Tower of London, after being apprehended at the Battle of Agincourt. Written in 1415, the greeting is part of the manuscript collection within the British Library in London, England.

In Great Britain, Valentine's Day became a lot more popular during the seventeenth century. In the eighteenth century, it became common for friends and lovers of all social classes to exchange small tokens of affection or handwritten notes. By the end of the century, printed generic greeting cards replaced handwritten ones, due to improvements in printing technology. This of course made it easier for people to express themselves, in a time when direct emotions were discouraged in society. In the 1840's, Esther A. Howland began the first mass-produced valentines in America.

As of right now, it's estimated that over one billion valentine's cards are mailed off each year. Hence, making Valentine's Day the second largest card-sending holiday of the year; falling second only to Christmas which has an average of 2.6 billion cards per year.

Surprisingly, statistics show that 85 percent of valentines are purchased by women. Valentine's Day is celebrated in many countries throughout the world. Valentines greetings were always popular dating back to the middle ages. The first written valentines were nonexistent until after 1400, at least as far as we've uncovered. The first commercialized valentine's day cards were produced in the United States, in the 1840's by Esther A. Howland. Her unique card designs using ribbons, real lace, and colourful pictures (known as scrap), earned her the nickname "Mother of the Valentine."

To this day all over the world, society continues to exchange gifts and affections on valentine's day. Yet the true history or the meaning behind it is often shrouded in mystery. A holiday that mixes a bit of Roman and Christian traditions, as it promotes the time of romance and love. Today, the Catholic Church recognizes three saints named Valentine or Valentinus. However, what gives the name such ancient rite to the holiday?

We may never know for sure as historians have been debating that for years. However, what is certain is that Valentine's Day has become not only deep and rich with tradition, but it's one of the few traditions most of the world openly embraces.

40 DAYS

In the Babylonian believe system it is said that Tammus/z, the son of Serimanus, wife and mother to Nimrod (note the similarity between Gaia and Uranus) was lethally injured by a boar while hunting.

Tammus/z died of his wounds at age 40 and his mother Serimanus declared a period of grieve and honouring Tammus/z, one day for every year he lived to celebrate the end of his life. The grieve part was turned into an orgy of sex and liquor and was then celebrated nonstop for 40 days and nights to celebrated his life.

The ritual survived up to today, it is celebrated and repeated around the world in order to celebrate and or to mark the last 40 days of a happening or time frame for individuals or groups of people. It is normally associated with liquor, late nights and an attitude of free spirit and sex on the 40'th day to mark the end of a time, for instance the end of University or school.

Interesting to note that we see 40 days occurring in other places in the Bible. With Noah's flood it rained for 40 days and nights, we also see the Satan tempting Yashua in the desert for 40 days and nights.

CHAPTER 6

The Conclusion

Adamites start spreading on earth

650

Noah 182

777

969

Sem

Gam · Kanaan · Nimrod

Jafet

Floud

Lamech 187

365

Mathusaleg 65

962

Enoch 162

Jered 65

895

910

Mahalalael 70

905

Kenan 90

912

Enog 105

930

Seth 130

Adam

| 0 | 100 | 200 | 300 | 400 | 500 | 600 | 700 | 800 | 900 | 1000 | 1100 | 1200 | 1300 | 1400 | 1500 | 1600 | 1700 | 1800 | 1900 |
| 4100 | 4000 | 3900 | 3800 | 3700 | 3600 | 3500 | 3400 | 3300 | 3200 | 3100 | 3000 | 2900 | 2800 | 2700 | 2600 | 2500 | 2400 | 2300 | 2200 |

Gisa Pyramid

People in UK

Egyptian dynasty   EARLY ERA   OLD   KINGDOM

Babilonian era starts

Chinese mythological period

Xia Dynasty

THE BIBLE

It helps us to look, appreciate and understand the following important biblical truths we have investigated up to now.

The earth is older than 6000 years and there are definitely huge similarities between science point of view with that of the Biblical statements concerning the "re creation" and the way the earth did and will get into a state of total chaos . . . again in future. These cataclysmic events correlate almost exactly with each other . . .

When YHWH created the heavens and the earth in the beginning, He created the earth in such a beautiful and perfect "Garden of Eden" state that the angels responded with joyful singing and shouting.

Before the Genesis account of the "Garden of Eden" where Adam and Eve were created, there was a previous "Eden earth" teaming with plants and animals in the Pre-Adamic Age. YHWH put Lucifer in charge of this Pre-Adamic "Eden earth", as the leading angel.

At this point it must be said that the Western nations tend to think that the Chinese and Japanese cultures (Eastern cultures) are much older than all other cultures, which are totally wrong and feeds the misconception about the Adamic creation.

The difference is that Eastern cultures moves effortless from historical fact to mythology to include it in their cultural time line, where Western cultures does not include mythology or pre Adamic events in there time line.

Therefore the misconception of the Chinese culture being so very old, when in fact their factual history started in line with that of Egyptian and Mesopotamian cultures.

This Pre-Adamic earth with its firmament (its heaven and atmosphere) was completely ruined, wasted, destroyed, flooded and darkened when Lucifer, who became Satan, sinned and led a rebellion against God with the following of a third of the angels in heaven. When exactly in the history of earth we cannot say, but we can guess with some sort of accuracy.

We are totally misled and wrong in our Hollywood perception of the Pre Adamic earth and its inhabitants at that stage, earth and the people living on it was highly developed, like today if not higher. The perception of individual small groups of cavers and ape like scavengers pre date this era and should not be confused with the 40 to 10 000 years before Adam. City's existed and international trade was booming between worlds and peoples. Communication, interstellular travel and extraterrestrial visitations were a common occurrence. It is possible that all this happened in ways we are all capable off but somehow lost the ability to make use of it anymore, telepathy, teleportation, time travel and shape shifting was normal and socially acceptable.

Certain technology's was absolute and they had the natural ability to do things that are unthinkable and unexplainable in today's world.

Once again our preset conceptions of "Aliens", which are little green men with slits for eyes, are totally misinterpreted. The word "Alien" means that something or somebody is "alien" to earth, in other words, not normally found on earth, or from somewhere other than earth, This then also means that our spirits are all alien to earth and that we need an earthly suit or package to operate on earth. You can figure that when we die we go back to our alien state into heaven, space or just a different dimension, still to complicate for us to figure. The Bible states that ELOHIM will come on the clouds from space . . . . alien? Angels and creatures visit us daily from heaven, space or from a different dimension. Could "Alien" also mean alien from our dimension?

The average percentage of paranormal and Ufo's sightings around the world currently stands on 1 every 4 minutes worldwide. Is this the product of our accumulative imaginations creating it in our subconscious?

Earth's geology and topography have been greatly impacted and shaped by the massive Pre-Adamic cataclysmic global judgement from YHWH's against Satan and his fallen angels, when YHWH violently cast them back down to earth.

After the Pre-Adamic earth in its Eden state, was destroyed (K-T Event), it remained for an unknown period of time as a wasted, iced up, flooded and dark *tartaroo* prison for Satan and his fallen angels. This was until YHWH renewed the surface of the earth and its firmament (its heaven/ atmosphere) again in time. Another era followed where animals and plants grew excessively large but not quite as large in the Jurassic. In this era we will put the Mammoths and Sable tooth tigers just to give it a picture of reference.

The devil and his fallen angels was living, ruling and running the earth before the Genesis recreation period in the Bible. Their mismanagement of earth and the fact that he was cast down to earth by YHWH was some of the main reasons for the earth to become desolate the first time.

The Biblical recreation of earth was one of many renewals of earth after natural or unnatural cataclysmic events. We cannot say how many times this has happened precisely but we know that Genesis was definitely not the first time, but the second last time.

At the Second Coming of YAHSHUA MESSIAH, there will be yet another last massive cataclysmic event. This will result in earth's geology and topography being greatly impacted and shaped once again. It will be in preparation for MESSIAH to establish His glorious Millennial Kingdom, and transform the earth's surface into a Garden of Eden once again for eternity.

The earth will be destroyed again by major cataclysmic events and according to scriptures hundred percent of life will perish in stages . . . . as it happened before, except his seed line that has accepted Him as their saviour, they will be saved from this event.

It is also important to remember that in this time before the Biblical flood there was no church, Bible or written religion to follow, for the normal man on the street. By the time of Noah 1900 years after Adam, the only thing that kept him genetically pure was the word he received by word of mouth from his elders. Remember that it was because he was genetically pure that he was chosen to man the ark and survive the deluge.

By saying this, we can state with surety that interbreeding with Neanderthal/Nephilim mongrels (**heylel** seed line) with the Adamic seed line led to the sinful and lawless situation on earth, leading to YHWH to decide on a flood to rectify the situation.

This is also stated in the book of Enoch.

This situation occurred before the Biblical creation of the Adamite and led to the earth becoming desolate and destroyed. Satan and his fallen angels carried on as before after the earth was restored with Adam, and nearly immediately went on as they did before.

We see in Genesis 1:24 (Revised Standard)

And God said, *"Let the earth bring forth living creatures according to their kind* . . . ."* Again a reminder not to manipulate or mix DNA.

In Lev18:23 we are warned against the "beast" which is the hybrid mongrels of Satan and his fallen angels, again the first warning is not to mix the DNA and to keep the gene pool pure:

"And you shall not lie with any beast and defile yourself with it, neither shall any woman give herself to a beast" . . . . why specifically woman and

not man . . . because the woman can reproduce the mongrel if it should happens . . .

Remember that up to 7 generations after Adam they still knew Adam personally, because of how long they lived.

They all became very old and if these patriarchs were sitting around a table you could easily account for thousands of years of wisdom around the table.

It was quite possible that Adam in person could sit down and tell tales about the garden of Eden and what happened in the time of his creation up to 7 generations later . . . . so to keep the bloodline pure was up to them spreading the word amongst each other.

In Ez. 34:8 and 25 it is said about his chosen seed: *"Because my seed have become **prey**, and my sheep have become **food** for the wild beasts"* . . . . Quite clear reference to the cannibalistic giants and mongrel seed line nations of Satan attacking the pure Godly DNA.

Also interesting to note that in Genesis 1:26 to 27 that man was made on the sixth day in His image, likeness . . . man was created male and female, in God's image, what is the image of God? God is in spirit . . . in other words man was created with male and female attributes as one being in spiritual form at first and afterwards in verse 2: 7 the body and soul was added to create a man able to **till** the earth, in verses 2:19 onwards male and female were separated as two . . . . would some people call this sequence of events up to male and female evolution or creation?

According to scriptures Enoch was the first man to develop writing and to have knowledge about the stars and other sciences. Considering the following figures of different life forms on earth. Adam had to identify and name them all, his knowledge and insight must have been tremendous and we can say with surety that before they committed sin that Adam and Eve was able to use 100 % of their brain capability, this was changed by

YHWH after they sinned and it was "down tuned" to a mere 10% as science has proven, up to today:

Vertebrates	
Amphibians	6,199
Birds	9,956
Fish	30,000
Mammals	5,416
Reptiles	8,240
Subtotal	59,811
Invertebrates	
Insects	950,000
Molluscs	81,000
Crustaceans	40,000
Corals	2,175
Others	130,200
Subtotal	1,203,375
Plants	
Mosses	15,000
Ferns and allies	13,025
Gymnosperms	980
Dicotyledons	199,350
Monocotyledons	59,300
Green Algae	3,715
Red Algae	5,956
Subtotal	297,326
Lichens	10,000
Mushrooms	16,000
Brown Algae	2,849
Subtotal	28,849
Total	1,589,361

Adam was created with extreme knowledge and he probably handed it over to Enoch. Adam must have had an extremely high IQ for naming all plants, animals and insects on his own, placing all in their correct categories of different phyla and orders . . . all living things . . . in the beginning Adam was created with all knowledge except the concept of right or wrong . . . all was right, there was no sin or wrong . . . . like the mind of a child . . . no wonder we get this scripture in the Bible:

Mark 10:15 (RS)

> *"Truly, I say to you, whoever does not receive the Kingdome of ELOHIM like a child shall not enter it?"*

It is also interesting to note that we read in Genesis 1:26 that YHWH never gave the stars, sun or moon to his chosen seed to rule over or to use them as gods. Instead he gave them the fish, birds, animals, and all living creatures, and the earth itself, to rule over, we see in Deuteronomy 4:19 (Revised Standard)

> *"And beware lest you lift up your eyes to heaven, and when you see the sun and the moon and the stars, all the host of heaven, you be drawn away and worship them and serve them, things which the lord your God has allotted to all the other peoples under the whole heaven".*

The sceptics can also debate that it was impossible for Adam to have named all the species since some are only discovered today, we can't say that for sure, maybe he did discovered them all?

. . . . But the theory stil stands that if that is the case that the genetically pure Adamite is still naming them today.

In Genesis 5 we have the descendants of Adam and then in Genesis 6 we have Noah building the ark. Not much is said Biblically in this small part but a lot happened that shaped our thinking and the way the world operates today.

First of all it tends to look like a short period of time from Adam to Noah, just half a page in the Bible . . . but in reality we are talking about 1900 years . . . . That is 112 years less than from the Crucifixion to now . . . . 2012.

THE NEPHILIM GIANTS

Genesis 6:1 (Living Bible)

*1 "Now a population explosion took place upon the earth. It was at this time that beings from **the spirit world"***

*2 "looked upon the beautiful earth women and took **any they desired** to be their wives". (Without consent means raped.)*

3 "Then God said, "My Spirit must not forever be disgraced in man, wholly evil as he is. I will give him 120 years to mend his ways".

*4 "In those days, and even afterwards, when the **evil beings from the spirit world** were sexually involved with human woman, their children became giants of whom so **many legends are told**."* *(Mythological beings and legends.)*

5 "When the Lord God saw the extent of human (offspring) wickedness, and that the trend and direction of men's lives were only towards evil" . . . .

Genesis 6:1-9 (King James Version) (KJV)

1 "And it came to pass, when men began to multiply on the face of the earth, and daughters were born unto them",

2 "That the sons of God saw the daughters of men that they were fair; and they took them wives of all which they chose".

3 *"And the* LORD *said My spirit shall not always strive with man, for that he also is flesh: yet his days shall be an hundred and twenty years".*

4 *"There were giants in the earth in those days; and also after that, when the sons of God came in unto the daughters of men, and they bear children to them, the same became **mighty men which were of old, men of renown".***

5 *"And God saw that the **wickedness** of man was great in the earth, and that every imagination of the thoughts of his heart was only evil continually".*

6 *"And it repented the* LORD *that he had made man on the earth, and it grieved him at his heart".*

7 *"And the* LORD *said, I will destroy man whom I have created from the face of the earth; both man, and beast, and the creeping thing, and the fowls of the air; for it repented me that I have made them".*

8 *"But Noah found grace in the eyes of the **LORD** ".*

Scientifically facts during and before the Adamic creation:

We had a cataclysmic event in Europe 40 000 years ago with the Campania Ignimbrite eruption in Italy. 20 000 years ago is where it looks like "MAN" can coin the term "modern man" for the first time. We have cave paintings 29 000 years before Adam of hybrids and demy gods.

Around 10,000 years ago (4000 before Adam) humans began to practice sedentary agriculture domesticating plants and animals. Interbreeding and gene manipulation between Neanderthal, Cro-Magnon, Archaic and modern humans occurred.(unknown period)

5000 before Adam a major ecosystem collapse Leeds to 135 Species of Mammals to go extinct (Mastodons etc). Looking at the evidence it is safe to say that there was great changes climatically during the 10 000 years before Adam.

We can be sure that a bunch of early humans, hardly clothed, armed with stones and sticks could not have been the sole reason for the extinction of 135 mammal species some larger and much more dangerous than the normal elephants and lions of today.

These early peoples could also not be held responsible (on their own) for the total collapse of the entire planetary ecological collapse, **again.** There is no evidence of huge populations or overpopulation in these times. Something or somebody else more plentiful or powerful must have had an influence leading up to these collapses or extinctions.

Unfortunately we have no written accounts or historical facts for this period so we must make use of science, common sense and the oldest historical writings known to us. We have now considered all the facts and myths, the earth became empty, that it was **heylel,** his fallen angels and their bastard malformed offspring, upon the earth before and after the Genesis recreation of ELOHIM that was to blame for this cataclysmic event as well as Noah's flood. The picture is getting clearer and we can start seeing the patterns of earth and the problem of interbreeding revolving and happening again and again.

> *"Everything that is, was, and what was will be again, nothing is new . . ."*

PLAYING WITH FIRE

The following report might just as well been tabled to **heylel** in the era's before Adam, it all correlates with what is happening today on earth.

Matthew 24:37 (Revised Standard)

"As were the days of Noah, so will be the coming of the son / lover of man"

"Prions are infectious pathogens that are made up mainly of a form of misfolded PrP proteins. Infections in different species go by different names, the most famous being "mad cow disease" in cows. In humans, it's called Creutzfeldt-Jakob disease and results in clumps of brain tissue dying resulting in dementia and other symptoms and eventually death.

Up until now, it has been thought that there existed a biological barrier that made it difficult for prions to pass from one species of animal to another, but that assumption has been based mainly on brain autopsies. In this new study, the researchers found that when prions from other species (elk, hamsters and cattle) were inserted into the brains of mice that had been genetically altered to express the human or sheep version of PrP, the transfer rate to the brain was very small (just 3 out of 43 cases) as expected. However, when they also autopsied other organs in the mice such as tonsils and especially the spleen they found that the prions had migrated in 26 of 41 cases. They also found that in such cases, the mice didn't display any symptoms of the disease which leads the authors to conclude that many more animals and humans likely carry the disease than has been thought.

The concern is that human carriers could be inadvertently infecting others through blood transfusions, organ donation or even via surgical instruments since prions have been found to be resistant to normal antibacterial processes. And if that is the case, it appears likely that at least some of those infected would eventually find themselves falling prey to Creutzfeldt-Jakob disease" (Medical science and technology feb 2011.)

We see in the reality of technological advancements that it evolves about 20 to 30 years after its creation by Science fiction writers. It is with un canning accuracy that these writers like Philip Dicks and others nearly without exception writes about futuristic technology just to see it realize in 20 or 30 years later?

Robots and humanoids start to blur the lines between reality and virtual fantasies. Technology is starting to talk about memory implants, a cyber experience you can purchase and implant or download into the brain to be recalled as reality, vacations, experiences etc. In today's world in 2012, it is frightening to see with what speed technology is moving forward where the virtual world via cell phones and electronic games is fast becoming a real addiction problem where people and youngsters lose themselves in the reality transformation of the virtual world.

The time spent in these alternative realities is becoming problematic and we can see that our technological enhancements are metamorphosing into an invasive technology for human kind. People lose control and their grip on reality is so fantasized that they have a hard time living life normally.

New mental disorders are added to the list of psychological illnesses daily and all because of the lack of normal life exposure.

Except for your DNA, it is mainly your exposure to reality that forms your memories and your personality as a person in becoming an individual. The less you are exposed, the less of everything you become. To create a mentally stable and physically balanced, fit human takes a lot of physical and mental exposure to life as a whole. The mental stimulation of peers, friends and family, forming your personality is vital to your existence and survival on earth later in your life.

Memories are about the only tangible thing you will have left in old age. Technology is and will undoubtedly be of great help and for the good of humanity, but it is almost a given that the negative side effects will lead to our fall as intelligent individuals.

Not even mentioning new gadgets and ideas and just looking at what's to happen to our minds we should see the intelegant individual disappearing from daily life in the near future, they will be so far and in-between that these people will be branded as outcast, mad or plain dangerous to the puppets living in virtual reality.

How much time does technology needs to produce our first cloned humans or humanoids, how much do they need or will it takes to create so close to YHWH that He would not be able to allow the situation to escalate any further on earth.

"Every living thing on earth uses DNA or RNA to carry its instructions for life. These two nucleic acids are built from different sugars: DNA from Deoxyribose and RNA from Ribose. Now scientists have shown that at least six other types of sugars can form nucleic acid backbones—and they can be used to store and retrieve genetic information. Called XNA's (for xeno-nucleic acids), the new synthetic chains could address important questions about the origin of life. John Chaput, a team member and molecular biologist at Arizona State University, poses an even more tantalising one. Can you create synthetic life with it? He asks. That is possible, but much further down the road"

Sarah Fecht. Popular Mechanics, RSA, August 2012, p13.

The Godly DNA will be literally out bred and out manoeuvred by society and the Satanic rulers of the time. For those with intellect and insight it must be clear that the end of our existing time in the present geological time frame are perilously close to the end as we know it as life on earth.

You should come prepared for the fight. It is said that only a couple, so few, that it would resemble a lonely flagpole on the barren earth in a desert, will qualify for the right to sit back and be of witness of what's to come. These events will not touch them, but they will be able to see it happen. These will be the people with the pure Godly DNA and that has renewed their life and has been reborn in YHWH.

You should not be surprised to stare cataclysmic events in the face in the near future as a reality. Do not run if you hear the news that the asteroid "Wormwood" or with some other closely related name has been sighted.

MYTHOLOGICAL GIANTS

It is clear that these Titans and gods were Satan and his fallen angels with their offspring.

To try and figure out which is which, or what name belongs to whom, is nearly impossible because of the incest and deliberate confusion in the seed line, "family tree".

Some of them existed before Adam and others came after.

Some of the main questions are why some were so large and tall, others had powers and some was hybrid between human and animals. The Asch tree nymphs were even hybrid with nature itself.

We do find their fossilised remains and their memories in folklore and especially in children stories today, where the untrained mind can be easily corrupted.

It is a scientific fact that they did walk the earth. Why where all the dinosaurs and plants so large . . . for what reason where they gigantic?

Science tells us that the earth experienced perfect conditions during the Mesozoic period and all life on earth bloomed and flourished so dramatically that they become really gigantic in all their forms and phyla.

Can we then say that the fallen angels and Titans were giants because of the earth's condition? That they co existed in the Mesozoic period . . . . why if you have magical powers do you need to be gigantic . . . ?

In an era where everything else are gigantic it makes sense that they were gigantic as well . . . We are in proportion to our present situation in relation to our current place in nature, it is quite obvious and simple.

This gives credence and helps to explain all the tales and fables about the Titans slaying mighty dragons and fighting gigantic beasts in the mythological tales.

We see the Biblical correlation that all the Titans was bond and expelled and thrown into Hayedes, the underworld, exactly the same as the fallen angels were bound and imprisoned under the earth the way the biblical history told us.

Is the word "Titans" just a renaming or synonym for Fallen angels or Satan? Maybe just spelled the other way round "snatit" to become satin or Satan?

The K-T event ended the Mesozoic period 65 million years ago and we see that we had another event hitting the planet 40 000 years ago in Europe with the Campanian Ignimbrite eruption in Italy.

It is in and after this event that science point to the first human like creatures "evolving" not quite human but close and changing for the first time. These creatures evolve to fit into their individual climatic circumstance, on the other hand the rulers of earth at the time intervened, forcing and practising gene manipulation and cloning on large scale on the human-like population of earth, enslaving them and trying to create "specific models" for "specific jobs". We credit these events with the major jumps between species.

We have seen a major ecosystem collapse 5000 before Adam. 135 Species of mammals go extinct 5000 before Adam. (Mastodons etc . . . Why?)

In this same period from 40 000 to 5000 before Adam, we see the offspring of the Titans called "gods" entering the mythological record . . . . perfect if we compare it with the same story of **heylel** and his fallen angels that was cast from heaven and bound under the earth exactly the same as the Titans.

We also see how Lucifer's reign on earth lead to the earth to become a wasteland . . . empty and desolated . . . . totally destroyed. His fall from heaven with his fallen angels after the war with YHWH and his righteous angels was the spark for the earth becoming empty again, barren as described in Genesis.

The correlation is immense, science, mythology and the Biblical facts fits together 100% if we let our brain except the fact that there was a world before the Biblical creation.

Killing of the firstborn or eldest son's "Cronus swallowing his children being afraid to lose kingship" is another correlation and trait that spilled over in actual history and into Biblical events. The Anak, Satan seed, trying to eradicate the pure seed line of Adam, Seth, Abraham, Isaac and Jacob, mentioned in numerous other events in the scriptures of the Israelites.

Looking at the traits of these "gods" I am convinced that they were wrongly named as "gods" and should have been called "**Devils**". No "god" in any other doctrine's or believe system was credit with vulgar acts like these.

It is clear that these Mythological Giants and creatures were one and the same as the Nephilim Giants (The fallen angels) under new hidden names.

1. The giants and their offspring where real and living creatures.
2. Some of them survived Noah's flood.
3. They had allocated living areas with cities and formed nations.
4. They had names and were renown in their time.
5. They had supernatural power and powers. Their wives became the first witches.
6. Some of their body's was completely different from human beings.
7. Some had animal characteristics build into their genes.

8. They must have had hugely overdeveloped lungs. (they were very loud)
9. Everybody was afraid of them.
10. They were all descending from **heylel** and his fallen angels.
11. Some of them were monstrous to look at and in there manner.
12. Adultery, blatant rape and murder was in there nature. (1 Sam 22;18)
13. These giant mongrels had their own gods. (1 Sam 17:43)
14. No laws or regulations applied to them.
15. The smallest was at least double the height of a normal human.
16. They were not part of the Biblical creation story. They were already there, before and after the Biblical recreation with Satan.
17. Their genetic line pre dates that of Biblical Adam.
18. The giants lived for very long times. (life expectancy up to 1000 years)
19. These nephilim could metamorphose or "shape shift" there body's. (Satan before Eve)
20. They inspired legends and fables.
21. Their existence inspired people to idolize them to "God" status.
22. Because the written language was lost and still in its redevelopment stages and the knowledge thereof not available to all, word of mouth was the caretaker of these new "gods" and their power and statue grew by the day among the peoples of the earth as the stories was retold and adapted at will.
23. Their names got new pronunciations and eventually some names change with time, but the golden thread remained.
24. They drank blood and practised bestiality. They were also successful in cloning, gene manipulation, copulating and producing offspring from any animals, producing half humanlike creatures or hybrids.
25. The moon, sun and stars were specifically given to them and other peoples on earth to worship.
26. These giants and their wives practised the cutting of roots, magic spells, producing the first "witch doctors" and black magic on earth.

THE PRE-ADAMIC THEORY
AND TIME LINE

13.8 Billion years ago:

YHWH ELOHIM start His creation, scientifically known as the "Big Bang" Trillions of pieces of matter scatter into space forming the beginning of the universe. Planets, stars, suns and galaxies form in the never ending expanding universe.

4.6 Billion years ago:

Our own solar system forms with the sun as epicentre, the Earth and at about 4.2 billion years ago the moon has formed. Earth is still in a molten to semi molten sate.

4.2 to 2 Billion years ago:

The earth cools down and the crust is formed. During this time Earth is being bombarded by meteorites and we see the Vredefort impact occurring in Southern Africa around the end of this period.

2 to 1 Billion years ago:

The ozone layer is formed and Oxygen starts to form and will increase to reach 30% of atmosphere at about 300 million years ago. Rodinia forms, and at 950 million years ago we get to the end of the Stuart-Varanggian ice age.

750 Million years ago:

Rodinia start to break up and move apart and we see the last polar shift occurring in our geological records.

600 to 300 Million years ago:

The end of the "snowball earth" effect and Rodinia reforms together to become known as "Pannotia". At about 550 mya "Pannotia" brakes apart to form two landmasses called "Laurasia and Gondwana". This is the start of the Cambrian where YHWH command life to explode onto the scene in nearly all its forms as it is today. Up to 300 mya, jelly's, corals, fish, insects and plants starts to flourish as the oxygen levels reach 30% of the atmosphere and we enter the Permian period.

250 to 65 Million years ago:

This era is accumulatively known as the Mesozoic and consists of the Triassic, Jurassic and Cretaceous periods. "Laurasia and Gondwana" reforms and becomes the new supercontinent "Pangea". We see all living creatures becoming gigantic; nature explodes into its splendour because of the near perfect climatic conditions. It is in this Era that we see Lucifer and his angels starting to populate earth as giant beings, living in harmony with all life forms ruling the earth. It is so perfect, you may call it paradise.

During this 200 million years Lucifer and his angels lives on earth, why, we don't know and the purpose might be seen in the fact that we will one day "rule" with Elohim.

They start building mega structures and possibly lives a type of life we can associate with other planets, Ufo's and other spiritual beings visiting from outer space. They start manipulating genes and Lucifer and his angels get cast down after the revolt in heaven.

The revolt in heaven between YHWH and Satan coincides or causes the K-T event at 65 mya leading to the destruction of earth and the death of 85% of all life on earth when a meteorite slams into the Yucatan in Mexico according to the best of our knowledge.

65 to 1 Million years ago:

Accumulatively known as the Tertiary it consists of 5 epochs known as the:

The Palaeocene Epoch—65 to 54 million years ago

The Eocene Epoch—54 to 38 million years ago

The Oligocene Epoch—38 to 24 million years ago

The Miocene Epoch—24 to 5 million years ago

The Pliocene Epoch—5 to 1.8 million years ago

The term Tertiary is also divided into two periods namely the Palaeogene and the Neocene which is the more acceptable way of mentioning this period today. Each epoch has unique characteristics for climate and geography. The plants and animals changed from epoch to epoch.

The beginning of the Tertiary Period was very warm and moist compared to today's climate. Much of the earth was tropical or sub-tropical. Palm trees grew as far north as Greenland! By the middle of the Tertiary, during the Oligocene epoch, the climate began to cool. This cooling trend continued and by the Pliocene epoch at the end of the Tertiary period, an ice age had begun.

Tectonic activity continued as Gondwana finally split completely apart, and India collided with the Eurasian plate. South America was connected to North America toward the end of the Tertiary. Antarctica—which was already separate—drifted to its current position over the South Pole. Widespread volcanic activity was prevalent.

The climate during the Tertiary slowly cooled, starting with the Palaeoncene, with tropical-to-moderate worldwide temperatures and ending before the first extensive glaciations at the start of the Quaternary.

The plants of the Tertiary period are very similar to the plants that we have today. The warm climate at the beginning of the period favoured dense forests. As the climate cooled open woodlands and grasslands became abundant. The grasses were important because they supported huge herds of grazing animals.

The extinction event (K-T) at the close of the Cretaceous period wiped out the dinosaurs, large reptiles, and many other species. This left room for new animals to develop. The mammals became the dominant animals. In fact, the Cainozoic era is often called the Age of Mammals. Most of the main groups of mammals were present by the Eocene epoch. With the dinosaurs and other large reptiles gone, mammals grew in size, numbers and diversity. They filled ecological niches in the sea on land and in the air.

Birds did almost as well as mammals during the Tertiary period. Many of the birds we know today were present. There were also many large flightless birds that are now extinct. These birds did particularly well before the mammals develop so many species. Fish species branched out during the Tertiary period. Sharks became more plentiful. Trout and bass evolved. Flowering plants means nectar for insects, the insect population increased in the Tertiary period. Bees and other insects that lived on pollen and nectar of the flowering plants prospered.

Heylel and his fallen angels are having a royal time in this period. Cloning and mixing, experimenting wildly with gene manipulation on all forms of nature and early ape like creatures as they appear during the Pliocene, these were the first hybrids forming mongrel slave nations for the Nephilim!

The Tertiary Period Ends With An Ice Age and Land Bridges. The cooling climate of the Tertiary Period led to huge glaciers at the poles. The mountains of the world were also covered by glaciers, including the newly formed Himalayas and Alps. The huge amounts of water locked up in the ice lowered the level of the sea and land bridges appeared:

Between Asia and North America

Great Britain and Europe

South East Asia and Borneo

This enabled migrations of both plants and animals across these land bridges.

The Tertiary period which had begun hot and humid, ended in a cold dry ice age

1 Million years ago to Adam

This is the period known as the Quaternary divided into the Pleistocene and the Holocene epochs.

During this period flourishing and then extinction of many large mammals accrued. Anatomically ape like mongrels appear into our time line. Quaternary Ice Age continues with glaciations, further intensification of Ice-house Earth (snowball earth) conditions prevailed. This was the dawn of human stone-age cultures, with increasing technical complexity relative to previous ice age cultures, such as engravings and clay statues of their giant and hybrid gods (e.g. Venus of Lespugue), particularly in the Mediterranean and Europe.

Lake Toba super volcano erupts 75000 years before present, causing a volcanic winter that pushes humanity to the brink of extinction. Pleistocene ends with Oldest Dryas, Older Dryas/Allerød and Younger Dryas climate events, with Younger Dryas forming the boundary with the Holocene.

50 000 we see the legend of Atlantis playing off, with huge technological advancements, like flying objects and visits from outer space.(Cayce)

40 000 years before Adam

Cro-Magnon man appears. Different peoples and small groups form naturally according to body form and natural ability's, slowly moving and spreading apart on earth. The fallen angel race make sure that these creatures get their regular dose of satanic DNA and experimentation leading to horrifying results is in the order of the day.

30 000 to 10000 years ago

Neanderthal man disappears. The last glacial period ends; rise of human civilization. Quaternary Ice Age recedes, and the current interglacial begins. Younger Dryas cold spell occurs, Sahara forms from savannah, and agriculture begins, allowing humans to build cities. Palaeolithic/Neolithic (Stone Age) cultures begin around 10000 BC, giving way to Copper Age (3500 BC) and Bronze Age (2500 BC).

We see the massive buildings or what is left of them been built and designed by these fallen giants, with their advanced scientific knowledge and great strength we see them building with huge, but in proportion to them, with stones and carved masonry, the great ancient remnants of cities and monuments we see today all over the world like the pyramids and at Baalbek.

By this time Satan and his fallen angels are thoroughly established either by myth or fact within the satanic communities on earth.

They became the main deity's and gods for these bastard seed lines created and cloned by themselves. Half human creatures and the mythological figures we see today in most cultures under new names in different languages, but more popularly found in the Greek and Roman mythology, exists in flesh and blood and roams the earth.

They are seen and treated by these peoples as gods and is being taken up into folklore and lifted to ultimate god status.

These fallen angels have unnatural powers and their scientific knowledge is unsurpassed by anyone on earth, at that stage, they enjoy the upper ranks of their self created situation and society on earth. They come and go and have the ability of flight, either naturally or by technology, witnessed or recorded by these primitive unschooled people captured for history by primitive drawings and cave paintings.

Because Satan and his fallen angels are originally not from earth (Alien) we may say or debate them to be extraterrestrial beings, manipulating the living creation on earth genetically producing offspring and creating giants as they go along. These acts also explain the animal brutality and occurring in unison with Ufo sightings.

Again this act and lawlessness on earth corrupts the whole ecosystem and YHWH decides to wipe them out in the near future in order to replace the "management" and control of earth with a Godly gene.

This gene will be able to create, have compassion, protect and respect nature, earth and YHWH.

10 to 5000 before Adam

Once again the situation on earth (scientific fact) coincides perfectly with the time frames of the Biblical recreation. Looking at the psychics in this time we note the following.

10,490 to 10,390 BCE: The construction of the Great Pyramid of Giza, which took 100 years according to Edgar Cayce, and was directed by Ra and Hermes. (Cayce 5748-6) The pyramids were built around 10,500 BCE and the Great Sphinx was built 100 years later; during the time of the "great eclipse" (Daan Akkerman).

10,360 BCE: Destruction of the Atlantean manufacturing city Marzeus and Terna (the Biblical "cities of the Plain") by the "Navaz" forces (naturally occurring energies) they had forgotten how to control. This caused the end of the knowledge and usage of advanced technology that was based on their science. (Oliver, "A Dweller on Two Planets")

10,360(?)-9,900 BCE: Greed, lust and corruption led to moral decline and the spiritual downfall of the golden age of Atlantis. Blinded by the fear for coming disasters, as retribution for their sinful lives, human sacrifices of innocent people became common in an attempt to atone for their mutual sins. (Oliver, "Dweller on Two Planets") Edgar Cayce also mentioned between 7,000 and 9,000 BCE as the timeframe of the decline of the golden age of Egypt.

5000 years before Adam

Mongrel nations multiply with no natural ability or intuition to create or care, the situation worsens, and a total moral collapse manifests in time. Cloned and diluted with satanic DNA, no one has the ability to avoid or soften the coming cataclysmic event.

These nations, their traits and manor, are described for us in Deut. 28:31 to 53.

They serve the moon, stars and gods created from wood and stone, a consortium of different demy gods. They are hard of face and not forgiving.

"A nation whose language you do not understand, a nation of stern countenance, who shall not regard the person of the old or show favour to the young"

"They will eat the offspring of your cattle and the fruit of your ground until you are destroyed, who also shall not leave you grain, wine, or oil, the increase of your cattle or the young of your flock, until they have caused you to perish".

They are destroying and corrupting earth. They do not protect or enhance. There is no creative spirit in them and they will devour without thinking or considering tomorrow or the consequences of their actions. They are without mercy, fairness or rational thought. Any sign of forgiveness, love or compassion are treated as a weakness. They think nothing of it to dominate the weaker, elder or those in need . . . not even until they perish. They see themselves as heroes, all of them. They are incapable to show, or to experience, shame. They are excessively loud, practise cannibalism, witchcraft and communicate with the dead as a believe system.

These nations will literally consume the flesh of the Godly DNA. They have an inherent natural hatred towards them as we see in Genesis 3:15

"And I will put enmity between thee and the woman and between the seed and her seed" (gene pool, offspring, DNA).

It is also against YHWH word for the seed of Satan to rule over the seed of Elohim, we see in Deut 17:15 . . . . *"you may not put a foreigner over you, who is not your seed".*

Satan was the ruler of the earth because it is said that he had a throne and subjects. Since he was cast down and lost his kingship and got it back after misleading Eve, so it is also indicates to be happening before the Genesis creation.

He wanted to climb up "above the clouds" also indicating that he was living on the physical earth below the clouds . . . . If this is so then the earth, clouds and stars where already in existence before Genesis . . .

The extinction of earth before Adam was decide by YHWH because of the sins of **heylel** and his angels towards YHWH and the fact that there interbreeding and genetic mixing led to malformed, mixed races, DNA manipulated creatures, mongrels and hybrids.

It reached a point (in wickedness and mismanagement) where nearly all mammals and various ecosystems collapsed to extinction, leading to the earth becoming "without form and void".

According to science we had a mass extinction 5000 before Adam where we lost most mammals like the Mammoths and sable tooth tiger type of animal's roaming the earth at that stage.

Now for the last time in pre history YHWH destroyed the earth with another cataclysmic event with its epicentre somewhere in the Bimini islands region. Earth enters another ice age. Nearly all life reaches extinction. In this last stage of our time line we see the sea level rise with 91 meters at the end of the Wurm/Wisconsin ice age covering earth globally.

The whole earth is thrown out of sequence and the rotation and wobble of earth is altered. Time is out of rhythm and day and night is not constant . . . . Earth became "without form and void", "shapeless and chaotic", "formless and empty" How long earth remained in this state is unclear but the table was laid . . .

All in line for the great Biblical re creation by Elohim where all these chaos was reformed into order and splendour.

Adam: 6 000 years ago

The "Cambrian explosion" where all life spontaneously occurred simultaneously without any evidence of evolution, created by ELOHIM is obviously our first creation that we have proof of.

Perfect conditions prevailed in nature. Time went by. There were no sickness and the climate was clean and perfect. Nature flourished and plants and animals grew out of proportionally large and plentiful. Some animals and different phyla adapted and changed minutely were necessary as climate forced it upon them.

It reached its climax in the Mesozoic era during the Triassic and coming to an end with the Jurassic period with the K-T event.

It is in this time that the UFO (extraterrestrial theory) starts carrying water, for these angels was from outer space, not from earth but "alien". During this time we see species mutate and we can argue the evolution of man as gene manipulation accoutred with the Homo erectus, ape like phyla.

Heylel, his fallen compatriots and some species survived the cataclysmic event and repopulated earth again. Remember that Satan and his angels are capable of living forever and they will be cast into hell with the coming of YHWH . . . . They could survive anything thrown at them.

The six day recreation of earth was planned by YHWH to put someone else in charge with a Godly spirit resembling YHWH to rule the earth from then on . . . . Lucifer lost control of earth via the creation of Adam.

Almost immediately Adam lost his authority "kingship" over the earth after Lucifer misled Eve and planted his own seed and adding to the existing gene pool in contrast with that of Adam trying to corrupt the seed line.

We can also debate that because Adam and Eve had superior DNA to anything else Satan had on earth, he saw a great opportunity to steel DNA from Eve via Cain to improve his own existing gene pool on earth, he used Eve to see if he could create something better than Adam, reclaiming his position of master and ruler on earth . . . . as it is today.

Heylel had offspring from Eve named Cain and therefore established his own living seed line on earth to be in eternal fight against the direct seed line of YHWH through Adam and Seth.

This led to the fact that for the first time in earth's history Satan could add Godly DNA to his seed line via Cain. The helter shelter recipients of this DNA are the reason to the individual brilliance we found among these nations.

It is also interesting to note that when Elohim created His own seed line on earth he established them in a separate area on earth called Eden. A special place created for their purpose and use alone. This area was protected by gates and Gerubs, ever wondered why . . . was it to keep Adam and Eve in, or was it to keep the satanic seed line out?

Isn't it strange that after they sinned that they were thrown out of this protection zone (protected, separate, holy) with the satanic seed on the outside never to enter Eden again but instructed not to corrupt their DNA while living intermingled with the satanic DNA line?

These two lines went their separate ways and we can see the Satanic seed line moving into Egypt (Amun/Amon) and Babylon (Nimrod/Serimanus) regions where nations start to create complex and different Babylonian type believe systems, greatly enhancing the mythological figures and hybrids to demi god status interweaved into their believe systems in one way or the other.

We see these figures today in the Greek and Roman mythology as myth and nobody takes them or their existence, seriously (men of renown).

I am not taking it further down into history and leave it up to the reader to make its own discovery on the questions that must be hanging in your thoughts, this book is not written to point the finger or identify any nation or group of people. It will be up to the individual to read and study the facts of what happened to these two seed lines further down the road of history, the evidence is well studied and available and doesn't need rewriting.

The main point is made, we have explanations for the mystic evidence that stare us in the face. With their buildings and mystery's, we understand how and why it came into being and we can now better understand what is coming.

The facts however are bombshells in their own right and people will try and discard them as fiction for the times we live in where it became a serious crime to categorise people according to their believe, DNA or social grouping. It is however clear that we will have to make use of these facts in order to establish, which is which?

This corrupt gene pool is still at work daily to try and corrupt the pure seed.

In time and with the knowledge increasing in these fields of natural sciences and mythology, we will get more and more matches and evidence to proof this theory, more archaeological evidence will became available and the picture will focus into clarity. If you compare the speed of technology growth with what is still needed for science to clone and create synthetic life, and calculate that into years left to go, I am sure that you will agree with me that scientifically, time is frantically running out, if not already.

It should now be clear to you that all the questions you had about life, myths, why, how and for what reason seems to fall into place with this theory.

This theory is supported Biblically as well as scientifically.

It is clear that gene manipulation and mutation of new unclassified species of human animal type hybrids will be occurring at the end of days as with Noah. We know that this is happening today.

We can see that race mixing wasn't supposed to be. Different peoples, types, colours and races that are geographically bunched together should stay together as far as possible.

It is clear that there are two opposing seed lines on earth. The one satanic and the other pure Godly DNA. It all started way before Adam and is continuing today.

We have looked and studied on all fronts, Biblical and scientific evidence is pointing to the fact that we are on the threshold of another cataclysmic event where earth will go through a major change, some will argue to prepare for this and get food and shelter ready, become more self efficient and rely on your own resources . . . . I say yes, you may, but after you fixed your life with YHWH, because all will be lost if you fail to be reborn in your ways and give your life to your creator and acknowledge Him.

This event will be the second coming of YAHSHUA MESSIAH. You will also not be able to do this if you are of the satanic DNA, but not to worry, there will be no natural hunger to get close to YHWH if you are from the satanic seed.

Then and only then will all your plans be successful to survive to coming events. It is only then that you will realize and come to the conclusion, that it doesn't matter very much since I am saved, all this need to know and "understand it all" is actually not of much use after all, but crucial beforehand to get to the understanding thereof.

It is important however to understand this theory and structure, so that it can stand as a blueprint base model to be perfected in time with new evidence as it becomes available, what should have been shelved and rejected in the past can now be boxed and filed correctly into this age old truth.

There is no single or other theory in existence today that fit or explain, all these otherwise contradictory evidence, and only contradictory, because of the lack of seeing the Biblical time frame as it should be seen in correlation to the sciences and mythology.

Whatever questions you throw at it, it explains it all.

Now I can hear you ask the last main very important question . . . where are they today?

The answer is in your heart, if you understand this theory and if it makes sense to you, if it is acceptable to you, you will be able to identify what DNA you are carrying in you? The traits of the mongrel seed line should be as clear as daylight to you, and you should easily be able to place yourself and other people around you into one of these two lines or categories.

It is wise to remember that you still need to be born again to inherit everlasting life to rule with ELOHIM for ever, maybe on another earth like planet, so perfect you may call it heaven?

It is only after a lifetime of assembling all knowledge that it doesn't matter to have it anymore.

Good and evil, it's all in the genes.

OTHER BOOKS AND REFERENCES
YOU MAY FIND INTERESTING

In the Bible

Teleportation. Acts 8:39-40, Ezek 2:3, 3:14-17
Parachuting. Acts 10:11
Cannibalism. Ps 79
Fingerprints. Isaiah 49:16
Hypnosis. Genesis 2:21
Telepathy. Acts 21:4
Meditation. Ps 4:5
Giants. Num 13:28, Genesis 6:4, 12:6, 14:5, Deut 1:27, 2:10-21, 3:11-13,
    Jos 12:14, 13:12
Identification of Gods seed to be hidden. Ps 83:3-5
Satan seed to misinform the world. 2 Peter 2:2-3
The Beast.(Satan DNA) Jer 7:20, 21:6, 27:6, 31:27, 33:10, Dan 4:15,
    Ezek 14:13-21, 29:8-11,
Jonah 3:8, Sag 8:10, 2, Pet 2:12-22, Judas 1:10-16, Cor. 15:32

Books to read:

Holy Bible, King James Version.
The last hours of Ancient sunlight. by Thom Hartmann.
The two Babylon's. by Rev. Alexander Hislop.
Eden the knowledge of good and evil. by Dr. J J. Pugh.

REFERENCES

9/2/2002: Added Ababua fragment. 8/21/2002: New Ohlone myth. 6/2/2002: Chippewa myth from Barnouw expanded and another added. 2/16/2002: New Roman myth from Frazer's *Golden Bough*. 1/16/2002: "Northern California Coast" identified as Kato and revised from Gifford & Block reference. 11/15/2001: New Tamil myth. 10/6/2001: New Hindu flood from Mahabharata. 8/30/2001: Reordered by language group; from Grinnell: new Pawnee myth; from Shaw: new Pima myth; removed duplicate Lenape myth. 7/6/2001: From Frazer: new Masai, Tchiglit, Orowignarak, Central Eskimo, Herschel Island Eskimo, Tlingit, Loucheux, Haida, Bella Coola, Kwakiutl, Lillooet, Thompson, Tsimshian, Smith River, Ashochimi, Maidu, Acagchemem, Twana, Cascade, Sarcee, Dogrib, Ottawa, Chippewa, Timagami Ojibway, Delaware, Cree, Pima, Zuni, Carib, Tarahumara, Cape Frio, Caraya, Murato, Canari, Macusi, Ancasmarca, Guanca; revised Kootenay, Kathlamet, Mandan, Montagnais, Chippewa, Muysca, Acawai, Ipurina, Araucania, Inca. 5/27/2001: From Frazer: new Greek, Arcadian, Samothrace, Gypsy, Hebrew, Hindu, Munda, Santal, Tsuwo, Bunun, Shan, Karen, Mandaya, Ami, Narrinyeri, Samoa, Nanumanga, Rakaanga; revised Chaldean, Zoroastrian, Bhil, Batak, Mangaia. 5/19/2001: Slightly revised Tinguian myth based on Cole reference. 5/16/2001: From *The Mythology of All Races*: new Altaic, Tuvinian, Yenisey-Ostyak, Russian, Buryat, Sagaiye, Samoyed, Kiangan Ifugao, Dusun, Dyak, Victoria, western Carolines, Havasupai, Sia, Mixtec, Maya; modified Persian, Muysca. 5/3/2001: Give Koran story more fully. 4/29/2001: Acawai, Colla, and 3 Inca myths and Gifford reference; slight amendment to Scandinavian myth. 3/31/2001: Sabo-Kubo myth and LaHaye/ Morris reference. 1/1/2001: Added revision history. Added Merriam reference and 3 Miwok myths from it; Bell reference and Yurok myth. 11/4/2000: H. Miller reference and Chaldean, Tahiti myths from there; revised a Hindu myth. ~2/20/2000: Extensive revision: added introduction and several new myths; revised most other myths.

Abrahams, Roger D. African Folktales, Random House, New York, 1983.

Adigal, Prince Ilango. Shilappadikaram (The Ankle Bracelet), Alain Danielou (transl.), New Directions, New York, 1965.

Alexander, Hartley Burr. North American, in Gray, v. X, 1916.

Alexander, Hartley Burr. Latin-America, in Gray, v. XI, 1920.

Apollodorus. The Library, Sir James G. Frazer (transl.), Harvard University Press, Cambridge, 1921, 1976.

Appadurai. Kumarikandam, Kazhagam Press, 1940.

Balikci, Ansen. The Netsilik Eskimo, Natural History Press, New York, 1970.

Barnouw, Victor. Wisconsin Chippewa Myths & Tales, University of Wisconsin Press, Madison, 1977.

Barrère, Dorothy B. The Kumuhonua Legends: A Study of Late 19th Century Hawaiian Stories of Creation and Origins, Pacific Anthropological Records number 3, Bishop Museum, Honolulu, HI, 1969.

Bell, Rosemary. Yurok Tales, Bell Books, Etna, California, 1992.

Berndt, Ronald M. and Berndt, Catherine. The Speaking Land, Inner Traditions International, Rochester, Vermont, 1994.

Bierhorst, John. The Mythology of South America, William Morrow, New York, 1988.

Bierhorst, John. Mythology of the Lenape, University of Arizona Press, Tuscon, 1995.

Brinton, Daniel G. The Myths of the New World, Greenwood Press, New York, 1876, 1969.

Brusca, María Cristina & Tona Wilson. When Jaguars Ate the Moon, and Other Stories About Animals and Plants of the Americas, Holt, New York, 1995.

Buchler, Ira R. & Kenneth Maddock (eds.). The Rainbow Serpent, A Chromatic Piece, Mouton Publishers, The Hague, 1978.

Buck, William. Mahabharata, University of California Press, Berkeley, 1973.

Budge, E. A. Wallis. The Book of the Dead, Arkana, London, 1923, 1989.

Capinera, J. L. (1993) "Insects in Art and Religion: The American Southwest", American Entomologist 39(4) (Winter 1993), 221-229.

Carnoy, Albert J. Iranian, in Gray, v. VI, 1917.

Chagnon, Napoleon A. Yanomamö, The Fierce People, Holt, Rinehart and Winston, 1977.

Clark, Ella E. Indian Legends of the Pacific Northwest, University of California Press, 1953.

Cole, Fay-Cooper, 1915. "Traditions of the Tinguian: A Study in Philippine Folk-Lore", Field Museum of Natural History, Anthropological Series 14(1), Publication 180.

Courlander, Harold. A Treasury of African Folklore, Marlowe and Company, New York, 1996.

Walter Burkert, Greek Religion

Dalley, Stephanie. Myths From Mesopotamia, Oxford University Press, Oxford, 1989. de Civrieux, Marc. Watunna, An Orinoco Creation Cycle, David M. Guss (transl.), North Point Press, 1980.

Demetrio, Francisco, 1968. "The Flood Motif and the Symbolism of Rebirth in Filipino Mythology", in Dundes.

Dixon, Roland B., Oceanic, in Gray, v. IX, 1916.

Dresden, M. J., 1961. "Mythology of Ancient Iran", in Kramer.

Dundes, Alan (ed.) The Flood Myth, University of California Press, Berkeley and London, 1988.

Edmonds, Margot & Ella E. Clark. Voices of the Winds, Facts on File, Inc., New York, 1989.

Elder, John and Hertha D. Wong, 1994. Family of Earth and Sky: Indigenous Tales of Nature from around the World, Beacon Press, Boston. Reprinted in Parabola 22(1): 71-73 (Spring 1997).

Eliot, Alexander. The Universal Myths, Truman Talley Books/Meridian, New York, 1976.

Erdoes, Richard and Alfonso Ortiz. American Indian Myths and Legends, Pantheon Books, New York. 1984.

Fauconnet, Max, 1968. "Mythology of Black Africa". In Guirand, Felix (ed.), New Larousse Encyclopedia of Mythology, Hamlyn, London.

Faulkner, Raymond (transl.). The Egyptian Book of the Dead, The Book of Going Forth by Day, Chronicle Books, San Francisco, 1994.

Feldmann, Susan. African Myths and Tales, Dell Publishing, New York, 1963.

Flood, Josephine. Archaeology of the Dreamtime, University of Hawaii Press, Honolulu, 1983.

Frazer, Sir James G. Folk-Lore in the Old Testament, vol. 1, Macmillan & Co., London, 1919.

Frazer, Sir James G. The Golden Bough, Wordsworth Editions Ltd., Hertfordshire, 1993.

Gaster, Theodor H. Myth, Legend, and Custom in the Old Testament, Harper & Row, New York, 1969. (Most of the flood stories in this work are taken from Frazer, 1919.)

Giddings, Ruth Warner. Yaqui Myths and Legends, University of Arizona Press, Tucson, 1959.

Gifford, Douglas. Warriors, Gods & Spirits from Central & South American Mythology, William Collins, Glasgow, 1983.

Gifford, Edward W. and Block, Gwendoline Harris. Californian Indian Nights, University of Nebraska Press, Lincoln, 1930, 1990.

Ginzberg, Louis. "Noah and the Flood in Jewish Legend", in Dundes; reprinted from The Legends of the Jews, vol. 1, Jewish Publication Society of America, Philadelphia, 1909, pp. 145-169.

Gray, L.H. (ed.), The Mythology of All Races, Marshall Jones Co., Boston, 1916-1920.

Grimm. The Complete Grimm's Fairy Tales, Pantheon Books, New York, 1944.

Grinnell, George Bird. Pawnee Hero Stories and Folk-Tales, University of Nebraska Press, Lincoln, 1961; reprinted from Forest and Stream Publishing Company, New York, 1889.

Hammerly-Dupuy, Daniel, 1968. "Some Observations on the Assyro-Babylonian and Sumerian Flood Stories", in Dundes.

Heidel, Alexander. The Gilgamesh Epic and Old Testament Parallels, University of Chicago Press, 1949.

Holmberg, Uno. Finno-Ugric, Siberian, in MacCulloch, C. J. A., ed., The Mythology of All Races, v. IV, Marshall Jones Co., Boston, 1927.

Horcasitas, Fernando, 1953. "An Analysis of the Deluge Myth in Mesoamerica", in Dundes.

Howey, M. Oldfield. The Encircled Serpent, Arthur Richmond Company, New York, 1955.

Judson, Katharine B. Myths and Legends of the Missippi Valley and the Great Lakes, A.C. McClurg & Co., Chicago, 1914.

Kahler-Meyer, Emmi, 1971. "Myth Motifs in Flood Stories from the Grasslands of Cameroon", in Dundes.

Kalakaua, David. The Legends and Myths of Hawaii, Charles E. Tuttle Company, Rutland, VT. 1972 (1888).

Kelsen, Hans, 1943. "The Principle of Retribution in the Flood and Catastrophe Myths", in Dundes.

Kolig, Erich, 1980. "Noah's Ark Revisited: On the Myth-Land Connection in Traditional Australian Aboriginal Thought", in Dundes.

Kramer, Samuel Noah (ed.). Mythologies of the Ancient World, Anchor Books, Garden City, NY. 1961.

LaHaye, Tim & Morris, John. The Ark on Ararat, Thomas Nelson Inc. and Creation-Life Publishers, Nashville/New York. 1976.

Leland, Charles G. Algonquin Legends, Dover, Mineola, NY. 1992.

Leon-Portilla, Miguel, 1961. "Mythology of ancient Mexico", in Kramer.

Lindell, Kristina, Jan-Ojvind Swahn, & Damrong Tayanin, 1976. "The Flood: Three Northern Kammu Versions of the Story of Creation", in Dundes.

Margolin, Malcolm. The Ohlone Way, Heyday Books, Berkeley, CA, 1978.

Margolin, Malcolm. The Way We Lived, Heyday Books, Berkeley, CA, 1981.

Markman, Roberta H. & Markman, Peter T. The Flayed God, HarperCollins, 1992.

Merriam, C. Hart. The Dawn of the World. University of Nebraska Press, Lincoln and London, 1910, 1993.

Miller, Hugh. The Testimony of the Rocks. Or, Geology in Its Bearings on the Two Theologies, Natural and Revealed. Gould and Lincoln, Boston, 1857. In MacRae, Andrew, n.d. Hugh Miller—19th-century creationist geologist, http://www.tiac.net/users/cri/miller_part7.html.

Miller, Lucien (ed). South of the Clouds: Tales from Yunnan, University of Washington Press, Seattle, 1994.

Mountford, Charles P. "The Rainbow-Serpent Myths of Australia", in Buchler.

Norman, Howard. Northern Tales, Traditional Stories of Eskimo and Indian Peoples, Pantheon Books, New York, 1990.

Opler, Morris Edward. Myths and Tales of the Jicarilla Apache Indians, Dover, 1938, 1994.

Ovid. The Metamorphoses, Horace Gregory (transl.), Viking Press, New York, 1958.

Parrinder, Geoffrey. African Mythology, Peter Bedrick Books, New York, 1967, 1982.

Plato. The Dialogues of Plato, vol. 2, B. Jowett (transl.), Random House, New York, 1892, 1920.

Poignant, Roslyn. Oceanic Mythology, Hamlyn, London and New York, 1967.

Platt, Rutherford H. Jr. (ed.) The Forgotten Books of Eden, Meridian, New York, 1927.

Roheim, Geza, 1952. "The Flood Myth as Vesical Dream", in Dundes.

Salomon, Frank & Urioste, George. The Huarochiri Manuscript, University of Texas Press, Austin, 1991.

Sandars, N. K. (transl.). The Epic of Gilgamesh, Penguin Books, Ltd., Harmondsworth, England, 1972.

Shaw, Anna Moore. Pima Indian Legends, University of Arizona Press, Tuscon, 1968.

Smith, George, 1873. "The Chaldean Account of the Deluge", in Dundes.

Smith, William Ramsay. Aborigine Myths and Legends, Senate, London, 1930, 1996.

Sproul, Barbara C. Primal Myths, HarperCollins Publishers, New York, 1979.

Sturluson, Snorri. The Prose Edda, Jean I. Young (transl.), University of California Press, Berkeley, 1954.

Tedlock, Dennis (transl.). Popol Vuh, Simon & Schuster, New York, 1985.

Vitaliano, Dorothy B. Legends of the Earth, Indiana University Press, Bloomington, 1973. von Franz, Marie-Louise. Patterns of Creativity Mirrored in Creation Myths, Spring Publications, Inc., Dallas, Texas, 1986.

Walls, Jan & Walls, Yvonne. Classical Chinese Myths, Joint Publishing Co., Hongkong, 1984.

Waters, Frank. Book of the Hopi, Penguin Books, New York, 1963.

Werner, E. T. C. Myths and Legends of China, Singapore National Printers Ltd, Singapore, 1922, 1984.

Westervelt, W. D. Myths and Legends of Hawaii, Mutual Publishing, Honolulu, 1987.

Whitten, Norman E. Jr. Sacha Runa, University of Illinois Press, Urbana, 1976.

Wilbert, Johannes. Folk Literature of the Yamana Indians, University of California Press, Berkeley & Los Angeles, 1977.

Zong In-Sob. Folk Tales from Korea, Routledge & Kegan Paul Ltd., London, 1952.

Cann, Rebecca L., Stoneking, Mark, Wilson, Allan C., "Mitochondria DNA and human evolution", *Nature*, Vol. 325, January 1, 1987.

Dorit, R.L., Akashi, H., Gilbert, W., "Absence of Polymorphism at the ZFY Locus on the Human Y Chromosome," *Science*, Vol. 268, May 26, 1995.

Brown, Michael, *The Search for Eve*, Harper Perennial, New York, 1990.

Sitchin, Zechariah, *The Wars of Gods and Men*, Avon Books, New York, 1985. Also, Sitchin, Zechariah, *Genesis Revisited*, Avon Books, New York, 1990.

Gardner, Laurence, *Genesis of the Grail Kings*, Bantam Press, New York, 1990.

Wikipedia, the free encyclopedia—Human—Mythology Mythology, Myths, Legends & Fantasies, Grange Books Catholic Online. Distributed by NEWS CONSORTIUM.

GOOGLE

"Egypt at the time of Ra-Ta"—by Ann Lee Clapp—see the website: www.huttoncommentaries.com, or see the book: "Edgar Cayce's Egypt"—by A.R.E

www.ufomystic.com/2008/02/21/cigar-ufos

www.wisdomofsolomon.com/psr73.html

www.hinduwisdom.info

http://nazcamystery.com

www.comicbookresources.com

Thom Hartmann, The last hours of ancient sunlight, Three river press. New York

The Laymans Parallel Bible, Zondervan Bible Publishers, Grand Rapids, Michigan